W9-DBG-792

Defining Moments

Dispatches from an
Unfinished Revolution

P<small>ETER</small> C. N<small>EWMAN</small>

VIKING

VIKING
Published by the Penguin Group
Penguin Books Canada Ltd, 10 Alcorn Avenue, Toronto,
Ontario, Canada M4V 3B2
Penguin Books Ltd, 27 Wrights Lane, London W8 5TZ, England
Viking Penguin, a division of Penguin Books USA Inc., 375 Hudson Street,
New York, New York 10014, U.S.A.
Penguin Books Australia Ltd, Ringwood, Victoria, Australia
Penguin Books (NZ) Ltd, cnr Rosedale and Airborne Roads, Albany,
Auckland 1310, New Zealand

Penguin Books Ltd, Registered Offices: Harmondsworth,
Middlesex, England

First published 1997

1 3 5 7 9 10 8 6 4 2
Copyright © Power Reporting Ltd, 1997

Printed and bound in Canada on acid free paper ∞

Canadian Cataloguing in Publication Data

Newman, Peter C., 1929–
Defining moments: dispatches from an unfinished revolution

ISBN 0-670-87604-6

1. Canada—Politics and government—1984–1993. 2. Canada—Politics and
government—1993–. 3. Canada—Economic conditions—1971–1991.
4. Canada—Economic conditions—1991–. 5. Canada—Social conditions—
1971–1991. 6. Canada—Social conditions—1991–. I. Title.

FC635.N49 1997   971.064'7   C97-930396-6
F1034.2.N49 1997

Visit Penguin Canada's web site at **www.penguin.ca**

This book is dedicated to
Dana and Brandi,
the world's most endearing stepdaughters,
who light up my life

By the same author:

FLAME OF POWER
Intimate Profiles of Canada's Greatest Businessmen

RENEGADE IN POWER
The Diefenbaker Years

THE DISTEMPER OF OUR TIMES
Canadian Politics in Transition

HOME COUNTRY
People, Places, and Power Politics

THE CANADIAN ESTABLISHMENT
Volume One: The Old Order

BRONFMAN DYNASTY
The Rothschilds of the New World

THE CANADIAN ESTABLISHMENT
Volume Two: The Acquisitors

THE ESTABLISHMENT MAN
Conrad Black: A Portrait of Power

TRUE NORTH: NOT STRONG AND FREE
Defending the Peaceable Kingdom in the Nuclear Age

COMPANY OF ADVENTURERS
Volume One of a history of the Hudson's Bay Company

CAESARS OF THE WILDERNESS
Volume Two of a history of the Hudson's Bay Company

SOMETIMES A GREAT NATION
Will Canada Belong to the 21st Century?

CANADA
The Great Lone Land

EMPIRE OF THE BAY
An Illustrated History of the Hudson's Bay Company

MERCHANT PRINCES
Volume Three of a history of the Hudson's Bay Company

CANADA 1892
Portrait of a Promised Land

THE CANADIAN REVOLUTION
From Deference to Defiance

"Canada's survival has always required the victory of political courage over immediate and individual economic advantage."

—George Grant

CONTENTS

FOREWORD

IN THE SWIRLING SPAN of time covered by this book, Canada came so close to breaking up that the margin of victory in the Quebec Referendum was the same as the number of fans who attended the 1995 Grey Cup in Regina, a few weeks later.

It was that close. And it still is.

As the universe rolls into the next millennium, Canadians feel trapped by the past and agitated with the future, while harbouring grave doubts about the present. Life seems as unpredictable as Preston Manning's haircuts. No one knows if the country will still be around to greet the year 2000.

Looking around, it's tempting to agree with would-be president Lucien Bouchard of the Quebec Republic, who maintains that Canada isn't a "real country." He has a point. Sometimes Canada seems more like the stuff of tabloids: A former Francophone prime minister in his seventies has a baby with a constitutional lawyer in her twenties and co-nurtures the child with a national columnist, who is campaigning to keep the British monarchy in business. A mad assassin leaps past snoring Mounties at 24 Sussex Drive and is stopped by the prime minister's demure wife wielding an Inuit carving. The Canadian army faces down Mohawks across drawn rifles and unsheathed bayonets, then disgraces itself by killing a Somalian teenager in cold blood. Meech and Charlottetown, formerly a muddy lake and a charming island town, become national curses. Pamela Anderson's mountains turn into gold mines, while the world's largest gold mine turns into a mountain of mud; and Ashley MacIsaac comes out of the closet just long enough for everybody to wish he'd go back in.

If the earth hasn't moved, at least it shuddered.

We make our way across the ponds of history in a sequence of leaps, from one defining moment to the next. This volume brings together under one cover some of the short pieces I've written over the past few years. In their selection, I have tried to capture those stepping-stones—large and small, bitter and sweet—which define that journey.

Only three years short of the new century, Canadians find themselves in a quandary: how can a people who took ninety-eight years to agree on the design of their national flag survive in an age of lightning change?

Defining Moments provides some answers.

AS THE COUNTRY EVOLVES from one incarnation to the next, the future is difficult to divine. But the odds favour change bordering on anarchy. The guitar armies of frenzied rockers, who play their angry songs to the swaying devotion of their fans, are expressing their communal determination to never again heed the sermons or accept the dictates of their elders. The young are on the way to founding a Digital Nation of their own—a post-modern Utopia where anything goes. It will be a brave new world where technology is power, interactivity replaces authority and the world off-line becomes an afterthought. (Couch potatoes will be road kill on the info highway.)

In this process, a generation gap is opening between television surfers and computer nerds. While TV continues to be the telescope through which most Canadians view the world, much of what they see is image rather than fact, perception instead of truth. The flickering TV or PC screen delivers little sense of history and less perspective on the future.

Occasionally, the avalanche of breaking news grows too complex or diffuse to be captured on film. Those endless TV reports outside the unity conferences at Meech Lake and Charlottetown and coverage of the 1997 election were good examples, since they provided little sense of history, and even less context. During the past decade, the way we work and play, live and learn has been turned upside down. Everything is up for grabs. Television and films can capture these frenetic changes, but only print can explain their meaning. Hence, this book.

The acceleration of history is not a comfortable ride for most Canadians. We may live in the age of computers that count milliseconds as eternities, but we still prefer to move as slowly as the seasons. We hardly ever rush to judgement. Instead, we stand back, yawn, scratch ourselves. Even when the continued existence of our country is at stake—as I believe it is—we tend to react by offering some tired remark, such as: "It is, eh ... so what else is new?"

That's not as glib as it sounds. This country wasn't born in a hurry, and despite the current crisis, it is not likely to disappear overnight. The best of our historical figures, including Canada's founding fathers, took their time, testing the waters, then testing them again, before deciding to jump in. We celebrate Canada Day every July 1st as if, on that magic moment back in 1867, the country emerged fully formed, with Canadians ready and eager to engage in the national pastimes of bitching and envying. In fact, only four provinces got to the Confederation party on time, and it took another thirty-eight years for five others to join the club—all except Newfoundland, of course, which waited forty-three more years. Just to be sure.

HISTORY HAS GROWN IMPATIENT. When the last Russian troops left East Germany, Boris Yeltsin flew to where the last Communist security troops were packing their knapsacks, and delivered a prophetic farewell address. "Today," he proclaimed, "is the last day of the past." He was right, except that his aphorism fits every leaf on every day-calendar since. The world is changing as we walk in it. Change is guaranteed—except from vending machines.

The Canada most politicians, professors, commentators and special-interest mavens are fighting to protect no longer exists. Meanwhile, the new country being born is still too much putty in too many hands to have taken on any definite shape or purpose.

THE PAGES THAT FOLLOW mirror both the recent past and the turbulent present. The book's opening section, Listening to the Country, reflects some of the excursions I have taken across this large land in recent years, from Resolute Bay in the North, to Clayoquot Sound in the West and Newfoundland outports, too small to have a name, in the East. Two very disparate Canadians—Florence Turner, an angry widow from Pickering, Ontario, and Irving Layton, an even angrier poet from Montreal—vent their rage at a country they never made.

Whenever Canada is examined as a society, it's almost always in terms of our identity crisis, bilingual dilemma or agonies as a pigmy-nation being trampled by the elephant next door. Yet what we really are is a capitalist society run by a cluster of interlocking élites.

While Canada's business future will clearly be based on international deal-making, that notion still bothers those traditional merchants who consider it risky enough to market their goods in Prince Rupert, Trois-Rivières or Gander. Many find the idea of selling their wares in the global village a remote and frightening prospect. They view international commerce as a cold, strange world, filled with unpronounceable names, guttural dialects, and power lunches of raw fish and monkeys' testicles.

At the same time, the nation's Velcro-walleted business Establishment are finding out that memorizing a few operative phrases in Cantonese is one thing, but learning to be philanthropic is quite another. Since the public sector went bust, business has taken over more and more of the social responsibilities that matter. That's a tricky recipe. Profit and compassion are a poor mix. In this book's second section, Giving Capitalism a Bad Name, I've brought together tales of some of the breed's less admirable practitioners.

In contrast, the section Good Men in Wicked Times picks a dozen characters who illustrate that good men are still with us, despite the wicked times. My honour roll includes such disparate heroes as Václav Havel, Vlád Plavsic, Jack Austin, Wally Berukoff, Michael Pitfield, Frank Giustra, Louis Riel, Jean-Jacques Servan-Schreiber and the Right Honourable Christopher Francis Patten. Heroes reflect the nations that anoint them, and Canada isn't very good at it. We tend to choose lost explorers or inventors who transferred most of their patents south of the border. When we pick such authentic heroic figures as Terry Fox, Dr. Norman Bethune and Tom Thomson, we minimize the risks, because they died at the height of their fame. I am glad to report that, with the exception of Louis Riel, my tiny heroic platoon is still alive and kicking.

Politicians of every stripe and motherboard get most of the blame for the mess we're in. That's probably not fair, since it's hard to imagine that any group of well-meaning men and women, no matter how inept, could have produced such dire results. Surely the destruction of Brazilian rain forests, Conrad Black, global warming and the passage of the comet Hale-Bopp must have had something to do with creating our political mess. Still, as the British philosopher-mathematician Bertrand Russell wisely noted: "Democracy is the process by which people choose the man who'll get the blame."

There is plenty to go around. Brian Mulroney, Kim Campbell, Preston Manning, Mike Harcourt, Jean Charest, Paul Martin, Glen Clark, Lucien Bouchard and Jean Chrétien are some of my targets in the book's next two sections, Absurdities & Other Diversions and Scaring the Horses. As I ponder their worth, it occurs to me that what binds together these and the many other misguided politicians we seem to spawn in these northern latitudes is not necessarily stupidity, but ignorance. They decide the nation's future, for example, on the results of high-and-mighty referendums. Yet such tallies are less than useless. As president of the French Republic, the late François Mitterrand pointed out: "In the course of a referendum, people do not answer the government's questions. They answer the questions they are asking themselves."

It is a tough time to be in politics. Everybody demands leadership, yet the same voters also want to be consulted, not just on the great issues, but on such mundane matters as the direction of sewer lines. "I've never been able to figure out," David Peterson, the former Ontario premier, told me shortly after his defeat in 1990, "the difference between making a very tough decision in politics, which you have to do, and arrogance. I guess the dividing line is that if people agree with you, you're a great leader, and if they don't, you're an arrogant son of a bitch, because you didn't listen to them. The truth is there has been an enormous amount of consultation going on all the time. We beat our brains out consulting, and people still said, 'You didn't consult with me.' What they were really saying was, 'You didn't *agree* with me.'"

THE CHIEF OCCUPATION OF CANADA'S politicians and under-employed academics for the past decade or more has been an exercise which falls under the loose heading of "Saving the Country." Canada's national unity problem is simpler to define than to resolve: How, precisely, can the federal and provincial governments respond, creatively and courageously, to the looming threat of Quebec independence?

As the King of Siam so aptly declared: "It is a puzzlement."

Since Canada was exhibiting all the public and private symptoms of a nervous breakdown, I went to see the country's leading
psychiatrist, Dr. Vivian Rakoff, who has twelve degrees and heads
Toronto's prestigious Clarke Institute. "It's quite bewildering," he
told me. "Here we are, one of the world's happy countries—not perfect, but essentially benign, welcoming and decent—and we seem
to be tearing ourselves apart, as though we were oppressed by some
offensive, outside regime. It's madness. One reason may be that our
politicians are not talking about anything that really affects us.
They're not talking about the price of sausages, going crazy or hy-
perinflation; they're talking about this funny, mixed-up, blessed,
pluralist mess of a society that most of the world envies and is desperate to get into, and that's about to tear itself apart, because of
some constitutional lawyers' problems."

Jean Chrétien is no help in resolving the impasse. He still reas-
sures anyone who'll listen that *his* Canada includes the Rockies,
Don Cherry, Newfie screech and Robert Charlebois. But that no
longer turns anybody's crank. Neither will the lame constitutional
solutions offered by the swarms of bureaucrats and Charter groupies
who inhabit the national and provincial capitals. Most of these
would-be wizards—pinched men and women with quartz eyes and
little pink hands—had their most lively instincts defanged long
ago. The hard ploughing involved in trying to keep this country together is described in Quebec on a Hot Tin Roof.

Trying to reinvent Canada before the next Quebec Referendum, due in the fall of 1998 or the spring of 1999, is like climbing
Mount Everest on a dinner date. It can't be done and shouldn't
even be attempted. But it can—and must—be tried.

To soothe the furies of Quebec's militant separatists and calm
the corresponding rage of western Canadian patriots will require
a subtle, highly sophisticated approach. That has never been
our strong suit. My own model of such finesse runs close to the instructions given to a group of French musicians by Jackie Gleason,
when he was recording the score for the film *Gigot*. Although the
comedian couldn't read music, he knew precisely the sound he
wanted from the many bands he conducted. "Tell them," Gleason
had his French interpreter explain to the orchestra. "Tell them, I

want the first note to sound like someone pissing off a cliff into a Chinese tea cup."

That's a tough assignment, especially on a windy day. But it will take some such delicate manoeuvre to resolve the present impasse.

At many levels and on many issues, Canada is at war with itself. That's a highly inflammatory situation. As any cop will testify, it's far safer to face down professional killers than to intervene in domestic quarrels.

DURING THE PAST DECADE, I have lost a number of friends, among them: Robertson Davies, George Hees, Peter Bronfman, Robert Bourassa, Andy Sarlos, Arthur Child and Bruno Gerussi. In Exits, I pay inadequate tribute to their memory.

The last two sections of *Defining Moments* deal with the future (Slouching to Millennium) and my home country, Canada (Bearing Witness for My Country).

History moves from one defining moment to the next, according to its own agenda. Nothing and no one stands still. To allow Canada, the bravest nation-building experiment ever attempted, to be consigned to the dustbin of history would be a crime. We must find a way to lighten the political load with common sense— and do so—as Jean Chrétien so endearingly puts it—"The better, the sooner!"

Defining Moments

I LISTENING TO THE COUNTRY

THE 1997 CAMPAIGN: POWER TO THE PEOPLE

THE 1997 CAMPAIGN may have been the dullest on record, but the June 2 results were electrifying. The election turned out to be a contest in which the verities of the past meant very little and the risks of the future meant everything. In the 11 hours it took 15 million Canadians to cast their ballots, something profoundly significant happened.

Faced with dreary alternatives, Canadians re-elected the Liberals but without the comfortable majority that would allow them to govern as they choose. Their obvious disillusionment with what was once Canada's "Government Party" was due in large measure to Jean Chrétien's sleepwalk through the campaign. Its two defining moments both involved the prime minister himself, and they were both downers.

The first was an opening day when he stood at Government House, and having been asked why he had called the election long before his term was up, he had to consult his notes for an inadequate answer. The other was on May 22 in Halifax, where he opened the country's first commercial virtual-reality installation by cutting a virtual-reality "ribbon"using a computer mouse. Chrétien had trouble working the tiny instrument and later confided to reporters that he has never used a PC. Now, prime ministers aren't supposed to be hackers, but not having an entry point into the world of RAM, megabytes, E-mail and the Internet isolates you from the mental space where most Canadians now live and work.

Being yesterday's man has nothing to do with age.

Seldom if ever before have Canadians voted for what they

already have, yet that was what the Liberals asked them to do. In past elections, the winning political leader offered a vision, or at least a plan, some sense of movement toward a better tomorrow. The Liberals offered nothing, and the fact that the voters responded with enough ballots to grant them the slimmest of majorities was only a kind of obligatory gesture by people who realized that, like it or not, we had to have a government.

It was one of the great ironies of the campaign that Chrétien, whose only reason for calling the election was to perpetuate his power before it vanished completely, had nothing new or interesting to say about national unity. As prime minister before and after June 2, he ought to have made that his lead priority. Now, the future of Canada rests on the shoulders of the man who panicked in the last Referendum. The same politician weighted down the already cumbersome process of constitutional reform with regional vetoes that will make fundamental changes next to impossible.

Bloc Head Gilles Duceppe's loosey-goosey leadership style, plus the fact that Jacques Parizeau lived up to his reputation for taking his foot out of his mouth only long enough to make the odd public statement, helped dilute the Bloc's following. But it would be wrong and dangerous to conclude that Quebec separatism is a spent force. Lucien Bouchard remains the most dangerous politician in the land, and he will no doubt take advantage of the confused federal scene to call an early election.

Against all odds, the voters boosted the feisty Jean Charest and saved the Conservative party from oblivion, allowing him the higher profile that will make him the contender to beat next time out. Charest's failure to make the dramatic breakthrough into Quebec that his valiant campaign deserved flowed from the fact that the PC organization on the ground was not strong enough to sustain his personal momentum. There hasn't been a viable Tory constituency organization in Quebec since Laurier's time at the turn of the last century.

Alexa McDonough's showing was particularly praiseworthy, because the election could have marked the end of Canadian socialism. Her success in bringing out more than her core voters proved that you can, in this country, still run a political party strictly on ideology. That's a refreshing change from the Democrats under Bill

Clinton in the U.S. and Labour under Tony Blair in the U.K., who had to betray their parties' founding principles to bully their way into power.

That doesn't explain Preston Manning's impressive showing. Alone of the leaders he ran a tough, policy-oriented campaign, and stuck to his divisive, anti-Quebec songbook throughout. His shock troops were humbled everywhere except in B.C. and Alberta, so that the party seems to be sliding back where it came from. Still, Presto's new prominence as leader of Her Majesty's Loyal Opposition will be his great test: can he turn himself into a statesman, or will Reform remain a populist protest movement with a preacher as leader and a Christmas cake full of nuts as followers?

The fact that Manning's hard-rock appeal won such a strong echo in British Columbia and Alberta will help the West be heard more loudly in the Golden Triangle (Ottawa-Montreal-Toronto) that still firmly rules this country. That's as it should be. But there was a warning implicit in Presto's western sweep. The overwhelming support of Manning's hard-rock platform was no accident. It accurately reflected western Canada's state of mind.

The overwhelming advantage of the 1997 election was that it taught the Liberals a lesson. No group of democratic politicians ought to aim at governing comfortably. The fact that Canada's voters undermined that comfort zone, allowing the Grits to remain in office but not exactly in power, is a triumph of public will.

Long live the Canadian voter.

CLAYOQUOT DREAMS

A FEW SEASONS AGO, I sailed with three friends around Vancouver Island, a journey touching some of the intertidal world's most wondrous coastline. An unforgettable incident during that voyage was gliding, late one Sunday evening, into a tiny cove just past Meares Island on Clayoquot Sound, north of Tofino.

We were exhausted from the day's long sail, clutching our mugs of tepid coffee as if they were Crusaders' chalices, anxious to drop anchor and be done for the day. I remember standing on the sloop's cabin-top, trying to judge depths and distances, reaching out to touch my boat's shivering mast with a lover's hand—tenderly yet loosely, feeling reciprocated confidence. There were birds everywhere, gulls being wafted upward in the nocturnal wind currents while cormorants flew overhead in long, trailing echelons. We felt as if we had drifted into a cloistered cathedral.

Until the next morning, that is. Dawn revealed that the shores of the cove we had so gently entered in darkness the previous evening had been clear-cut. Our cathedral had been desecrated. We found ourselves anchored in a barren, ugly place that resembled nothing so much as the cone of a burnt-out volcano.

It is from this highly subjective viewpoint that I judge the current controversy about the woods companies being permitted to cut trees in Clayoquot Sound. They should on no account be allowed to touch a single tree, bush or weed.

This dispute is not, as MacMillan Bloedel Limited would have us believe, about cutting old growth to provide wood for the construction industry. This dispute is about values. What kind of society do we want to perpetuate in these northern latitudes? Is the short-term gain of harvesting wood for profit worth giving up a way of life? It all depends on your point of view. Like most city-dwellers,

I never gave trees a second thought until I moved to British Columbia a dozen years ago.

It was only when I witnessed the devastation of clear-cutting first-hand—it's not like giving the landscape a crew cut; it's more like deliberately devastating it to shoot a World War I film about trench warfare—that I realized what was involved. A tree is not a vertical stick with green fuzz at the top, it's part of a local and regional eco-system whose value is beyond calculation. The pulp-and-paper firms and their lobbyists maintain that's stupid, because trees are a renew-able resource. They plant millions of saplings every year and take countless TV pictures of the tiny, perfect plants becoming less tiny perfect trees to prove it.

They're wrong for one simple but telling reason: Trees are re-newable. Forests are not.

It takes literally centuries for bunches of trees to turn them-selves into fully integrated forests. The process involves not just trees, but the quality of the underbrush, nature's ponds and the animals that make the forest their home. The few existing rain forests still remaining on this earth are a precious and highly finite commodity. Cameron Young, a British Columbia environmental-ist, has predicted that unless we act immediately to stop clear-cuts, by the year 2010 the Pacific coast's temperate rain forests will have disappeared. He estimates they are now being decimated at the rate of 26 million cubic metres a year, so that within seventeen years, the original growth will all be gone. The companies dedicated to cutting these venerable plantations maintain that old trees die from natural causes and that they are merely managing the forests. Not so. The forests are being liquidated.

The environmentalists out there on the front lines, daily facing down the RCMP and the loggers, are reviled as being radicals and tree huggers. If defending the eco-system that contributes so much to our well-being is judged to be a radical and undesirable act, then we're all in deep doo-doo. But, yes, they're tree huggers.

And so am I.

There is nothing quite so glorious as hugging one of those first-growth giants that still stand tall in the dwindling pockets of British Columbia's untouched forest. When we sailed to the Queen Charlotte Islands two years after our Clayoquot adventure, I recall being part of a human chain at the edge of an unnamed inlet on the east side of Moresby Island, where it took seventeen of us, hands joined, to surround this big mother of a tree. Old-timers like that deserve all the hugs they can get. Bill Reid, the great Haida sculptor, caught that feeling when he wrote: "I would like to think that the people who call these bountiful islands their home, they and their peers will have more than nostalgic memories of how it used to be, upon which to build their own vision of the past. I would like to know they can go to at least one sacred place that has not been crushed by the juggernaut of the subduers and that they can create their own myths of a living culture."

Old trees even contain their own music.

I remember hanging out with a Vancouver musician named Michael Dunn, who shapes guitars out of weathered logs. "You need old growth for the sound boards," he told me, "because the grain is tighter and the chemical composition stronger. In the ancient forests, trees had to fight for survival under fairly harsh conditions. The newer, commercially grown trees mature under ideal conditions, producing more growth rings, but they don't have the strength, quality or consistency."

Loving forests is very much within the Canadian tradition. The wild land's moods, seasons and weathers were the original chronometers by which we measured our lives. We first lay claim to citizenship by planting settlements on the shoulders of our shores, the elbows of our rivers and the laps of our mountains—testing nature rather than trying to conquer it.

It is the land—which really means its forests—that has anchored our sense of who we are and what we want to become. The shape and growth of our landscape has been the most potent influence on the formation of the Canadian character.

Let's not flatten it.

3

LISTENING TO THE COUNTRY

THE RECENT DEMISE of Toronto's primary literary imprint, Coach House Press, was widely lamented as a body blow to Canadian culture. It is as if the disappearance of this venerable and eminently worthy publishing house symbolized the end of the Canadian dream.

I don't think so.

Our culture—the reason we're Canadians rather than Tutsis, Hutus or Americans—is only vaguely connected to those latte-blitzed downtown Toronto publishers who slouch around Prego's, confidently setting the national agenda. The country's culture isn't reckoned by how many angels dance on Margaret Atwood's head.

Our true culture—as opposed to the intellectual pretensions that serve mainly to camouflage it—is much closer to the ground, nurtured within each of us, central to everything we do and think. It defines who we are, what we feel, how we live and love, what makes us laugh or cry. "It is the way we know ourselves and each other," says Bernard Ostry, the communications guru who is one of its more down-to-earth proponents. "It is our web of personal relationships, it is the images that allow us to live together in communities. It is the element in which we live."

Summer is the best time to observe Canadian culture at ground level. The music festivals that enliven the country's parks and meadows serve as a kind of tuning fork, resonating with the country's mood, giving off the beat and harmonies that reverberate with the true pitch of the people's vibrations.

My wife, Alvie, and I recently spent most of a weekend at the Mountain Music Festival in Merritt, a lumber settlement of 7,500, nestled into the Nicola Valley, some 270 km northeast of Vancouver. In its fourth year, the festival, which attracted an impressive crowd estimated as high as 65,000 over its four days, featured some of the best of current Canadian as well as imported country music, including the legendary Johnny Cash.

Country, which in simpler times used to be called cowboy music, is easy enough to parody by picking such absurd song titles as "If the Phone Don't Ring, You'll Know It's Me," or "I've Got Tears in My Ears from Lyin' on My Back Cryin' Over You." The late Steve Goodman, a wonderfully witty Chicago troubadour, once combined the essential elements of country songs in one verse of his classic, "You Never Even Called Me by My Name."

> Ever since the dog
> Got drunk and died,
> And Mama went to prison
> Ain't nothin' around this farm
> That's been the same
> And you know when Mom broke out
> Last Christmas
> She drove her getaway laundry truck
> Right into a train.

At their best, country musicians sing and play in search of their own humanity; we listen to their songs and see inside ourselves. That's why their music and audience reaction to it tend to reflect people's vital concerns. Their feel for what really matters rings truer than the earnest computer readouts of Messrs Gallup or Reid.

What the country singers are pushing these days are the traditional virtues of faith and compassion, the idea that the only journey that counts is from the depths of one being to the heart of another, that love is like money, you can't give it away if you've never had it, and, oh yes, that love is as good as it gets. Lucien Bouchard, Jean Chrétien, Preston Manning, the National Debt and Coach House Press are off the song sheets.

One of the hottest Canadian country artists right now is Duane Steele, from Hines Creek, Alberta, whose "Anita Got Married" tops the charts on the Canadian country music scene, both in the number of radio plays and on the New Country Network video channel.

After his appearance at Merritt, I spent a couple of hours chatting him up aboard his band bus, a vintage vehicle that once housed a young Elvis Presley and a middle-aging Leonard Cohen, during their Canadian tours. The interview with Duane Steele (whose real name is Duane Bjorklund, but none of the A&R men could pronounce it) wasn't hard to arrange. He happens to be my brother-in-law.

At thirty-three, Steele has been on the road with a series of bands since he formed Northern Sunrise at age fourteen and later achieved a measure of renown as leader of Rock'N'Horse, which earned him a Juno nomination. On the basis of his current success, he has been signed to a long-term recording contract by Mercury/Polydor in Toronto. "I've learned a lot on the road," he says, "trading emotions, telling people, 'I'll show you mine if you tell me yours'—that's the way new songs get born.

"Right from the time I was very young, listening to country music in northern Alberta, I felt that the lyric and content of the songs really got to people, which is why I developed such a passion for it," he told me. "It reaches those who might not otherwise be touched with words and thoughts, because they might not be reading books or newspapers. Country music is a great base for relating to people's problems and convictions. At the time you're feeling the emotions of a country song, you're not worried about political ideologies or national unity. It means more to have your personal life intact."

Steele defines country music simply as music of the country. "We used to be stereotyped into one strain of cowboy music, which related only to working with cows or horses," he says. "In the 1960s and '70s the hurtin' and cheatin'–type songs were the order of the day, and although we still tend to write about relationships, we also celebrate people's lives. The Canadian element in my songs is the fact that I grew up with Gordon Lightfoot ringing in my ears and spent my life absorbing the country."

Dang good thing, too.

4

SALVAGING THE CBC

THE UNDERSTANDABLE FUSS caused by the Juneau Committee's silly recommendation that Canadians be dunned nine dollars per household to support the country's public broadcaster obscured the report's worthy purpose: to document why we need the CBC, and prescribe how it can become relevant again.

The funding proposal—which was dreamed up by some rocket scientists at the Toronto accounting house of Ernst & Young who had never heard of the phrase "politically viable"—would have, if implemented, only yielded $150 million more annually than the CBC's current, reduced revenues from the federal tax pool. The only hypothetical advantage of the scheme was that it would have granted the network what it has always dreamed of: long-term funding independent of the vagaries of governments of the day. It was not to be.

A possible alternative to the doomed Juneau approach might be to place a levy on private broadcasters, getting them to finance the CBC, in return for becoming exempt of Canadian-content rules. But a much sounder solution would be to hold the Liberals accountable for the promises they made in their Red Book that got them elected in the fall of 1993. On page 89 of that document Jean Chrétien was very specific: "A Liberal Government," he pledged, "will be committed to stable multi-year financing for national cultural institutions such as the CBC." Three months later, then Heritage Minister Michel Dupuy was even more specific when he named Tony Manera the CBC's new president. "The Government," he wrote in his appointment letter, "considers the stable multi-year funding for the CBC is the most effective way of establishing its return to a healthy financing position. I am, therefore, pleased to confirm that the Government is prepared to commit itself to such a plan and to affirm that it does not intend to impose new reductions on the CBC over the next five years."

Thirteen months after that, Dupuy's department informed Manera that the Liberals had gone back on their pledge and were reducing the CBC's budget by more than $300 million in the next three years—on top of the $120 million cuts imposed by the Mulroney government. Contrary to the government's repeated promises to allow the people's network the fiscal freedom to do some sensible long-term planning, the Liberals hung the CBC out to dry.

That betrayal suggests that the Chrétien government has lost faith in the CBC as the country's key national cultural institution and is conspiring to weaken its operations to ensure its early demise, or condemn it to the kind of half-life of the National Film Board.

That's a serious situation that demands immediate action. Certainly, English-language CBC television has been losing its audience appeal. Even a decade ago it was commanding nearly a quarter of its available audience; now less than 10 per cent of its potential viewers tune in, and with drastically reduced revenues, program quality is bound to suffer. The argument is made that the CBC is dead anyway, that it cannot—and probably should not—survive in the 500-channel universe which technical wonks point out is right around the corner.

The opposite is true. "The very power of the 500-channel universe to fragment Canada makes the CBC imperative," insists former CBC president Manera, and he is right. We need the CBC more than ever, because with all its faults it alone provides the electronic bridge that allows the country to speak to itself.

It's fashionable for right-wing critics to make fun of Canadian patriots who equate the national destiny with the fate of the CBC. They make their case against public broadcasting in terms of the poor cousin that the CBC has become. But they're dead wrong in terms of what this country's public broadcaster could be and should be. Even at its worst, like Adrienne Clarkson's self-indulgent irrelevancies, CBC is the only TV medium we've got that can claim significant nation-informing potential.

A good example of how the CBC can redeem itself has been the hairy saga of its late-evening news, which lost its magnificent mandate in 1992, when the network's programmers moved it to a 9 p.m. time slot and ditched "The Journal," the best program in the CBC's history. Two years later, having lost much of their audience, they reversed themselves and moved the news back to its original time at 10. Since then, under Tony Burman's inspired direction, "Prime Time News" has regained most of its significant following, and is once again setting the national agenda.

The importance of TV as a force in nation-building can hardly be exaggerated. With our kids watching 900 hours or more of TV a year—and at least 80 per cent of it spreading the gospel of the American way of life—we must maintain a vibrant indigenous alternative.

The first step: no more commissions of inquiry. The CBC has been examined so often that a quick solution to its cash woes might be to transfer costs of the studies into its broadcasting budget. There's virtually no chance of resurrecting the national broadcaster with its current mandate, which has been made deliberately vague enough to be meaningless. Five years ago, Marcel Masse, who has since come out of the closet as a full-fledged separatist as head of the PQ's Paris office, severed the link between the CBC and serving a national purpose.

Placed in charge of Canadian culture by Brian Mulroney, he used the guise of a review of the Communications Act to eliminate the CBC's previous mandate "to promote national unity." Even though he admitted he was doing so because the directive was "a blatant and unacceptable propaganda tool for strong federalists," no one in the Tory cabinet tried to stop him. "I have removed the obligation to promote national unity," Masse boasted at the time, "because it is, first, maintaining this political value artificially and, second, it was a constraint on freedom of expression."

That was hogwash then and it's even worse hogwash now.

5

THE LAMENT OF
FLORENCE TURNER

SO PREOCCUPIED HAVE we become with resolving the national debt
crisis, fighting the Quebec Referendum and debating the merits of
multiculturalism, that no other issue is granted much meaningful
space on the national agenda.

Yet there are millions of English Canadians with deep roots in
this country who don't believe that political correctness is the ultimate virtue, and given the opportunity, long to speak out about
what's bothering them, in the hopes that someone might be listening. They aren't the silent majority exactly, because nobody knows
how many of them there are or what they believe. (Pollsters cut off
their respondents abruptly at age sixty-five, presumably on the
theory that senior citizens are incapable of summoning up any
worthwhile opinions, since they spend all their time knitting, lawn
bowling or drooling.)

That's not necessarily so. After one of my columns attacking
Quebec separatism, I received a letter from Florence Wright Turner
of Pickering, Ontario, a Toronto dormitory community, where she
has lived for the past eight years. A spry eighty-two, she dearly
loves Canada, but is mad as hell at France, and doesn't intend to
take it any more.

"You must be wondering," she wrote, "if these are the ravings of
a senile old lady. Well, let me assure you that is not so. I'm angry.
Very angry, as I expect millions of other Canadians are too. They
talk about it but they won't speak out publicly. So it's time for me
to be heard."

What enraged Mrs. Turner so much was the visit of Quebec

Premier Jacques Parizeau to France, and how he was fussed over by high government and private-sector officials, several of whom pledged diplomatic recognition for his independent republic, once the Parti Québécois leader realized his dream of destroying Canada.

"I want to remind France," Mrs. Turner told me in a later phone call, "that the citizens of Canada's provinces gave their blood and their lives in two world wars to save the hide of a country that now shows its gratitude by assisting those who would break up Canada. Citizens of this country came forward in droves to help save France and thousands of crosses in Flanders Field bear the names of loyal Canadians.

"I ask France," she challenged, "how grateful are you to those who were downed in aircraft or drowned in ships trying to get supplies to feed you and arms to help you fight for freedom? What right have you even to listen to a politician who is betraying the rest of Canada?"

That kind of rhetoric, harking back eighty years to the trenches of the First World War, seems so outdated that it can be written off as irrelevant. But it wasn't then and it isn't now. Florence Turner's career was ruined by that distant war. She's not asking for compensation or apologies. She merely wants to be heard and understood. "Why are we all so frightened?" she asks. "Why are Canadians so reticent about expressing their feelings? There must be many others who feel the way I do, but they only talk to each other. I'm speaking out."

Born in 1912, two years before hostilities broke out, Florence dimly remembers her father, two uncles and even the minister of her family's church enlisting to fight that war to end all wars, and her father lifting her up on his horse as they rode to Toronto's old Union Station and the train that took him away. "I was excited but unaware of the true facts of what I was seeing," she recalls.

Her father, Frank Wright (Florence's maiden name), had enlisted in a special regiment financed by Sir John Craig Eaton, who had promised his men that after the war they would each have a job, as long as Eaton's stores existed. Wright fought as a private in the Canadian Expeditionary Force in the mucky hell that was Ypres and Vimy Ridge, and came back a broken man. His lungs had been decimated by the mustard gas used by the Germans, his health never recovered from the dreaded trench fever caused by the constant immersion in the mud-filled dugouts where he had spent most of four agonizing years. (True to its proprietor's pledge, Eaton's retained a job for him, though he could only fill it part-time.) Eaton's kept its word in those days.

Frank Wright spent most of the rest of his life in and out of Toronto's Christie Street Veterans' Hospital. "It hurts me to remember," Florence told me, "how hard it was for Dad to breathe, how there was no money in the house because he could never be relied on to work a complete year, due to his poor heart and lungs."

Florence was forced to become the family breadwinner and could never complete her formal education. As a teenager she had published some poetry, and in her early twenties started writing music; in fact, she became one of the youngest members of the Canadian Composers Guild and had a minor hit with a ditty called "Alone, Watching the Lights on the Hudson." Hollywood's Famous Music Corporation, then a subsidiary of Paramount Pictures, offered her a contract to write some musicals, but she had to stay home to look after her father. Instead of following her ambitions she took on menial jobs to support the family, scrubbing neighbours' floors for fifty cents an hour, parcelling at Eaton's in the daytime and being a Woolworth's sales clerk at night. "I had no choice," she bitterly recalls. "What could I do?"

She did a lot, actually, eventually getting into politics and becoming fifth vice-president of the PC Party of Ontario, and successfully selling real estate. When she hit eighty, Florence decided it was time to start recording again. She now writes for a group that includes Deann deGruijter, one of the stars of the Gershwin hit *Crazy For You* who are planning to record her ten best compositions. (She also wrote a poem about Meech Lake, but it stays in the cupboard.)

Her father's fate never stops haunting her, and she will not forgive France for so easily betraying his memory. "Maybe I'm some kind of radical," she confesses with a twinkle in her voice. "But I just can't help looking at things as they should be, instead of the way they are."

6

GREAT BORDERS MAKE GOOD NEIGHBOURS

WE OFFHANDEDLY CALL it the 49th parallel. Yet the boundary that divides Canada from the United States runs along that oft-cited latitude only from the Ontario-Manitoba border to White Rock in British Columbia. The more populated parts of Vancouver Island and the Gulf Islands on the Pacific side, the most heavily urbanized areas of Ontario and Quebec (including Toronto, Ottawa and Montreal), plus much of the Maritime region lie well south of that symbolic dividing line.

The border, punctured by about 130 crossing stations, has no real topographical, ethnic or economic justification. Still, that boundary is the most important fact about this country. It defines not only our citizenship but how we behave collectively and what we think individually.

It determines who we are.

That isn't true of Americans, who seldom contemplate their northern boundary. To them, it is a barely relevant mark on high-school maps, as arbitrary and untroubling a point of demarcation as the equator or the horse latitudes. That's why Americans treat Canada like the attic of their national mansion, taking the un-crowded garret above them for granted, unless once in a while Canadians make too much noise to be ignored. Yet throughout the histories of the two countries runs that common link, and what has happened can best be assessed by the movement of people, goods and ideas across the border.

The curious fate of Ta-Tanka I-Yotank illustrates the differences between the surprisingly diverse societies that straddle that boundary. Better known as Sitting Bull, the great Sioux warrior had valiantly prevented the U.S. cavalry from capturing lands previously granted to his people by the government in Washington, when they proved valuable to new settlers. On June 25, 1876, his warriors wiped out an invading troop of 240 mounted soldiers led by Lt.-Col. George Custer (despite what the history books claim, he never did make general) in the valley of Montana's Little Big Horn River. Tagged as "the most dangerous man in North America," Sitting Bull and 5,000 of his supporters crossed the border at Wood Mountain into what is now southwestern Saskatchewan.

They were met by Insp. James Morrow Walsh of the North West Mounted Police, who rode alone into their war camp, wearing his resplendent scarlet jacket to stress the contrast with the dark-blue tunics of the cavalry. He sternly explained that the Indians could stay only if they obeyed Canadian laws. "They had been told by their grandfathers that they would find peace in the land of the British," Walsh reported to Ottawa. "They had not slept sound in years and were anxious to find a place where they could feel safe." Sitting Bull remained on the Canadian side of the border for a peaceful half-decade, returning to North Dakota in 1881, where he again placed himself in jeopardy and was gunned down by government agents a few years later.

Many similar incidents hint at how two very different societies were evolving on separate sides of the border. The Americans really did have a Wild West, with saloon duels, professional gunfighters, crooked sheriffs, lynching posses, marauding vigilantes and "Injuns" killed for target practice. ("Snipin' redskins to watch 'em spin" was one American mountain man's description of the sport.)

While we certainly exploited the Indians, that kind of shotgun individualism had few parallels in Canada. Our frontier was first explored in the early 1800s by the professional fur traders of the Hudson's Bay and North West companies, whose slogan was "never shoot your customers." They treated the Indians more as a free labour force. The natives killed the forest animals, skinned them and hauled in their pelts. Then, switching from suppliers to customers, they traded for axes, guns and blankets. The Americans had sixty-nine Indian wars, the last skirmish in 1890; we didn't have any, though we brought the aborigines such white-man's gifts as smallpox, syphilis and, worst of all, liquor.

The Canadian frontier was settled while the Canadian Pacific Railway was being built—linking up Central Canada with British Columbia in 1886—and that rapacious enterprise was immediately followed by that most quintessential of Canadian institutions, the bank branch. The process was policed every tidy step of the way by the Mounties, who not only upheld the law but confiscated the six-gun before anybody had much chance to use it. By the time most settlers arrived, they found themselves in a field-office corporate environment that demanded deference to well-entrenched authority.

The Americans had to fight for their independence (1775–1783), then wage a civil war to restructure their society (1861–1865); we won our freedom in 1867 after dispatching an alcoholic prime minister, Sir John A. Macdonald, to bargain with British diplomats who wanted to rid themselves of the burden of administering a troublesome colony. Those diverse beginnings still colour our nationalities. Our inglorious and relatively orderly past endowed most Canadians with such a passive sense of patriotism that collective survival, rather than individual excellence, became our ideal. We grew up with, and still practise, such sombre virtues as the notion that there is nothing more satisfying than a hard day's work well done, that it is always best to be close with one's money and emotions, and that even flashes of pleasure and moments of splendour must appear to look accidental and barely welcomed.

While our founding document, the British North America Act, smugly projects our highest aim as the muffled hope of preserving "peace, order and good government," America's revolutionary spirit proudly ricochets in a Declaration of Independence that proclaims the new nation's goals as "life, liberty and the pursuit of happiness." With no manifest destiny to spur us on but only the neutral imperative of survival, we huddle, coldly comforted by our freedoms—*from*, rather than leaping to exploit any freedoms *to*.

What sets us apart from Americans is that there is no process of becoming Canadian that amounts to an identifiable conversion. It just seems to happen inadvertently and is most clearly recognized in hindsight. There is no "Canadian" way of life and little pressure for uniformity. The miracle of it is that anyone, be they originally French, English, Scottish, Ukrainian, Italian, German, Sikh, Tamil or even Newfie, can become Canadian without ever ceasing to be themselves. That's very different from the United States, where the highly marketable American Dream continues to circumscribe its true believers and bedevil its malcontents.

Unlike Canadians, Americans are obsessed with their self-imposed burden of saving the world for democracy. In that context, Canada has always presented a natural target for the champions of America's manifest destiny. The Yanks have invaded us five times (1775, 1776, 1812, 1866 and 1870), including some halfhearted efforts by drunken Irish settlers who felt that Canada belonged to them. In a more serious gesture, during the War of 1812 the Americans offered to free us from the yoke of the British motherland. But we bravely fought to repel the would-be liberators, staunchly preferring to remain colonials. British soldiers fighting on behalf of the colony even burned down the White House.

What the Americans have always wanted is to control our resources and the profitable parts of our economy without the trouble and expense of colonial administration. They are in the process of achieving just that, indirectly, through the recently signed Free Trade Agreement, the latest of several attempts on both sides of the border to unite the two economies. The main reason Canadians must now tread carefully is not because the American economy is so much richer and bigger than ours, but because it operates on a different ethic, born out of our separate histories. "Americans like to make money; Canadians like to audit it," wrote the literary critic Northrop Frye.

Even though our businessmen make bold and brash pronouncements in support of free enterprise, they don't really practise it. At the first sign of trouble, they rush to Ottawa begging for government benefits, which last year totalled $30 billion. American business is much more aggressive and ready to take risks.

In the final analysis, it is only by preserving our differences that two distinct societies will continue to share the northern half of this continent.

Canada may be a loose federation of wildly diverse regions on the margin of the civilized world. But if there is a quiver of common intent that holds us together, it is the conviction that no matter how tempting it may be, we do not want to be Americans.

The 49th parallel must endure.

7

DASHING A PEOPLE'S DREAMS

GREAT ART, REALLY great art, whatever its format, must be guided by an invisible hand: the spontaneous blossoming of humanity caught in a moment's creative impulse. That's even more true of a great people, like Newfoundlanders. Spontaneity is their middle name.

To be a Newfie is to be a survivor. A survivor, not with any negative connotation of trying to outlive others, but in an exhilarating, nose-thumbing sense of tempting the fates that have never stopped trying to bring them down.

Now, that great spirit—that feeling of Darwinian pride that has allowed Newfoundlanders to claim with brassy validity that they are a race apart—is in serious jeopardy.

They are about to become an endangered species. Dash a people's dreams often enough, and you eventually kill their culture, which has depended for its sustenance on perpetuating the way of life that gave it birth.

The human tragedy currently playing itself out on The Rock has no precedent in Canadian history. It threatens not only the livelihood of 30,000 jobless fishers and cannery workers and their families, but it could be the end of a unique way of living. Fishing, as anyone knows who has done it even as a sport, is a serious business that gets into your blood, doubly so if your living depends on it. Rick Cashin, the former union official who headed the Atlantic Fisheries Task Force that issued its eloquent report last year, put it best when he wrote: "The sea is to those who fish what land is to those who farm. The relationship of the harvester to the elements—the sea or the land—is more than economic; it is organic. It is how one gains a sense of place, of belonging and of accomplishment."

It's not news that there are no cod to be caught off Newfoundland—or any other part of the Atlantic coast—because of over-fishing. What's new is that Cashin's gloomy prediction—that after five years of abstinence the industry would once again be able to provide at least 13,000 jobs—has turned out to be wildly optimistic. Instead, according to new estimates by a committee that includes Newfoundland Premier Clyde Wells and Federal Fisheries Minister Brian Tobin, less than half those jobs (6,700) will be realized. In other words, the ground fisheries are not just dormant but dead for the foreseeable future as a major source of employment. (When the industry was operating at a more or less normal level, the Atlantic provinces had 64,000 registered active fishers using 28,000 boats, with another 60,000 plant workers processing the catch in eighty plants.) The 27,000 Newfoundlanders currently getting emergency relief through Ottawa's $772-million assistance program are living on a knife edge. The program is due to run out and even if it's extended, as it will be in a modified form, Canadian taxpayers cannot be expected to carry the province for ever.

The loss of jobs isn't equivalent to a factory closing in Ontario or a sawmill bankruptcy in British Columbia. Most of Newfoundland's outports depend entirely on the fishery, so that collapse of the resource means ruin of the community. And that, in turn, will mean the enforced resettlement of its people. It's a deadly concept that to the Newfies who have lived through its previous manifestations echoes of the "holocaust." Although the rest of Canada hardly noticed, between 1946 and 1975, the inhabitants of some 314 small communities were "resettled." That's a polite word for the agony of being wiped off the maps by bureaucratic edicts issued in Ottawa and St. John's, with compensation of as little as $400 paid to house owners and families that were uprooted and forced to move into larger centres, or more frequently, to emigrate to an uncertain future in Upper Canada. To be poor with the high-spirited dignity only the Newfies can muster is one thing; to be forced out of your birthplace and have to sever your essential touchstones is quite another.

Apart from the obvious difficulty of finding alternate employment in a shrinking economy while equipped with few transferable skills, Newfoundlanders face a severely limited job market. Even Hibernia, one of the country's few mega-projects, will produce only

1,000 new permanent jobs in the province. Nor will it add to tax revenues; 97 per cent of the project's oil royalties will flow directly to Ottawa.

The value of any culture ultimately depends not on good books or great art, but on the passage of a people's seed from one generation to the next, on their link to the soil and the sea. Their life-force is expressed less in words than in deeds—the compassion and humour they feel for one another when there is nothing else available to share.

That's what is really at stake in Newfoundland these days. And that's why Canadians who live away from The Rock should not begrudge the relatively modest extra tax burden to keep our most vibrant culture alive and kicking.

8

THE UNKNOWN ELEMENT

WE HAD DROPPED anchor at Whaletown and the *Indra* tugged softly on the anchor rode, her mast sweeping the sky in the slow arcs of an indolent summer afternoon. We sat in the cockpit watching the intertidal ballet—the alternating sequence of beaks and upturned duck bums, the whiskered snort of a curious harbour seal, gulls bleating derision at a preening eagle. Whaletown is a tiny notch in the rocky southwest coast of Cortes Island, three days' hard sailing north of Vancouver. In 1869 and 1870, the Dawson Whaling Company's harpoon masters set off from here into Georgia Strait aboard the schooner *Kate* and came back with catches large enough to produce 13,000 gallons of whale oil. Ever since, the little outpost has been rehearsing to become a ghost town.

There was another vessel anchored near us that afternoon. We watched its owner, who looked as though he surfed for a living, washing his deck. He in turn watched us. He said nothing for a long while, studying our stern and the white lettering— TORONTO—that identified our hail port. Amused, he shook his head and quipped: "You must have had a hell of a time getting through Rogers Pass."

We had, of course, trucked the *Indra* across the country, but the remark was not as outlandish as it sounded.

I was deep into research for my history of the Hudson's Bay Company at the time and had discovered that, except for Rogers Pass, it is indeed possible to cross most of Canada by boat—if not aboard the *Indra*, certainly in a canoe. The early fur traders of both the HBC and the North West Company developed watery transcontinental highways from the Mackenzie River through the fur-rich Athabasca region down into Lake Winnipeg, and then out to Hudson Bay and the North Atlantic; or through interconnected lakes and rivers into Lake Superior and on to Montreal and the St. Lawrence.

While that 3,000-mile journey entailed many portages around rapids, waterfalls and beaver dams, it had, incredible as it may sound, only one land gap: the twelve-mile hike at Methy Portage in northern Saskatchewan, at the watershed between east and west. It was this intricate network of water-roads that maintained the fur trade as North America's dominant commerce for nearly two hundred years. The water route also created the notion in its travellers' minds that what later became Canada was possessed of a natural geographic unity.

We have, in the intervening years, come to believe that the dominant gene of our nationhood is possession of land, claiming citizenship by right of having stood up to our geography's chill and vastness. A.R.M. Lower, the great Queen's University historian, raised the worship of soil to near-theology with his *cri de coeur*, "From the land ... must come the soul of Canada." Mordecai Richler's Duddy Kravitz whined that in this country, "A man without land is nobody."

Maybe. But I suspect that water has been at least as important to our psyche, and the evidence isn't hard to come by.

During the ten dozen years since Confederation we have auctioned off major chunks of our resources and our real estate—our land—to the highest bidders, first to the British, then to the Americans. At the same time, our culture has been subverted and just about pecked dry by Madison Avenue; militarily, we have become a client state of the Pentagon; just about everything that turns a profit in this country has been taken over by foreign-owned multinationals.

This massive sell-out raised so little concern that, back in the early 1970s, when Walter Gordon, Abe Rotstein and I founded the Committee for an Independent Canada, we could barely gather a quorum and received virtually no support. While Brian Mulroney was dismantling the remains of the Foreign Investment Review Agency and the National Energy Program, most of us were too preoccupied with whiffs of rancid tuna to mount a meaningful protest.

It is not much of an exaggeration to suggest that selling off the land-based assets that are supposed to be the sacred repository of our identity, of our very soul, ranks somewhere equal to curling as a national pastime. We have casually allowed outsiders to reduce us to the status of squatters on our own land, and anyone who dares object is either ignored or relegated to being considered a marginal kook.

But let an American icebreaker point its reinforced bow into the Northwest Passage, let a Portuguese fisherman dip his nets in *our* waters, or let anyone suggest that we export a drop of the stuff, and this country is up in arms. Mention that the Americans are poisoning our lakes with acid rain and Canadian urbanites get ready to march on Washington.

Simon Reisman, Canada's free-trade negotiator who has been charged with selling Canada's birthright, formally defended himself in public only once. Accused of having advocated the sale of water from James Bay as the ultimate "sweetener" in any deal with the Yanks, he could smell the lynch mob and dashed off a letter to *The Globe and Mail* denying any intention of even considering such a devilish idea. Although he had been actively associated with the Great Recycling and Northern Development (GRAND) Canal Company, which had this objective in mind, Reisman swore the basic loyalty oath of patriotic Canadianism: not even if whipped with beaver tails would he trade away our water.

In his emphatic denial, Reisman was voicing a common reaction. The late General A.G.L. McNaughton, former chairman of the Canadian section of the International Joint Commission, the body charged with regulating cross-border exports, let loose a flourish of rhetoric against American attempts to grab Canadian water that still stands as the basic doctrine on the issue: "This is a monstrous concept, not only in terms of physical magnitude, but also in another and more sinister sense, in that the promoters would displace Canadian sovereignty over the national waters of Canada, and substitute therefore a diabolic thesis that *all* waters of North America become a shared resource, of which most will be drawn off for the benefit of the midwest and southwest regions of the U.S. where existing desert areas will be made to bloom at the expense of development in Canada."

Just about every federal politician charged with the disposal of our natural resources has since made similar affirmations. The

Pearson administration's northern affairs minister, Arthur Laing, flatly declared that "diversion of Canadian water to the U.S. is not negotiable. There is no such thing as a continental resource. *We* own it." The Mulroney government's environment minister, Tom McMillan, went even further. Not only was he opposed to the export of water, he went on record as being against transfers between domestic watersheds, including those designed solely to meet Canadian needs. Even one of Canada's most parochial provincial politicians adopted the same protective attitude. W.A.C. Bennett, the B.C. premier who treated the sale of his province's resources like loss-leader barbecue sets in his Kelowna hardware store, was enraged at the idea of bargaining away our liquid dowry. "British Columbia," he declared, "will sell the U.S. hydroelectric power, but not water. Even to *talk* about selling it is ridiculous. You do not sell your heritage."

Water is indeed one of the few commodities not being sold across the 49th parallel at the moment. The only exceptions are a few local arrangements between border communities, such as the daily 20,000 gallons that Coutts, Alberta, pumps to Sweetgrass, Montana. Water is such a heavily charged emotional issue that merely introducing the topic into the free-trade negotiations could have scuttled the whole exercise.

None of this makes sense. We not only enjoy a clear domestic surplus, but per capita we have more usable water than any nation on earth. Seven of the world's fifteen largest lakes are in Canada; we have so many bodies of inland water, in fact, that no complete inventory is feasible—although 563 lakes with surfaces of at least 38 square miles each have been tallied. Estimates of our renewable fresh-water supply range as high as 10 per cent of the planet's total. And unlike the other raw materials we sell, water is a renewable resource. (One factor that reduces the value of our water is that so much of it is in the wrong place. Nearly two-thirds of our rivers drain to the North, away from population centres.)

Obviously, water is much more than just a tasteless liquid when it comes to quenching our psychic thirst. The novelist Clark Blaise described "the parenting effect of water on the Canadian imagination." Dr. Peter Pearse, the University of British Columbia resource economist who chaired the recent Inquiry on Federal Water Policy, has attempted to understand this strange mystique. After touring the country listening to scores of witnesses, Pearse concluded that, for most Canadians, water—and more particularly its inviolate retention within our borders—has become more of a moral than an economic issue. "We tend to think that it's an opportunity when foreigners want to buy our other natural resources, even when they are not renewable," he told me. "But the talk of exporting water raises all kinds of apprehensions. Perhaps it reflects a cultural perception that water is the essential element within the Canadian ambience. We identify water as a critical part of our mental and physical landscapes."

"Water is very special to Canadians," I was told by Dr. Derrick Sewell, the country's leading expert on water usage who now teaches geography at the University of Victoria. "There is no Indian word for wilderness, because while we may regard it as something separate from us, for them the wilderness is everything—their dwelling place and source of food, part of their being. To some degree, Canadians view water with that kind of internal attachment."

Certainly, our affinity for water has deep historical wellsprings. The first visitors here were after fish, not empires; as they worked the Grand Banks off Newfoundland they gradually began lengthening their sojourns by setting up camps ashore. Canada was first explored by water, instead of on horseback, because the animals, even when available, could not move easily or find enough nourishment in the Precambrian Shield. How the continent was first mapped by various navigators pushing up the St. Lawrence and elsewhere in search of the Northwest Passage is a familiar story, but even the academic history of this country had nautical beginnings. As early as 1686, in Quebec City, the Jesuits taught classes in hydrography to professional St. Lawrence River pilots.

The first water-driven grist mill was built on the Lequille River in Nova Scotia as early as 1607. The technology spread steadily westward. By 1836, there were six hundred mills in Upper Canada. Lumbermen pushed in on the heels of the fur trade, using many of the same waterways to float their logs to market, down the basins of the St. John, the Miramichi, the Saguenay and the St. Maurice, and along the lush valleys of the Ottawa. The chief market for most of the timber was Britain, cut off by continental wars from its traditional Baltic sources of supply. One imaginative provisioner to the Royal Navy, Charles Wood, of Port Glasgow, Scotland, decided to evade the English import tax by building huge wooden vessels at shipyards near Quebec City, sailing them across the Atlantic, then breaking them up for their timbers. The first of these behemoths, the 301-foot barque *Columbus* (3,690 tons), launched on July 28, 1824, was the biggest ship of her day. The even larger *Baron of Renfrew* (5,880 tons) hit the slipways in 1825, but she was wrecked in the English Channel through pilot error.

That was long ago. Now that we have no merchant marine, and a navy that relies on grey paint to hold most of its ships together, it's easy enough to forget how deep this country's nautical traditions run and what a dominant maritime power we once were. During the last half of the 19th century, Canada ranked fourth among the world's shipbuilding and ship-owning nations. The tidal terminals of every river and nearly every creek that empties into the Atlantic were crowded with angular silhouettes of the great wind ships. During the late 1870s Canada built and manned a fleet of 7,196 salty thoroughbreds (with a total of 1.3-million tons) that made their owners so rich they formed their own banks and insurance companies. Yarmouth, now a sleepy harbour in southwestern Nova Scotia, boasted more per-capita tonnage than any other centre on earth, with 2,000 ships, most locally built, on local registers.

These early watery adventurers were not limited to the East Coast. Paddle-wheel steamships provided the first mass transportation across the Prairies (even the Riel Rebellion's battle of Batoche was partly a naval engagement), and the Great Lakes swarmed with so many vessels that there may be as many as 10,000 shipwrecks on their polluted sandy bottoms. In one year alone, 1869, an amazing 121 ships went down. The prodigious inland shipbuilding effort required to back this armada included construction of major tonnages in some highly unlikely places. The *St. Lawrence*, launched in Kingston in 1814, for example, was larger and more powerful than Lord Nelson's flagship *Victory*. Boasting 112 guns and manned by a crew of 1,000, the fully rigged ship established British control of Lake Ontario in the latter stages of the War of 1812, but by the 1830s was sold for small change as a floating wood-storage shed. Except for a temporary upsurge during the Second World War, when Canadian shipyards built 878 naval and merchant vessels and the Royal Canadian Navy swept the North Atlantic, not much remains of our nautical past.

Water intrudes into Canada's economic history in more subtle ways. The three main developments that allowed Ottawa to consolidate its political control over the northern half of the continent—construction of steam-locomotive railways to the Pacific, the application of steam power to ocean navigation and the wave of industry-related canal building—were all forms of water-based technologies. Growth of the pulp-and-paper industry, the milling processes that allowed large-scale mining to become economical and, above all, the generation of hydroelectric power that industrialized Canada's agricultural base, all depended on adequate water supply.

During the first two decades of this century, Canada objected when the Americans diverted water from Lake Michigan to flush organic wastes from Chicago's huge abattoirs down through the Mississippi River system, and we raised hell again during the First World War when Buffalo and Syracuse demanded more than their share of the electricity we developed on our side of the Niagara River. The export of water in the form of hydro power has since become a routine transaction, with about 40-million gigawatt hours (10 per cent of our output) surging across the border. With the impending collapse of the U.S. nuclear industry, American utilities are looking at our electrical sources with renewed envy. At least three projects worth a total of $8 billion are early development possibilities.

But it is the debate about exports of raw water that sets off most of the howls. The grandest and dumbest of all the half-dozen schemes hatched by American engineers to drain our lake and river basins was the North American Water and Power Alliance (NAWAPA) project dreamed up in 1964 by Ralph M. Parsons & Co., a Los Angeles consulting firm. That $100-billion undertaking would have involved diverting Alaskan and northern Canadian waters into California and the eastern U.S. through a 500-mile Rocky Mountain trench and a ditch across the Prairies. Despite initial murmurings of approval by some American congressmen, the plan collapsed under its own impracticability.

NAWAPA's Canadian equivalent is the GRAND Canal

Company's proposed $100-billion diversion of fresh water from James Bay into the Great Lakes system, to stabilize water levels and irrigate crops in the U.S. and Canada. Tom Kierans, the visionary Newfoundland engineer who conceived the idea, believes it's technically feasible. So far, despite a grant from the National Research Council, it has won few supporters. Kierans (Eric's cousin) is realistic about the Canadian aversion to exporting water, but warns that we should negotiate while there are still options. "Of course, the United States will not simply come and grab our water," he explains. "They'll find another rationale—like saving us from the Russians."

When set against most estimates of future fresh-water requirements south of the border, that prophecy makes sense. The impending crisis in U.S. water supplies has to do with inadequate conservation and antipollution control (a quarter of America's 65,000 community water systems are seriously contaminated); depletion of the Ogallala aquifer (the chief underground water source that stretches from Texas to South Dakota); and huge jumps (to 1.5 million cubic metres per day) in home and industrial consumption. A presidential task force has predicted that one-fifth of the United States will face a chronic water shortage by the year 2000, when obtaining adequate water will become a critical American issue. Unlike energy, which can be obtained from many sources, water to fill gaps in U.S. water supplies can be pumped in only by importing it from Canada.

The lone Canadian politician who has spoken out on the issue is Alvin Hamilton, the agriculture minister in the Diefenbaker government. The most articulate voice has been that of Roy Faibish, once Hamilton's executive assistant, who has since advised two Canadian prime ministers and later became a television executive in England. "I have been trying since 1956," says Faibish, "to alert parties and people in Ottawa to how important water is and will become in the context of U.S.-Canadian economic and military relations, particularly during the last decade of this century and the first decade of the 21st. The U.S. south and southwest will not be able to develop without it. It will be impossible for Canada to say 'no' to the export of fresh water when it is needed to sustain human life. It may be easier to say 'no' when it is used for industrial and military purposes, but I doubt it."

Faibish sets the problem in a global context: "Canada will only be able, in the long run, to say 'no' to water export if it fills up its empty spaces with 40 or 50 million people. The strategic planners sitting in Peking, Moscow, Washington, Paris and London are looking at Canada—with our space, fresh water, energy, minerals, protein, wood fibre and so few people. Either we start exporting our water or else! In 1900 we said we'd never export electricity. Eventually we did. And so it will be with water."

9

LIVING UNDER
THE MIDNIGHT SUN

CONSIDER FOR A MOMENT the plight of Resolute Bay.

Perched on the southwestern tip of Cornwallis Island in the Eastern Arctic, hugging the 74th parallel and barely 500 km from the North Magnetic Pole, Resolute has the worst climate and the worst economy in the country. It resembles a white moonscape; signs of abandoned hopes include boarded-up houses, burned-out cars and the cannibalized carcasses of dead Skidoos.

This is a land of ice, not snow, and what snow there is (thirty inches a year) falls in relatively moderate July and August. Mean temperature (and it is mean) even during April, when I flew in for a brief stay, was −36°C but it has been known to drop below −50°C. The sky is an eerie whiter shade of pale, and the permanently frozen ground has the texture of pitted pewter. Except for the black dots of ravenous crows hovering over the garbage dump and the thick-furred dogs huddled in the curves of snowdrifts, there are few signs of animal life.

Walking about Resolute can get tricky, because ice storms can instantly obliterate the sight of your own boots as you stumble from one overheated habitation to the next, sucking breath out of the dry polar air. The social highlights of the year are the High Arctic Dive in early August, when hardy locals swim off ice still floating in the harbour (last summer a cavorting walrus joined the festivities), and the annual Sunrise Party held in the first week of February to celebrate the end of the twenty-four-hour winter darkness that pervades the tiny community from early November.

Resolute is an accident. In the summer of 1947 the U.S.

icebreaker *Edisto* was escorting a merchant ship assigned to unload material for a weather station at Winter Harbour on Melville Island, but the ice closed in early that year. The ships dumped their cargoes where they were stuck—which happened to be Resolute Bay. Within three weeks U.S. Navy engineers had bulldozed a 600-foot gravel airstrip and erected the weather station. The Canadian government eventually took over the installations, determined to turn the tiny outpost into the transportation hub of the Eastern Arctic. With the bravado that only Ottawa bureaucrats who have never been north of Kingsmere can muster, a town planner from Sweden named Ralph Erskine was hired to design a townsite for 3,000. He produced elegant drawings of three-storey apartment buildings in a horseshoe shape to form a windbreak for the single-family units in the middle. He planned a huge shopping centre, complete with domed indoor park. An underground sewage disposal system was actually built; it promptly froze solid, as did its accompanying water pipes, but not before the territorial government spent hundreds of thousands of dollars trying to fix them. The first unit of the apartment buildings was finished on schedule for $1.2 million and was furnished with luxurious Scandinavian-design accoutrements. It was occupied off and on for several years before the plumbing gave out; this was mainly because its citified architects had installed all the water pipes in the north wall, which is the most exposed to the elements. The complex has stood there, empty, ever since.

Another Ottawa brainwave was to populate the settlement with Inuit from Port Harrison, Quebec, and Pond Inlet, N.W.T. The move was supposed to improve their trapping prospects, but that particular directive never got through to the animals, and the newcomers have been scratching around for a living ever since. (In the 1979–80 season, the last figures available, Resolute listed thirty trappers; only seventeen of them earned more than $600.) The main cash crop is the "grey market" in hunting musk-oxen and polar bears, both semi-protected species. Native hunters are issued tags for a limited number of kills and they in turn sell them, for more than $10,000 apiece, to outsiders who consider stalking these magnificent animals a great blood sport. This season Resolute Inuit have a quota of thirty-eight bears, and two German hunters have already paid $20,000 to local guide Sam Idlout and his dogs to take them on the trail. A pair of American hunters paid $18,000 for a musk-ox expedition.

When I was there, Resolute's mayor, George Eckalook, was not available for comment because during my visit he was out driving the settlement's only garbage truck, but I talked to Elizabeth Allakariallak, a bright and articulate Inuit who is the local social welfare officer. She estimates that more than a hundred Inuit have left Resolute and that only a third of the 190 who remain can find work. Only one Inuit (Simeonie Amarualik) is still carving soap-stone. "The back-to-the-land movement is very strong here," Allakariallak told me. "We want to go where there are fish and caribou. We still don't know why we were moved here—probably to provide cheap labour for local mining operations, but those jobs never materialized either."

She is as puzzled as the visitor about the empty government apartments which dominate the Resolute skyline, a massive monu-ment to the proposition that even crime wouldn't pay if the gov-ernment ran it.

Despite the high unemployment rate and the increasing loss of skills needed for surviving in a most inhospitable climate, the Inuit remain proud and independent. Only seven families are currently accepting full welfare. A couple of years ago the local Bay store burned down, and its credit records were destroyed in the blaze. Within hours every Inuit in Resolute had reported his debts to the store manager—and the total tallied precisely with the company's estimates.

The Inuit are there to stay. "Resolute has to survive because it's our home," says Allakariallak. "When you're born here, you stay with it. I tell you, we don't have much choice."

10

CANADA'S FEISTY CONSCIENCE

ACCORDING TO KEITH Spicer's first declaration as head of the Citizens' Forum on Canada's Future, he wants our destiny articulated by poets, not the professors and politicians who brought this country to the brink of disintegration. So it seems entirely appropriate to seek the wisdom of the man Northrop Frye described as "the best English-language poet in Canada," the literary genius who comes as close as anyone to being our poet laureate, Montreal's Irving Layton.

The author of fifty-four books translated into seven languages, twice nominated to receive the Nobel Prize for literature, Layton lists his favourite recreation as "polemicizing," a search for ways to perpetuate his faith as "a freethinker." His seventy-eight years have not slowed him down exactly: instead of being a firecracker trying to explode every social shibboleth within range, he has become a cannon, aiming big shots at big targets.

We meet at the Hostaria Romana, a downtown Montreal pasta joint he describes as having "exquisite food, served as if the guests are royalty." The spaghetti Bolognese turns out to be mediocre, but the conversation is wonderful.

"Civilization has never been in greater danger," Layton begins, characteristically dismissing the comforts of understatement. "But I don't regard that danger as a menace or a bad thing. On the contrary, with danger, you have the possibility of change and hope, an opportunity to do something different. Everything becomes negotiable, because there's the possibility of doing things in a fundamentally new way. Too often in the past we've drawn back and resisted the opportunity for genuine improvement."

Unlike most Canadians who tend to blame everything from the Expos' losing streak to the latest snow flurry on the politicians, Layton just thinks they're irrelevant. Brian Mulroney he kisses off as "basically a good guy whose heart is in the right place, but who lacks the intelligence for the job." He is convinced that Jean Chrétien lacks the character, stamina or personality required by the Canadian crisis. "You've got to have not only the right man but the right moment," he explains. "This is the right moment, but we don't have the right man." Robert Bourassa he praises as a "cool-headed economist who understands that the most important thing is to feed and clothe people, so you can't go wild with your nationalism."

Only Pierre Trudeau brings down the poet's wrath. "He thinks he's a visionary," Layton charges, "but a certified visionary must understand the elements he's working with, and Trudeau ignores the French-Canadian fact. He has always struck me as being very opinionated, highly dogmatic and, above all, arrogant. His pit-bull attitudes are based on his inability to listen; he feels so superior to everybody, because of his training as a Jesuit and his mixed background as an Anglo. In short, his class and his education mitigate against him."

Partly because he has travelled and read so widely, Layton views Canada's current crisis from a world perspective. "I see the quest for independence—whether it's in Eastern Europe or in Quebec—springing out of the alienation of the individual from a world he never made. I see modern man as being alienated from God, from nature and, finally, in this last stage, from himself. We feel afraid, forlorn and comfortless, seeking a touch of warmth, like lost sheep plunging back into a flock that follows no direction."

Such an apocalyptic view seems hard to justify, but Layton is adamant in his prognosis. "I can't help feeling," he gloomily predicts, "that we're now in a situation analogous to the fourth or fifth centuries, during the fall of the Roman Empire, when the barbarian hordes were knocking on the gates. Those barbarians were external. Ours are internal in the sense that they're our own citizens who have shaken off the restraints of civilization. It's even true of the arts. Will we ever see another Milton, Shakespeare, Racine or T.S. Eliot? Forget it. That kind of greatness is gone forever, destroyed by technology and the forces of so-called education. If you want great poetry today, you don't go to the poets who are all busy writing their sweet little lyrics, God bless them. If you want great poetry today, you must go to films and music."

Curiously, Layton's pessimism does not include the future of Quebec, because he feels its society is firmly rooted in a distinct history, religion, language, literature and memory. That's where the grievances and the difficulties come in, he believes, because English Canada lacks such unifying anchors. This doesn't only mean English Canada will have a tough time facing the determined collective will of French Canada, but that those of us outside Quebec are much more open to the destructive forces of the modern world. "Menaced by the Anglos, the French Canadians pull in," he explains, "because they feel they're protecting something valuable against the onset of mediocratization and homogenization. English Canadians don't have much intellectual baggage whatsoever, none at all, really. So they have very little to protect and not much will to fight back."

The third glass of sparkling wine has grown warm between us, and the waiters, who look like cashiered mutual-fund managers, seem silently to be agreeing with Layton. But the poet ends the interview on an up note.

"I have two deities," he says. "My main deity is chance; the other is love. I'm a great believer in chance. I was born circumcised, which gave me the vanity and egotism of a saviour, and made my mother favour me. I was the only one in her brood of seven who attended high school, because our family couldn't afford the fees. She felt that if I turned out to be the Messiah, I should know the English language, history and so on. I've been a great believer in chance ever since."

Layton hints that Canada may be salvaged by just such a chance.

I can't resist. Surely, as a putative Messiah, he is the one who can save the country.

His eyebrows shoot up; he's not sure whether I'm joshing him. "I don't think you can save it," he says, sadly adding, "and I don't think I can save it."

Then he reconsiders. "I shouldn't be overcome by such modesty all of a sudden," he says. "Maybe after I've had another drink ... "

II | GIVING CAPITALISM A BAD NAME

11

THE SULTAN OF SANCTUARY COVE

AUSTRALIA DOESN'T FIGURE very large in the quirky world of jazz lore. With the possible exception of the Australian Jazz Quartet, no Aussie group has made much of an impression this side of the Pacific. But those of us who favour the underground legends of that swinging subculture can never hear the word "Australia" without enjoying a quiet giggle about the Daly-Wilson Big Band.

A group of hip young guys who started out as a rehearsal group at Sydney's Stage club in 1969, the Daly-Wilson band produced six gold records, and its version of "Kanga: Tie Me Kangaroo Down" remains a classic.

They toured the big cities and the outback, making great music and raising hell. But times and tastes changed, and eventually people stopped showing up. During an all-night, post-concert drunk, co-leaders Warren Daly and Ed Wilson decided the best way to save the band was to get audiences to come out to *see* them, as well as hear them. According to their impeccable Australian logic, marinated by Gilbey's and Lamb's, that meant only one thing: they would play bare naked. They did just that, and for all I know, the nineteen nude musicians are still on the road somewhere on the Gold Coast, blowing their horns and having the time of their lives.

I was reminded of that story when I spent a morning with Michael Gore, an Australian entrepreneur passing through Vancouver, who told me that he had hired the Daly-Wilson band for the opening ceremonies of a luxury $340-million subdivision he built in Queensland. Gore, who is planning major investments in British Columbia, never does anything by halves; the other featured entertainers at his gala were Frank Sinatra and Whitney Houston.

Gore, fifty-two, is an outsized character who lives without

recognizing any of the ordinary limits of speech, dress or behaviour. He is a former racing driver (the kind who likes to rip his competitors' door handles off), process server and encyclopedia salesman, who was once taken to court for selling "holy dirt from Lourdes." He has modelled his life on George "Old Blood-and-Guts" Patton, the unorthodox American Second World War general who harangued his troops, yet whose ruthless drive and disregard of military rules won some notable campaigns. Gore has seen the Hollywood film about Patton, starring George C. Scott, at least a hundred times and starts each morning by listening to recorded excerpts from the general's pre-battle pep talks.

Gore's dress code is late 1950s safari-guide khakis with open shirt, topped by a bronzed face and a Cheshire grin. "I don't perm my chest hair and don't wear gold dicks around my neck," he says, redundantly explaining: "I'm not with the establishments of this world. I'm not frightened of sticking my arm down the shithouse to unplug it. I believe that's what's always carried me. Some of those public-company types are as slick as snot on a doorknob. But you turn them over and they aren't worth the price of Paddle-Poop."

Authentic Australian gibberish.

If Gore is aware that not all people talk like him, he shows no sign of it. Thus his analysis of business trends Down Under: "The Australian economy has turned to shit in a hand basin. I decided I would rather go off and seek other opportunities. I'd been working on a video program that teaches illiterate kids how to read. I've put about $8 million into it. I thought I might go to the States, look around, find some finance, put that together, and I was talking about it to Ian Thomas [a Vancouver real-estate consultant] in Australia, Christmas of last year, and Ian suggested I try Vancouver."

Gore is in Vancouver with his third wife, Karen, who is a sports psychologist, and their nine-month-old twins, Ashley and Bryghton. "I didn't like the smell of the Vancouver Stock Exchange and didn't want to get on the treadmill of parties and clubs, meeting people and being at the forefront of the publicity thing again. I just wasn't ready for it," he says. "Karen and I talked about it and then I thought, 'I don't have the desire any more to work 120-hour weeks.' I know I'm good and I know I'm clever at what I do, but what I really need is to get together a group of people who are not interested in building paper empires. I can get benefits out of their respectability and capitalize on their talents. I'm going to put a company together and give each one of them a good stack of equity up front. But I'll want their hearts, minds and undivided attention. I'm talking about seven-year deals. I can provide several hundred million dollars' worth of cash, at very, very low interest rates, and I want to run such an enterprise and make money out of it. I'm no longer interested in fighting the establishment, or going to big lunches in $3,000 suits. I don't want to read 300-page reports. I want to read 3-page summaries. Of course, I only pretended to read the 300-page reports all my life, but now I want to say up front, 'I don't want to read that shit.'"

He is not overly impressed with Canadian business tactics. "I sat down with the head of Woodward's department store just before he got the ax," Gore recalls, "and he was talking about what a great opportunity there was for somebody to buy Woodward's. Having walked through some of the stores, I thought, 'You're blind.' I mean, there's no joy in the staff, nobody wants to work, nobody wants to put any effort into it. Why the hell do they think places like The Future Shop are doing so well? Because they get enthusiastic people selling and putting in the effort."

Gore's move into the Australian big leagues came in 1983, when he switched from selling cars and got into boat building with Hong Kong partners. While aboard his yacht, searching for a place to erect a boat factory, he found Hope Island, a mangrove swamp twenty-five minutes north of Surfers Paradise. He bought the land for $3 million, intending to use ten acres for the factory and sell the rest for $4 million. A week later, he discovered that Australian tycoon Alan Bond owned the property next door and had been trying to get it rezoned for seven years. Gore decided that the only way to hasten a positive ruling was to come up with something so impertinent, so preposterous, so impossible that the local government might believe in him.

That was how the idea of building "the ultimate resort" was born. The Queensland government passed a special act of parliament, the Sanctuary Cove Act, which spared Gore the worry of local government regulations and turned the land into a private fiefdom. The resort was to include 1,400 luxury houses, four man-made harbours, a country club, two golf courses, a tennis club, a huge shopping village, a 500-room Hyatt hotel and a 400-berth marina with room service. Guarded by a $4-million security system, the project quickly became a *nouveau riche* ghetto. Its social tone was set in an ad published by Gore to attract clients: "The streets these days are full of cockroaches and most of them are human. Every man has a right to protect his family, himself and his possessions. To live in peace and safety. Sanctuary Cove is an island of civilization in a violent world, and we have taken steps to ensure it remains so."

To open his "ultimate resort," Gore staged the "ultimate event"—a $15-million spectacular, including not only Daly-Wilson, Sinatra and Houston, but Arnold Palmer on the golf courses and Hana Mandlikova and Jimmy Connors on the tennis courts. Altogether, 900 performers took part over five days—with programs running twenty-four hours per day. "It was a celebration of the best entertainers and best sporting stars, to emphasize that the best talent goes with the best resort," Gore recalls. "I got Sinatra, not because I'm a fan of his—I'm not—but because he's the best. I didn't give a bugger when he arrived or if he played golf or what, as long as he was on stage and did a bloody good job. I certainly didn't expect him to take Twinings tea and cucumber sandwiches with me on my patio."

On January 5, 1988, the night of the Sinatra concert, Gore stood up in front of 70,000 people and thanked the politicians and real people who had helped make the project possible. "After I got off the stage," Gore remembers, "the chairman of the public company that had been my partner came over in an absolute rage with all his henchmen around him, and said, how dare I get up in front of all those people and not tell them how good he was. I said, 'God, fuck me, you're my partner, for Christ's sake. I mean, how much money are you going to make out of this thing? What do you want me up there talking about you for?' It just was not relevant to what was going on."

They had a very public falling-out. At the same time, Gore's second marriage was failing, and he was about to be charged with tax evasion. But first, he had to steer Frank Sinatra safely past the news conference he was due to give before heading back to America. "Sinatra," he recalls, "was absolutely paralyzed by the press, especially the Aussie media. I told him, 'Listen Frank, I'll tell you what I'll do for you. I'll run the press conference. I'll guarantee there won't be any trouble.' And he said, 'Michael, can you promise me that?'

" 'Absolutely, Frank, I know Australians better than you, and I know bloody journalists.' So I went out, and in the courtyard of a house that we had built for Sinatra's dressing room—which was up for only thirty-six hours—I agreed we'd let one hundred journalists in. I put the newspaper blokes with the girls at the front, and I put in some raised areas for the photographers. At the back, I had a large raised platform for the television people. I got them all in there twenty minutes before the press conference started, and I said, 'Now fellows, any talk about prostitutes, molls, illicit affairs of Mr. Sinatra, whether he's bald, whether he reads cue cards, anything, I'll stop this fucking conference. Do you understand me? And the reason I'm going to stop it is because the power lead that feeds every single camera you've got here and all those fucking lights is between my feet. I will simply reach down and pull the fucking thing apart and that will be the end of you. Okay?' "

The next day, Gore sold his interest in Sanctuary Cove to his partners for $35 million and prepared to face the tax fraud charges, which had to do with the import and export of luxury boats by one of his subsidiaries, Southern Cross Yachts. "At one point in the trial, I was convinced I would go to jail. I had to talk to my son and tell him I might be gone for a while," he remembers. "When the judge came in on the last day of the trial, I was doodling on a business card, writing down all the various sentences I could have gotten. I had it narrowed down to a custodial sentence with about seven months inside."

To his surprise, he was fully acquitted, but his marriage by now was really on the rocks. "On the day I won the trial at the Supreme Court in Australia," he recalls, "my lawyers were all in tears, and I was in tears. My wife was sitting up in the back of the court, and we were going through terrible times at that particular junction. I looked around and she was crying, too. I got a big lump in my throat and walked up and put my arms around her and I said, 'Well, darling, there's a chance for us yet.'

"She said, 'What are you talking about?'

"I said, 'Well, all our people are crying, I'm crying, you're crying.'

"She said, 'I'm only crying because you're not going to jail.'

"I knew I had real problems then. So I just lavished money on her. I mean insane money, millions of dollars, just pissed up against a wall. Fucking Arab horses and stud farms, jewellery and art. She had a Ferrari and a Range Rover and a Nissan. I mean, it was just insanity. I actually sat down with her and said to her, 'Jenny, you can live your life any way you like. You could go anywhere, do anything, you have your own business—she had several businesses that I had funded and set up for her—there are only two things I ask: that when you do come home, you come home to me; and that whatever you do, you don't do anything that embarrasses me.' And I was quite happy with that. I would have lived quite happily with that.

"My wife was insanely jealous of me being the centre of attention. I would walk down the street, people bloody talked to me. I mean, people still stop me in Vancouver who know me from Australia and talk to me. She hated it. She'd say, 'Who the fucking hell do you think you are, Marlon Brando?' And she used to say, 'You seek these people out, you look for somebody that recognizes you just so they'll talk to you.' And the truth of it was that I didn't want that.

"So, in the end we jumped into my jet with her mother and our son, and I'll never forget that trip as long as I live. We went to Singapore and I bought four fur coats for her and two for the mother. We spent $300,000 U.S. in diamonds. We flew from Singapore to Bahrain, where there was this gold market and we bought heaps of fucking useless gold. Then we went to Rhodes and the island of Lindos and bought some more fur coats there. We went to Barcelona and bought truckloads of leather goods. We went to Paris and bought Christian Dior and Louis Vuitton. I mean, I spent about $700,000 in four days.

"Finally we flew down to San Francisco and booked into a hotel to stay there for the night. We were going to go on to Honolulu and home the next day. We had some dinner, and we were sitting in our suite. I asked her if she'd enjoyed the trip. She said, 'Yes, it was marvellous. But I really do want a divorce.'

"I said, 'Okay.' Well, there was no point. During that trip I had started to think, what the hell AM I? All I am is a money machine. I mean, money didn't change my attitude to life, but all of a sudden hers had changed dramatically, and I just wasn't interested. As God is my judge, I met Karen [his present wife] three months later, and it just fucking happened. That's the way it was."

Michael Gore never went bankrupt but his companies did, and he left Australia a trifle hurriedly, in the summer of 1992. The Aussie buccaneer has yet to choose what investment path he will follow in Vancouver or where he will permanently settle down, but he is determined to invest the considerable funds he claims to have at his command in these northern latitudes.

The naked big band can't be far behind.

12

THE DISMAL SCIENCE

THERE'S AN APOCRYPHAL story making the rounds these days about the darkest days of the Cold War, when every Revolution Day the Soviet Union would show off its latest means of mass destruction to the world by staging an elaborate military parade past the Kremlin. From a cement balcony, the country's leaders, awkwardly muffled against the cold, would take the salute, figuratively thumbing their noses at what then was a highly nervous, not as heavily armed western coalition. On one of those occasions, long after the rows of tanks had rumbled by and the newest missiles had been towed before the reviewing stand—right at the tail end of the parade—there was an old car occupied by two middle-aged men in untidy suits, waving to the crowds.

Leonid Brezhnev, then in charge of things, turned to an aide and furiously demanded what the jalopy and its funky passengers were doing in his parade of deadly weapons. "They're economists, Mr. Chairman," was the hasty explanation. "You'd be surprised what damage they can do."

Most Canadians would agree with that harsh verdict on a much misunderstood profession. Never have we as a people been so worried about our economic future, or felt so frustrated by the inability of professional economists to explain exactly what's going on—or to predict what's going to happen next. And with good reason.

The terrible truth is that economists don't know. Canada—and the industrialized world, for that matter—have never found themselves in a fix quite like this before. There are no precedents from which to divine the future. Despite the hopeful mutterings of baffled economists—whenever some Statistics Canada index edges up a couple of tiny notches—that at last there's "light at the end of the tunnel," we're so deep into the tunnel that if there is a light at all, it's probably some poor guy, just as lost as we are, flashing an S.O.S.

Despite their inherent caution and their stubborn assurances that we're not in a Depression, economists do recognize some startling similarities between the Calamitous Nineties and the Dirty Thirties. Both decades were sobering-up periods for previous orgies of irresponsible spending and borrowing. In the 1920s, gullible investors bought swampy real estate in Florida; in the 1980s, equally gullible investors purchased highly levered office buildings in Toronto. Both decades were populated by high-flying gamblers who masqueraded as conservative businessmen. The 1920s had Ivar Kreuger (the great match king who committed suicide when his empire collapsed); we have Bob Campeau and Paul Reichmann, whose fiscal manipulations turned greed into an art form. Their demise, like the numerous millionaires who bit the dust in the thirties, hurt many innocent people—not to mention bankers who suddenly discovered that their prized collaterals had become worthless.

"To claim that this is not a Depression because the statistics are not as horrendous as in the 1930s misses the point," insists Dominik Dlouhy, a leading Montreal-based investment strategist. "At that time, the public sector was very small, whereas now governments have captured a large and growing percentage of the GDP, financed by ever higher taxes and borrowings. To claim that this is not a Depression because unemployment, economic and human suffering are not as severe as in the 1930s is like saying that the Persian Gulf war was not a war because millions were not killed in the trenches, as they were in the First World War."

The Depression was also a time of mass unemployment and currency manipulations and devaluations. Already last year, central banks in Norway, Sweden and Finland gave up their efforts to defend their domestic currencies, and more countries are sure to follow that dismal lead, possibly including Canada. It was, of course, the advent of the Second World War that snapped the economy back to life, but that was preceded by a recovery in property markets, as owner-occupied homes became all the rage.

The reason economists have so much trouble trying to figure out how we get out of this recession is that it's so different from the seven others we've experienced since 1945. Most of the previous downturns were deliberately brought on by the Bank of Canada to dampen inflationary pressures and rebalance supply and demand. They lasted an average of 11.8 months and reversed themselves when low inventories kicked in renewed industrial production and reduced interest rates prompted refreshed consumers to start spending again.

The current cycle (and it still is a cycle; there *will* be an upturn) was triggered by our inability—as a nation, as corporations and as individuals—to service the debt we had accumulated.

Dlouhy and others have pointed out that the army of Canadian unemployed is about the same size it was in the Depression (three million) even if unemployment insurance and welfare payments have made their plight slightly more bearable, and that corporate profits have collapsed to the same levels as 1932. Economists assign most of the blame to federal politicians for not even trying to balance the budget. Canada's total national debt first topped $100 billion in 1982. It has since doubled, and doubled again. Due to reach $500 million at some point in 1993, that national burden is rapidly reaching unmanageable proportions. Other than the standard remedy of inflating (or deflating) our way out of this muddle, Dlouhy suggests in a thoughtful article in *Investors Digest* that we either call in the International Monetary Fund and let them run the country for a while, or better still, float a conversion loan that would switch our debt into new bonds with 21st-century maturities bearing interest rates as low as 1.5 or 2 per cent.

Whether or not some kind of conversion loan or some other unconventional instrument is used to tame our national debt, 1993 will be the year Canadian politicians will finally realize that none of the traditional policies and instruments work any longer. What this country needs more than anything else is a new way of looking at itself and its problems.

If we can achieve that kind of breakthrough, any economist whose black art tries to harm us will be as powerless as Brezhnev's missiles.

13

GIVING CAPITALISM
A BAD NAME

As THE NATIONAL finances continue to deteriorate, it has become obvious that more and more of Canada's social and economic infrastructure will have to be supported by the private sector. That's why it's doubly awkward that recent disclosure of executive salaries brands most of the men (and few women) who command the country's major business enterprises as selfish beasts collecting obscenely swollen pay packets that have little connection with the success or failure of their efforts.

While blue- and white-collar workers are being asked to forgo raises or to cut back their incomes, their bosses keep raking in more and more dollars. Apart from the dismal ethics of this game, the fact that compensation is unrelated to profit means there is little incentive for higher productivity, and no motivation for our industrial leaders to try harder.

Almost the opposite is true.

No Canadian company whose executives weren't actually jailed suffered a more humiliating downfall than Royal Trust, which went from ranking among the continent's highest-rated financial institutions to virtual bankruptcy in twenty months. Yet Hartland MacDougall, chairman of the board who presided over this self-inflicted carnage, was handed a combined salary, bonus and severance package of $2,853,846 for 1993, when his company was folded into the Royal Bank. Although Royal Trust's fifty main executives had boasted in the good years that their compensation was tied directly to their sterling performance, when they had run their once-great enterprise into the ground, the loans they had taken out to finance their share purchases were forgiven and they lost none of their bonuses.

Similarly, Marvin Marshall, the CEO of the real-estate firm Bramalea Ltd., was paid an impressive $971,225 in 1993, the year his company lost a howling $90.6 million.

The rocket scientists who run Hamilton's Dofasco Inc., which once was the pride of the Steel City, awarded themselves $4.3 million in salaries and $1.6 million in bonuses for making the brilliant decision to purchase Sault Ste. Marie's debt-ridden Algoma Steel Corp. The move cost Dofasco an out-of-pocket loss of $713 million. (Japanese steel executives regularly commit suicide for losing a quarter as much.) Being rewarded for losing money on that grand a scale is particularly rotten, because at the same time its executives were collecting their booty, Dofasco was laying off its mill workers and other employees as part of its "urgency economy measures."

At Canadian Pacific, which has been able to weather most past economic downturns, in one recent year chairman and CEO Bill Stinson was paid $1,181,895—a 31 per cent increase from the previous year, although his company's profits were down 52 per cent. Meanwhile, Varity Corp., the pitiful Buffalo-based remnant of the agricultural implements empire Massey-Ferguson, once Canada's mightiest and most profitable manufacturing enterprise, was being run by Victor Rice and Vincent Laurenzo for a combined compensation of $4.7 million. (Although their faltering enterprise had been saved by taxpayer-financed handouts from Ottawa and Queen's Park, they moved Varity's headquarters across the border. That way their salaries are paid in U.S. funds.)

Some of the worst examples of how executives are overpaid comes to light in the pay packages they're able to negotiate even before joining a company's payroll. Stephen Banner, who joined Seagram's as an executive vice-president in 1992, was paid a signing bonus of $4 million plus 50,000 Seagram shares, plus $7.4 million for the half-year he put in between June and December. Stephen Bachand, who switched to Canadian Tire in March 1992, was handed a starting bonus of $3.9 million (plus his $1.2-million salary), not to mention a $1-million interest-free loan to purchase a home and stock options worth $2.1 million by the end of 1993. The jury is still out on his performance, but that wasn't the case with Paul Penna, who until recently ran a money-losing operation called Agnico-Eagle Mines out of Toronto. The company's charter was less concerned with mining than with providing Penna a $5-million bonus if he was ousted—even though his company has posted nothing but losses since 1988.

There are exceptions to this style of unbounded greed, of course. Paul Desmarais, for example, chairman of the mighty, Montreal-based Power Corp. of Canada, paid himself a relatively modest $1.66 million, though his firm's net earnings were a healthy $200 million. The executives of a few companies that have fared badly in the recent recession were conscientious enough to voluntarily not accept any bonus in 1993. Bell Canada Enterprises CEO Red Wilson, as well as David Jolley and David Galloway who run Torstar Corp., which owns *The Toronto Star* and Harlequin, were conspicuous in this small field.

Sometimes getting rid of a bum executive is more expensive than keeping him. When Paul Stern was dismissed as CEO of Northern Telecom last year, he left with a $3-million cash compensation package, plus another $5.5 million in stock options. The Keystone Kop duo that almost succeeded in drowning Montreal's once-profitable Domtar Inc.—James Smith and Raymond Pinard—collected a combined bonus of $1.9 million for 1991, even though they left at the same time 1,300 salaried employees were being laid off.

This sordid tally is not only bad for shareholders; it's bad for business. If the leaders of our vaunted private sector aren't careful, Canadians will soon begin to realize their ethics stink as high as those of the politicians.

14

THE HIGH COST OF FREE TRADE

THE NEVER-ENDING SEARCH for a quick fix that would allow Canadian manufacturers unlimited access to the U.S. market is reviving the issue of a U.S.-Canadian trade agreement.

None of the basic arguments for or against such a fateful pact have changed significantly since Canadian voters soundly defeated the idea in the 1911 election, but the current circumstances are vastly different. It is a topic that has always intrigued businessmen in this country. Vice-presidents (marketing) love to savour the sales-graph-busting prospect of serving more than 200 million cash-happy consumers, instead of being restricted to 30 million penny-pinching Canadians.

The notion was simplistic enough to have attracted what was laughably called Ronald Reagan's brain-trust advisers who in their 1980 Republican platform boasted that the macho candidate would unite this continent from the Coppermine River to the Yucatán Peninsula in one huge economic unit. The theory was that more efficient reallocation of natural and secondary resources would make us all richer and happier. Canadians were expected to rally to the cause.

Reagan has since been diverted by more TV-appealing concerns, like Grenada's threat to take over the universe. But a growing number of thoughtful Canadians, in and out of government, remain convinced that doing away with all barriers to the more than $100 billion in Canada-U.S. trade is the way to go.

What's new about the current debate is that, without too many people being aware of it, Canadian tariff protection is rapidly approaching zero. At the last Tokyo round of GATT negotiations, it was agreed that by 1987 Canada's duties on industrial products will be reduced by 40 per cent, leaving only a 10 per cent tariff wall between us and the Americans. "Further moves in this direction," says Prof. Abraham Rotstein, a University of Toronto economist who presented a brief to the Macdonald commission on the issue on behalf of the Canadian Institute for Economic Policy, "are fuelled by economic illusions of the United States as the land of 'greener pastures' and gloss over the difficult problems of our branch-plant economy. Calls for freer trade divert attention as well from the main economic challenge of developing an industrial policy to deal with high unemployment."

To smooth out the transition, Ottawa has devised a sector-by-sector free-trade approach, with such items as urban mass-transit equipment, textiles and petrochemicals leading the way. The problem with all this, as Rotstein and others have pointed out, is that at the same time as our industries would gradually be gaining access to U.S. customers, their manufacturers would be swamping our markets, bolstered by the built-in price advantage of longer runs and larger promotional budgets. (Of the many production factors, only two—marginally lower wages and proximity to raw materials—favour some Canadian locations and sectors.) Canada's only long-term experience with sectoral free trade has been in the agricultural implements industry, which has been duty free since 1944. The result has been a dramatic shift of manufacturing to south of the 49th parallel.

Unlike most free-trade negotiations, the ultimate shape of the U.S.-Canada economic relationship will not be determined by market forces alone. Because nearly half of our secondary manufacturing is owned by Americans, goods move across the border at internal transfer prices rather than at competitive rates. According to a recent federal government report, "Heavy U.S. ownership in Canadian industry would, through the operation of boardroom prejudices, result in Canadian production being relocated in the United States even in those instances where Canadian production costs were lower." Rotstein says that 56 per cent of our exports to the United States take place between firms in which one partner has at least 5 per cent of the equity of the other. "It is Alice in Wonderland economics to expect branch plants in Canada to compete with their U.S. parent companies on their home ground. Indeed, the reverse phenomenon is more likely: free trade will encourage the dismantling of Canadian branch plants, and our market will be served either from the United States or from relocated production in Southeast Asia."

High-minded pledges supporting free trade don't really mean very much on either side. Just recently Ottawa slapped an extra 7.7 per cent tariff on U.S. stainless steel, following a similar move by Washington last July. At one point, there were sixty-three protectionist bills before Congress that would restrict Canadian exports. When we still suffer from double-digit unemployment, it is much too risky to negotiate a free-trade pact that could devastate our manufacturing sector.

In the background is the memory of former U.S. Secretary of State George Ball's prediction in his book *The Discipline of Power*: "Sooner or later, commercial imperatives will bring about free movement of all goods back and forth across our long border; and when that occurs, or even before it does, it will become unmistakably clear that countries with economies so inextricably intertwined must also have free movement of the other vital factors of production capital, services and labor. The result will inevitably be substantial economic integration which will require for its full realization a progressively expanding area of common political decision."

Any such harmonization of our two countries' economic policies is bound to eat away at our sovereignty and reduce the already shaky vitality of Canadian nationhood.

15

DON'T PUT NAFTA IN YOUR OIL LAMPS

JEAN CHRÉTIEN WON the 1993 election on three main pledges: that he would ground the National Defence Department's luxurious VIP helicopters; review and probably reject the deal privatizing the Toronto airport; and renegotiate the North American Free Trade Agreement so that it reflects Canada's national interests.

He kept the first two promises, though the navy will eventually require a fleet of alternate choppers and Pearson International Airport will ultimately need alternate administrative arrangements. Despite the controversies they triggered, these were relatively minor issues with few long-term consequences.

But NAFTA is forever.

The deal's impact will be nothing less than to place this country into the jaws of a magnet that will reorient our economy and our society. Whatever elements of Canadian life still functioning along their historical east-west axis will be twisted into north-south channels. That will include highways and truck routes, what's left of the railways and future telecommunications systems. Instead of perpetuating the nation's founding metaphor of Canada as stretching from coast to coast, NAFTA will force our defining horizons to face south.

We have become the citizens not of a country but of a continent which boasts 363 million consumers and a gross domestic product that at $7.5 trillion is $1.5 trillion larger than that produced annually by members of Europe's vaunted economic union. It all sounds dandy until we do a reality check. Just how much influence will we have in this new constellation of political and economic forces? Judging by

Chrétien's failure to alter a single comma in the NAFTA agreement that he was pledged to change, the answer seems to be—roughly none.

If under the original Canada-U.S. Free Trade Agreement we were limited to the influence of a mouse scratching the imperious hide of an elephant, under NAFTA, we are about to assume the clout of a flea. The reason for this reduced status—and the comparison may not hold because determined fleas can make even big guys squirm—is that the Mexican deal is only the first step in a set of alliances being planned by Washington to transform the hemisphere into its own giant day-care centre, with the kid-nations all dancing for the Yankee dollah.

This is no distant, empty theory. Negotiations to admit Chile into NAFTA are already under way, while Mexico—with the blessing of the U.S. State Department—has signed bilateral agreements with such future NAFTA partners as Guatemala, Honduras, El Salvador and Costa Rica, while also discussing extensions to Colombia and Venezuela. It's all somehow reminiscent of the colonial impulses first enunciated by the Monroe Doctrine, which was basically aimed at giving Washington sway over anything that moves between Alert, at the frozen edge of Ellesmere Island, and Tierra del Fuego, on Cape Horn, the windswept tip of South America.

Even after he won his 1993 majority, at his first post-election press conference, Chrétien was insisting that he would delay NAFTA's implementation unless he got some meaningful concessions from the Americans on the treaty's provisions dealing with energy, water exports, government subsidies and the indiscriminate application of countervailing trade sanctions.

Selling Americans our water, which next to Shania Twain and k.d. lang may be the most precious asset we have left to offer, is the ghost issue of North American trade agreements. The NAFTA and FTA accords don't omit Canadian water as a permitted export commodity, yet Canadian officials keep denying they gave away a single drop of the stuff. More dependable is the word of U.S. chief negotiator Mickey Kantor, who flatly insists that water is part of the deal.

On energy, Chrétien wanted nothing more than the same protection clause the Americans signed with the Mexicans that allows them to retain control over their oil and gas supplies at times of international shortages. In contrast, during such emergencies Canadians will have to go without and place fulfilment of existing contracts to U.S. customers ahead of any oil and gas required for domestic use—no matter how cold the winter. (Last year we exported 2.1 trillion cubic feet of natural gas and 804,000 barrels a day to the U.S. as part of existing long-term contracts.)

On other outstanding issues, working groups have been set up to harmonize definitions of national subsidies and to try and find some method of preventing the Americans from slapping anti-dumping and countervailing import duties on our goods. The authority of these extra-parliamentary bodies is dubious, their mandate vague.

Apart from such administrative considerations, NAFTA's most severe impact on Canada is bound to be on industries with heavy labour contents. Mexican wages are 10 per cent or so of comparative Canadian pay scales, with unskilled workers getting 60 cents an hour, while auto-part makers earn $1.55, compared with $14.71 in Ontario. Andrew Jackson, senior economist with the Canadian Labour Congress, estimates 371,681 jobs will be threatened by the relocation of manufacturing plants to Mexico, once the NAFTA treaty becomes law on January 1, 1994.

Part of President George Bush's motive for initiating the NAFTA process was that failure of the Mexican economy would have led to huge immigration problems for his downhome Texas economy. As it is, an estimated 300,000 Mexicans now move into the U.S. every year. ("Why aren't there any Mexican teams in the swimming and running games?" went a joke going the rounds at the Los Angeles Olympics. The answer: "Because any Mexican who can swim or run already lives in the United States.")

NAFTA is a lousy treaty and Jean Chrétien should sign it in shame. Yet again, a Canadian political leader finds himself trapped between the inevitable rush of history splitting the world into trading blocks—and the frightening reality of how that process will constrict Canada's economic prospects.

The P.M. ought to have stood his ground and kept his promise.

16

YOUNG KEN

HE MOVES THROUGH life with studied gracelessness, doing none of the things one would expect a man of his means and opportunities to venture and enjoy. Deferential to the point of absurdity—and stingy to a point far beyond that—Ken Thomson has turned self-effacement into an art form.

His astonishing communications empire swirls about him, throwing off $4.4 million a week into his personal dividend account, employing 105,000 on four continents, and threatening to become the world's largest multi-media oligarchy. It already ranks fourth—after Germany's Bertelsmann, Capital Cities/ABC and Time Warner Incorporated. Thomson publishes 175 newspapers (with a daily circulation of 4.5 million)—more than any other firm—and circulates or sells an incredible 40,000 other editorial products, including 145 magazines, 188 weeklies, and assorted books, directories, newsletters and software packages.

There's no corporate kingdom quite like it anywhere. Besides his publishing holdings, Thomson owns a real-estate arm (Markborough, with assets of $2.3 billion) and an overseas travel subsidiary that operates 40 per cent of England's package tour business and five hundred Lunn Poly "holiday shops." He also is sole proprietor of Britannia Airways, the United Kingdom's second-largest airline, which carries about six million passengers aboard forty jumbo jets. (Sixteen more are on order.) Because the Thomson companies' debt ratios are unusually low and their credit lines are virtually unlimited, they are in the enviable position of being able to buy any $5-billion property that comes along. And they have.

By mid-1991, Thomson's personal equity holdings were worth $7.7 billion, which, according to the July 22, 1991, issue of *Forbes* that annually ranks the wealthy, made him the world's eighth-richest individual. The listing placed Thomson well ahead of Gerald Grosvenor, sixth Duke of Westminster, who is England's richest man, and such celebrated moneybags as Italy's Giovanni Agnelli, Hong Kong's Li Ka-Shing, the Gettys, the Rothschilds and the Bronfmans. He also happens to be—by quite a wide margin—the richest Canadian.

Unlike these and other worldly figures who qualify as rich and famous—and behave as if they were—Thomson acts as if he lived around the povery line. He leaves few public clues to his private thoughts or personal motivations. Compulsively shy of personal publicity and seldom interviewed except about his art (and for this book), he would much prefer to be invisible, and he in fact almost is. "The lowest profile," he contends, "is the very best to have."

Although he seems scarcely aware of it, Thomson is caught in a time warp between the high-tech world of his communications conglomerate and the unbending Baptist ethic of rural Ontario where he simmered up. "We were raised on the principle that you kept yourself to yourself and that only the members of your close family were your true friends," recalls his niece Sherry Brydson, who grew up with Ken. "You played it close to your chest and believed that only with family could you let your hair down. Ken has taken it a step further. He's got to the point where he doesn't let his hair down with anybody."

Even in his dealings with longtime business colleagues, Thomson demonstrates that air of impenetrable reserve. It is entirely in character that his office, on the top floor of the Thomson Building at the corner of Queen and Bay streets in downtown Toronto, has a moat. Public elevators run to the twenty-fourth floor, but only pre-screened and thoroughly vouched-for visitors are allowed into the private lift that ascends to the twenty-fifth level shared by Thomson and John Tory, his chief corporate strategist.

Thomson's office houses part of his art collection, including most of the 204 canvases by the Dutch-Canadian artist Cornelius Krieghoff that he owns—hanging there, looking as uncomfortable as nuns in a discotheque.

Gathering Krieghoffs is Ken Thomson's most visible passion, but his real cultural hero is a somewhat less exalted artist in a very different discipline: Clarence Eugene "Hank" Snow, the Nova

Scotia–born country singer. Thomson used to regularly visit Hank at the Grand Ole Opry in Nashville, owns all his records, has been to Snow's house in Tennessee and once presented him with a gold Hamilton pocket-watch that had been a family heirloom.

Ken Thomson's psyche is so difficult to penetrate because he behaves like an actor, able to detach himself from whatever crisis might be occupying his mind. Occasionally, very occasionally, an emotion will flicker across his shuttered face, only to be withdrawn quickly, like a turtle's head popping back into its protective shell.

Exceptions to such Bermuda Triangle reticence come unexpectedly.

A FEW SEASONS AGO, Posy Chisholm, a sophisticated and vivacious Toronto socialite who looks smashing in hats, has a profoundly developed sense of the absurd and possesses a remarkable memory, found herself at Heathrow, about to board British Airways Flight 93 to Toronto. When she spotted Ken, the two acquaintances decided to travel together, though Chisholm first had to trade down a class, wondering why Thomson was too cheap to travel in style and comfort.

"You know why I'm flying home?" Thomson asked, when they were settled in their narrow seats.

"No, I don't, not really," Posy replied.

"To give Gonzo his evening meal," the press lord matter-of-factly explained. "I've been away from my dog for five days now, and I miss him so terribly. We were half an hour late leaving London, and I'm really nervous they might give him dinner without me."

"Oh, Ken," Chisholm tried to reassure her agitated companion, "they'll make up time across the ocean."

"Gonzo is crazy in many ways, but very, very lovable," Thomson went on as Posy, crammed into a steerage seat beside the fretting billionaire, began looking longingly down at the heaving Atlantic. "Gonzo is the sweetest dog. He's everybody's pal, especially mine. He's a Wheaton terrier, the colour of wheat, off-white. Actually, he's got a little apricot."

"How about some champagne, Ken? No? Oh well ..."

"Gonzo leads a good life. I plan my trips abroad around him. I never go to annual meetings unless I've got him covered. I couldn't put him in a kennel; he's a member of the family. He seems to have an understanding of what's happening all the time. We communicate. We know what the other is thinking. We love each other."

"I suppose you take him walking ..."

"Oh, I take him out all the time. Early in the morning, late at night, and every time I can in between. If I can't get home for lunch, my man goes up and walks him. He might be there right this minute. Gonzo's got to have his exercise."

"Doesn't he have a garden?" asked Posy, grasping for relevance.

"He doesn't want to stay out all day. Gonzo's a people dog. He likes walking in the park and then he wants to come back inside."

It was going to be a long flight.

Chisholm remembered a friend joking that if she was ever reincarnated, she wanted to come back as Ken Thomson's dog. So Posy told him, hoping the idea might amuse the single-minded tycoon.

"Well, she'd be well looked after," was the earnest reply. "I tell you, Gonzo is a big part of my life. I know that sounds awfully funny. But it's a fact. I think of him all the time. I look after him like a baby."

"What about your wife—does Marilyn love Gonzo too?"

"One time, I was looking at Gonzo, and I said to Marilyn, 'Geez, he wants something.'

"She said, 'We all want something.'

" 'Yes, but he can't go to the refrigerator and open the door. Gonzo can't tell you he's got a pain in his tummy. We've got to look after him, anticipate everything he wants. It might be a bit of food he needs, maybe to go out or just a show of affection.' "

At this point Thomson leaned forward to emphasize the significance of what he was about to reveal. "I tried to figure what Gonzo was really after," he confided. "It's a game we play."

"So, what did Gonzo end up wanting?" Posy Chisholm halfheartedly inquired—purposefully fumbling under her seat, hoping that was where they kept the parachutes.

"A bikkie!" exclaimed the world's eighth-richest man. "That's what Gonzo wanted—a bikkie!"

There followed a lengthy silence. Thomson seemed satisfied

there was little point trying to top that remarkable bit of canine mind-reading.

About half an hour out of Toronto, he started to get restless because the 747 had been unable to make up the original delay and was not going to arrive at 17:35, as scheduled. He put on his coat and complained so bitterly he might miss getting home in time for his dog's feeding, that Chisolm suggested she take his luggage through customs and drop it off at his house—while he dashed through the terminal, bound for Gonzo.

KEN THOMSON SIGHTINGS are like that. If he knows and trusts the person he's with, he will talk about his dog or his art collection, but that's it. Unlike nearly every other rich and powerful individual of even a tenth his wealth and influence, he leaves few contrails. "The smartest thing those who have more than anybody else can do is not to flaunt it," he says. "It's resented and it's in terribly bad taste. It shows a poor sense of priority.

"Everybody has their own ways of doing things," he allows. "It's all a matter of temperament. A lot of people who make money fast spend it fast. It's very difficult to live a simple life and love your dog as much as I do. I spend as much time as I can with my family, walking Gonzo, watching a fair bit of television. I like to get in my car and fill it up with gas. So if you add up running the business with all the personal things I do, there's not an awful lot of time and energy left after that. I am as happy as can be."

Walking your dog and filling your car with gas may well be the path to eternal happiness, but those who know Thomson best insist that he is not as content as he claims. "He's not a man doing his choice of things," insists his niece. "If he had two or three brothers, he would never have chosen—or been chosen—to run the family empire. I get the impression of someone doing his duty. He is intensely loyal and was very attached to his father, so when my grandfather said, 'I'm going to start a dynasty and you're going to carry it on,' Ken said, 'Right.' It didn't really matter that he might have preferred to be the curator of an art museum—and now he's training his son David to take over, just as his father wished. He's doing it with goodwill but not much joy. Every morning when he wakes up he must say to himself, 'I'm unhappy being a businessman, but wait a minute, it's bringing me all this other stuff like my art collection that I couldn't otherwise have—so it's a trade-off.' "

Everything Ken Thomson says and does underlines that he's fundamentally decent, that he would be quite happy to have his epitaph read: "What a Nice Guy." He really *is* a nice guy, but he is much more than that—and despite his pose as the ultimate *innocente*, his self-assurance can be devastating. For instance, he readily conceded to a *New York Times* reporter in early 1980 that "there is a limit to how many papers one man, or company, should own," insisting that his own firm had yet to grow to such "ludicrous" extremes. "We will know ourselves, if and when we do," he reassured the dubious Commissioners on the 1980 Royal Commission on Newspapers. Thomson then owned forty daily and twelve weekly Canadian newspapers, one of the largest concentrations of press ownership in any democratic country.

The best evidence of Ken Thomson's success in perpetuating his anonymity is that most Canadians, even fairly sophisticated businessmen, still regard him as the youthful and untried inheritor of the publishing empire built up by his father, Roy Thomson. They dismiss the current press lord as "Young Ken," an immature figurehead whose main accomplishment was to be his father's only son.

"Young Ken" is in fact seventy-four years old.

"I'm not young any more, but I don't really mind being called 'Young Ken,'" says he. "My dad was such an unusual individual that nobody can expect to be anywhere near a carbon copy of him. He was one of a kind. He channelled his ambition in a single direction and everything emanated from that. Now it's a different world we live in."

Ken has force-fed his father's business empire from annual revenues of $725 million in 1976, when he took over, to $11.5 billion a decade and a half later. The total equity value of the companies he controls has sky-rocketed from less than $1 billion to more than $11 billion, exponentially surpassing Roy Thomson's impressive rate of annual growth and ranking second only to Bell Canada in terms of market capitalization of Canadian corporations.

In 1989, following sale of the Thomson Group's North Sea oil holdings for $670 million, its publishing assets were combined into an umbrella organization (the Thomson Corporation). Ken uncharacteristically boasted that it would allow him to set his sights on any target. "I can't imagine any publishing company anywhere in the world that would be beyond our ability to acquire," he gloated.

Ken Thomson leads a double life, and enjoys neither. In England—and most of non–North America where titles still mean something—he is Baron Thomson of Fleet of Northbridge in the City of Edinburgh, the hereditary peerage bestowed on his father on January 1, 1964, two days before he lost his Canadian citizenship for accepting a British title. "I regret giving up Canadian citizenship," Roy Thomson said at the time, "but I had no choice. I didn't give it up. They took it away from me. They gave me the same reward you give a traitor. If I had betrayed my country, that's the reward I would get—taking away my citizenship. Canada should allow titles. If you get a title from the Pope, there's no trouble accepting that."

What happened was that Roy Thomson turned down Prime Minister John Diefenbaker's 1959 offer to appoint him Governor General of Canada. "It wouldn't have suited me very well because I'm too much of an extrovert for that," Roy declared at the time. "I can't conceal my feelings very easily. I talk too much, everybody says, but I talked myself into more deals than I ever talked myself out of, so I'm still ahead of the game. At any rate, it worked out for the best. Since then, I've got a hereditary peerage. And I'm a Knight Grand Cross of the Order of the British Empire, that's a GBE, which is the highest degree of the Order of the British Empire. That entitles you to be 'Sir.' If I hadn't got a peerage I'd be Sir Roy, so I'm right at the top of the heap."

During their visits to England, the present Lord and Lady Thomson live in a four-bedroom flat (purchased for $180,000 in 1967) in Kensington Palace Gardens, off Bayswater Road. It was used for interrogating high-ranking Nazi officers during the Second World War. A secluded street with extra police protection, this is where many of the ambassadors to the Court of St. James have their residences. While abroad, the introverted Ken and Marilyn Thomson of Toronto are transformed into the introverted Lord and Lady Thomson of Fleet, using their titles, with two sets of clothing and accessories as well as stationery and visiting cards. "I lead a dual life and I'm getting away with it!" Thomson delights. "It actually works."

One place it doesn't work is in the House of Lords. Ken has never taken up his father's seat in Westminster's august Upper Chamber, nor does he intend to. The older Thomson glowed with pride the day he received his title. After celebrating by queuing up at Burberrys for a cashmere coat reduced from the British equivalent of $150 to $80, he had his official coat of arms carved on his office door (it features the bizarre image of a beaver blowing an Alpine horn under the motto "Never a Backward Step"). When one elderly London dowager persisted in calling him "Mr. Thomson," he barked: "Madam, I've paid enough for this goddamn title, you might have the good grace to use it."

Having been elevated to the House of Lords, Thomson seldom attended its sessions and didn't particularly enjoy himself when he did. "I've made a lot of money, but I'm not the brightest guy in the world, by a hell of a long ways," he once commented. "I've found that out since I've been in the House of Lords. About 90 per cent of the things they discuss there, I'm a complete ignoramus about. I've got a one-track mind, but I bloody well know my own business.

"For Dad, the title symbolized what he had achieved from nothing, and he made me promise I wouldn't give it up," Ken recalls. "He told me he'd like to see me carry it on because he rightly suspected I was the type of person who might not want to. I remember telling him, 'Well, Dad, I think you're a little naughty to ask me to do that. Because everybody should have the right to make his own decisions in this world. But after what you've done for me, if you really want me to, I'll make you that promise.' Now, I didn't promise him I'd use the title in Canada or that I'd take up my seat in the House of Lords. So now I'm happy to have it both ways."

Another of the inheritances from his father was the attitude that while making money was holy, spending it was evil. The Thomson style of penny-pinching—father and son—goes well beyond sensible parsimony; it combines Ebenezer Scrooge's cruder instincts with a cold and mean view of life that transcends commonly accepted behaviour. "Nobody has any sympathy for a rich man except somebody that's richer again," Roy once ruminated. "I

mean, hell, I eat three meals a day and I shouldn't. I should probably eat two. And I only have so many suits of clothes, and I'm not
very particular about my dress anyway, and I can't spend, oh, not a
small fraction of what I make, so what the hell am I doing? I'm not
doing it for money. It's a game. But I enjoy myself. I love work. I
like to be successful. I like to look at another paper and think, Jesus,
if only that was mine. Let's have a look at the balance sheet."

Roy Thomson's approach to spending was best summed up in
the marathon bargaining sessions he staged when he was renting
space for his Canadian head office at 425 University Avenue in
downtown Toronto. The landlord, a hyperactive promoter who had
a tight-fisted reputation of his own to uphold, despaired of reaching any reasonable rental agreement because Thomson's offer was
so far below rates charged for comparable space elsewhere. When
the press lord finally wore him down, the building's owner gasped
in reluctant admiration, "Mr. Thomson, you really are cheap!" To
which an indignant Roy Thomson responded, "I'm not cheap!
You're cheap! I'm cheap *cheap!*"

The photographs of the original Lord Thomson weighing his
baggage so he wouldn't have to pay extra on his economy flights
across the Atlantic, going to work on London's Underground, or
lining up for cafeteria lunches created a comic mask that somehow
took the hard edge off his business deals. His outrigger spectacles,
with lenses as thick as Coke-bottle bottoms, magnified his glinting
blue eyes as he peered at the world with Mister Magoo–like good
humour, hiding his touch of icy cunning. Thomson carefully cultivated the image of himself as the living embodiment of the profit
motive on the hoof. Seated next to Princess Margaret at a fashion
show, he spotted a lamé gown on one of the models. "My favourite
colour," he told the Princess. "Gold!" During Thomson's 1963 encounter with Nikita Khrushchev, the Russian dictator teasingly
asked what use his money was to him. "You can't take it with you,"
said Khrushchev. "Then I'm not going," shot back a determined
Thomson.

Ken Thomson's scrimping habits are equally mingy, if less well
known. Although he is a member of six of Toronto's most exclusive
clubs—the York, Toronto, National, York Downs, Granite and
Toronto Hunt—he prefers to lunch by himself at a downtown

yogurt bar, if he's not home walking Gonzo. He does most of his shopping on department-store bargain days.

Murray Turner, a former Hudson's Bay Company executive who knows Thomson slightly, was shopping in the Loblaws store at Moore and Bayview when he heard a shout, "Murray! Murray!" and saw Thomson beckoning to him. As he reached the side of the world's eighth-richest man, it was obvious that Thomson could hardly contain himself. "Lookit," he exclaimed, "lookit this! They have hamburger buns on special today. Only $1.89! You must get some." Turner looked in disbelief at Thomson's shopping cart, and sure enough, there were six packages of buns, presumably for freezing against a rainy day. "I'd walk a block to save a dime at a discount store," Thomson readily admits.

On the same day he spent $640 million on a corporate takeover, Thomson met George Cohon, the Canadian head of McDonald's, and asked him for a toy Ronald McDonald wristwatch. Cohon sent him one of the free timepieces (used mainly for internal promotions), but the very next day Thomson's secretary was on the phone claiming the watch had gained four minutes over the past twenty-four hours and asking where his Lordship could get it fixed. Cohon ordered another watch sent to him, but the messenger had strict orders to bring back the original gift.

The press lord appears to dress well (his shoes are from Wildsmith's on London's swank Duke Street), but his suits are made for him by a cut-rate tailor in Toronto's Chinatown at $200 apiece from the discounted ends of bolts he picks up during his journeys to Britain. In Toronto, he lives in a twenty-three-room mansion behind a set of handsome gates at the top of Rosedale's Castle Frank Road, built in 1926 by Salada Tea Company president Gerald Larkin. A prime example of Ontario Georgian-style architecture, the dwelling is rundown, its curtains left over from its first owner. The Thomsons (Marilyn's parents live with them in a coach-house) usually eat in the kitchen to save electricity, and the family is unable to retain housekeepers because of the low pay. Even the help's food is rationed. Most cookies are kept in a box with the Thomson name lettered on it. A strict allocation of two of Mr. Christie's best is placed on a separate plate to feed the rotating parade of cleaning women.

Besides the London flat, the only other Thomson residence is in Barbados, where he owns the Southern Palms Hotel. To maximize profits, Ken and Marilyn stay in a third-floor walk-up apartment whenever they visit, instead of occupying one of the more luxurious main-floor suites. Toronto travel impresario Sam Blyth has occasionally booked them aboard West Indies cruises on a travel agent's discount.

Thomson owns a Mercedes 300-E but usually drives his ancient Oldsmobile ("it clunks around but it's the car that Gonzo prefers") and once purchased a red Porsche turbo. ("Honestly, not one of my more practical expenditures. I was thrilled at first but I hardly use it—I've probably driven not more than twenty-five miles in it this summer.") The Thomsons seldom entertain and seldom go out. When they do, preparations include discreet calls to find out precisely what other guests have been invited, whether anyone will be smoking or drinking, and how soon they might comfortably leave.

There is much argument among his headquarters staff over how much cash Ken Thomson actually spends per week. Some insiders claim it's twenty dollars; others insist it's at least forty dollars. No one bids any higher. He has credit cards but seldom, if ever, uses them. "It's an idiosyncrasy," says John Tory, his chief confidant. "It's just very difficult for Ken to put his hand in his pocket and spend money. Yet he's extremely kind and generous. When we're rushing to a meeting and we're late, if he sees a blind man, he'll stop, miss a couple of lights and help him cross the street." Tory didn't need to add that the blind man gets no money. Thomson himself won't discuss his spending habits. "I agree with my father that you should use only a small portion of your money on yourself and that you have some kind of obligation to do something useful with the balance. He thought the most beneficial thing you could do with money was to invest and reinvest it, to keep it growing—and so do I."

Like son, like father.

THE SAGA OF ROY Herbert Thomson, whose father was a Toronto barber, quit school at fourteen to become a five-dollar-a-week clerk and in 1931 purchased a fifty-watt radio station in North Bay, Ontario, and another later at Timmins—so he could sell the radio sets he was lugging along country roads—is one of the sustaining legends of Canadian capitalism. Less well known is the way the hardships of the Great Depression permanently imprinted themselves on generations of the Thomson clan. "I'm still horrified by people who don't make soup stock out of meat scraps," says Ken's niece, who spent her youth in the communal Thomson home at Port Credit, just west of Toronto. "And if you were making a custard with three egg yolks, you could have knocked me over with a feather the first time I saw a woman throw the egg whites down the drain. That just wouldn't occur to me; the whites are tomorrow's dessert. You used everything and got into the rhythm of making your own jam and freezing your vegetables." (At about that time Roy's daughter Irma had to canvass funds from neighbours to get the roof of the Thomson house fixed because Thomson refused to spend the money.)

The Port Credit household, which for a time included not only Ken but also his sisters, Irma (Sherry's mother) and Phyllis Audrey, and most of their children, was run according to stern, puritanical precepts. "Granddad loved us very much," Sherry recalls, "but the affection was always very gruff. It was a staunch, didn't-come-from-much kind of family, so that signs of affection came out almost by accident, as asides." She remembers her mother being locked out by Roy, the family patriarch, if she ventured home after midnight. This was not when Irma was a teenager but well into her thirties, divorced, with a nine-year-old daughter, and dating again. Luckily the family had German shepherds and a dog porthole had been cut into the sunroom door. Irma's dating partners still recall having to push her, 1940s dirndl and all, through the dog door after they had bidden their goodnights. "They could only do that in the summer," according to Sherry, "because in other seasons, the ground got too wet. When I became a teenager I was locked out by my mother in turn, and had to climb up the trellis."

Young Ken had attended elementary school in North Bay, where he worked summers as a disc jockey in his father's radio station, CFCH. His main job was to play background noises meant to evoke the crowd sounds and clinking glasses of a ballroom, while big-band dance numbers were on the air, but he also fell in love with the music of Hank Snow and dreamed someday of actually meeting him. When the family moved to Toronto, young Ken was enrolled in Upper Canada College. After an unsuccessful year at the University of Toronto, he joined the Royal Canadian Air Force but was never promoted beyond Leading Aircraftman, the equivalent of a lance-corporal in the army, spending most of the war as an editorial assistant on *Wings Abroad*, a propaganda weekly. He took his discharge in London and spent two years at Cambridge, though the university had no discernible effect on him. After spending a year on the editorial staff of his father's Timmins *Daily Press*, he moved back to Southern Ontario where Roy Thomson had acquired the Galt *Evening Reporter* as one of four dailies he picked up in 1944. His five-year apprenticeship there was an important formative influence, as were the weekends he spent at the Port Credit house.

Roy Thomson had moved to Scotland in 1954 but returned to the family homestead in summer and at Christmas. The elder Thomson held court while watching the TV set in front of him, listening to the radio beside him, petting the Scottie dog at his feet, eating fruit from a bowl with a little paring knife, all the while reading a murder mystery.

Young Ken loved frightening his nieces and nephews, especially when they slept in garden tents during the summer. "He'd put a sheet over his head and ghost us," Sherry recalls. "Or he'd hide behind a bush and make fake owl noises. But we always knew it was him and we'd yell, 'Oh Kenny, stop it!' He was very much the tease."

By the late 1950s, Roy Thomson had not only acquired the prestigious *Scotsman* but had also won control, in what was the world's first reverse takeover bid, of the huge Kemsley chain that included London's influential *Sunday Times*. Roy's lucky streak broke in 1967, when he acquired *The Times*, Britain's great journal of record. *The Times* may not have lost its lustre under Thomson, but it lost him bags of money. (The extent of *The Times* authority was best summed up in a *Punch* cartoon, depicting a secretary walking into a British company president's office to announce: "Sir, the gentleman from *The Times* and the press are here.")

Thomson had by this time become a fixture among British press lords. He could always be depended upon to say something mildly outrageous and to pose for yet one more photograph showing off his skinflint habits. "They say business is the law of the jungle," was a typical sally. "I think it's the law of life. If you want to prosper, you've got to be ambitious. You've got to be ready to sacrifice leisure and pleasure, and you've got to plan ahead. I was forty years old before I had any money at all. But these things don't happen overnight. Now, how many people are there that will wait that long to be successful, and work all the time? Not very many. Maybe they're right. Maybe I'm a bloody fool. But I don't think I am."

American tycoons J. Paul Getty and Armand Hammer approached Thomson in 1973, offering a 20 per cent share in their Occidental consortium preparing to drill in the North Sea where Phillips Petroleum had already found valuable indications. Roy bet his family's (as opposed to his company's) fortune on the play, though oil was then worth only $3.60 a barrel. When Occidental struck the giant Piper field and later the Claymore—and prices climbed to $14 a barrel—Thomson almost overnight earned $500 million.

"Most people would say, 'I wouldn't want to do what you've done, even for your success,'" Roy reminisced in one of his last interviews. "They'd say, 'You've missed a lot out of life and success hasn't made it all worthwhile.' But it has to me. It's just a matter of ambition and determination, you keep plugging away. I learn more from my failures than I learn from my successes, because I learn bloody well not to do them again. Nothing has ever happened to me in my life that hasn't been for the best. Now I accept death. I lost my wife. I lost a daughter, but those things, I mean, you can't measure them in terms of happiness or success or failure. I'm a very imperfect individual, and I've done a lot of things I shouldn't have done, but I honestly am not a person who caused anybody any suffering if I could help it."

Henry Grunfeld, former chairman of S.G. Warburg, the London merchant bankers who had helped finance Thomson, remembers his last conversation with Roy in the bank's Terrace Room at its Gresham Street headquarters. "It was about three weeks before his death and we both knew it was the last time we would meet. He told me he was worth about $750 million, or whatever it was, and complained bitterly how much he wished he could have made a billion. 'Why, haven't you got enough, Roy?' I remember asking, especially since he was so obviously very ill. He looked surprised, as if he had never considered the question, and shrugged, 'Henry, it's just for the fun of it ...' It was pathetic."

Thomson died on August 7, 1976, and Ken was suddenly in charge. His father had passed away both too soon, because the younger Thomson was not ready to take over, and too late—because Ken was by this time fifty-three years old and had spent most of his adult life following his father a tactful step behind like a commercial version of Prince Philip. Inheriting a father's business is difficult; succeeding as powerful and articulate an individual as Roy Thomson—recognized as a folk hero of capitalism—was impossible. Ken tried valiantly to turn himself into an extrovert but quickly conceded that it was mission impossible. "The nice thing about my dad was that he was so unusual. No one in his right mind could expect me to be the same. I'd be happy to go unnoticed. I've tried to be a good, sound businessman in my quiet way, but I can't say I've been a slave to business. I've tried to strike more of a balance between my personal and business lives." His father's friend and adviser, Sidney F. Chapman, summed up the situation more succinctly: "When you live in the shadow of a legend, you don't go flashing mirrors."

Ken's first major decision was to cut family ties with the The Sunday Times and The Times, where union problems had forced suspension of publication for eleven months. During their twenty-one-year stewardship the Thomsons, father and son, had poured at least $2 million into the properties without any significant return. Their loyalty to those great institutions without any apparent fiscal controls was totally out of character. Thomson sold the two papers for the value of the land and buildings to Rupert Murdoch, and gradually moved his businesses back to Canada.

The company owned forty-three daily and eleven weekly Canadian newspapers at the time. They ranged geographically from the Nanaimo Daily Free Press on Vancouver Island to the Evening Telegram in St. John's, Newfoundland. What they had in common, apart from ownership, was a blandness so pervasive that no self-respecting fish could bear being wrapped in one of their pages. "Disliking Ken Thomson, let alone detesting him, is wholly impossible," confessed Richard Gwyn, a leading Canadian commentator who once worked for him. "He radiates niceness from every pore, down to the holes in the sole of his shoes. He's self-effacing, shy, unpretentious, soft-spoken. He peppers his conversations with engaging archaisms, like 'golly' and 'gee whiz.' But then you stop feeling sympathetic, because you realize that his innocence is just a synonym for timidity. And you realize at the same instant that the reason Thomson newspapers are bland is that they are led by the bland."

The Thomson operational code had been set down by Roy and it didn't initially change much under Ken. Both Thomsons regarded editors as expendable eccentrics and Clifford Pilkey, then president of the Ontario Federation of Labour, once called their company "a vicious organization, certainly not compatible with what I describe as decent, honourable labour relations." Reporters did not receive free copies of their own newspapers, and earnest bargaining went on to deprive delivery kids of half a cent in their meagre take-home pay. Most positions had fixed salary limits, so that anyone performing really well would inevitably work himself or herself out of a job. In pre-computer days, Thomson papers sold their used page mats to farmers as chicken-coop insulation and Canadian Press teleprinters were adjusted from triple to double spacing to save paper. Each newsroom telephone had a pencil tied to it, so there would be no wasteful stubs floating around. "God help us if they ever realize there are two sides to a piece of toilet paper," one publisher was heard to whisper at a management cost-cutting meeting. In a thesis he wrote for the Carleton School of Journalism, Klaus Pohle, the former managing editor of the Lethbridge *Herald*, documented the Thomsonization of his former paper, coining an appropriate name for an increasingly frequent process.

In the winter of 1980, Thomson had used some of his North Sea oil proceeds to purchase, for $130 million, a major Canadian newspaper chain, FP Publications Limited, but that projected him into new and unfamiliar territory. FP had fielded an impressive Ottawa news bureau under the capable direction of Kevin Doyle (later the editor of *Maclean's*) that included such stars of Canadian journalism as Allan Fotheringham, Walter Stewart and Doug Small. The bureau regularly beat the Parliamentary Press Gallery to the news, but it didn't fit in with Thomson's usual barebones operation. When FP's Edmonton bureau chief, Keith Woolhouse, who was working out of his one-bedroom apartment, asked for a wastebasket, Thomson's executive vice-president, Brian Slaight, wasn't going to stand still for such an outrageous request. Doyle tried to diffuse the situation by offering to send out an extra waste-basket from the Ottawa office.

"Is it excess to the Ottawa bureau?" Slaight, ever the champion of independent editorial control, sternly demanded.

Doyle, about to break the news of Prime Minister Pierre Trudeau's resignation, calmly replied, "Well, if you mean, do we *really* need it, no, I guess we don't."

At last, a triumph for head office. Slaight could hardly contain himself. "We have a truck that goes from Ottawa to Toronto to Winnipeg, then on to Edmonton. If we put the wastebasket on the truck, it will hardly take up any room, and won't cost us a cent!"

So the wastebasket jauntily journeyed across the country, and it took only a week and a half to reach its destination. But the Edmonton bureau's troubles were far from over. Woolhouse wanted to rent an office and needed furniture. Slaight vetoed the initial $1,600 estimate but later approved a bid of $1,100 from a local re-possession centre. That didn't save Woolhouse. He permanently blotted his copybook by purchasing his pens and paper clips on the open market instead of from the repossession house. The Edmonton bureau was soon closed, as was the entire FP news operation.

The FP purchase had also thrown the Thomson organization into the unusual position of having to operate newspapers against local competition, especially in Ottawa, where its *Journal* was up against the Southam-owned *Citizen*; in Winnipeg, its *Free Press* was head to head with Southam's *Tribune*; and in Vancouver its *Sun* had to compete with Southam's *Province*. That ran strictly against Thomson's publishing philosophy, which perpetuated his father's dictum that what's important "isn't the circulation of one's own news-paper, it's the circulation of the opposition's. Even being second-largest is no good. Only the largest is worth buying." The dilemma was neatly resolved on August 27, 1980, when Southam closed the Winnipeg *Tribune* while Thomson shut the Ottawa *Journal* and Southam bought out Thomson's interest in the Vancouver *Sun*— throwing 800 employees on the street. The Ottawa move was particularly puzzling because the *Journal*'s circulation had climbed

25 per cent in the previous six months and its advertising linage was the highest in eight years. But looking back on that Black Wednesday, Thomson wouldn't change a thing. "Nobody likes to see people lose their jobs," he says. "We didn't take any satisfaction in that. But the situation at the *Journal* was hopeless and it was never going to get any better. We couldn't give the paper away for a dollar. We tried nine different buyers. Nobody else wanted it. Somebody had to draw the curtain. So when Gordon Fisher of Southam told us he was going to close his paper in Winnipeg, he suggested we close them both on the same day. I thought it was a good idea because I knew if he closed his paper first, people would come to me and ask, are you going to close yours, and I didn't want to lie to them. So when he said, 'Why don't we do it the same day?' I said, 'Oh boy, we'll be in real trouble—but let's do it.'"

Trouble came in the form of a royal commission, headed by Tom Kent, a former *Economist* and Winnipeg *Free Press* editor, who labelled the Thomson publications as "small-town monopoly papers that are, almost without exception, a lacklustre aggregation of cash-boxes" and suggested the organization be forced to sell its flagship publication in Toronto, *The Globe and Mail*, purchased in 1980. The recommendation was not followed up, but the hearings brought into the public consciousness Thomson's utilitarian code of editorial independence. "We operate our newspapers in a highly decentralized manner, delegating operating authority to publishers," Ken Thomson told the Commission's opening session. "We have vested in our publishers the responsibility and the autonomy to decide what news, information and comment should be published daily in their newspapers." That was true enough, and there was no more eloquent witness to that philosophy than Harold Evans, the former editor of both *The Times* and *The Sunday Times*, who wrote in his memoirs that the difference in ownership between the Thomsons and Rupert Murdoch was "a transition from light to dark." Neither of the Thomsons has, in fact, cast much of an editorial shadow over their publications. The problem is that editorial budgets ultimately decide any publication's content, and that was—and is—how the Thomsons exercise control. Since the Kent hearings, John Tory impressively improved both the Thomson papers and the working conditions under which they're produced.

The severest test of Thomson's hands-off attitude was the *Globe* story about the newspaper closings written by Arthur Johnson, quoting the press lord's heartless comment on the plight of those who had lost their jobs: "Each one has to find his own way in this world." Johnson firmly stuck to his version, but Thomson categorically denies having made the comment. "I explained for twenty minutes how we had gone way beyond our statutory obligations in severance arrangements, but that we were not prepared to see the company's assets dissipated because we didn't have the guts to face up to the flak. I never said anything about everyone having to make his own way in the world, even though that quote will go down in history with me. I would never say that. I know I'm not brilliant, but even I can figure that one out." He didn't phone the *Globe* to complain, but six weeks later he met publisher Roy Megarry at a Royal York Hotel reception and let him have it. "Jesus, Roy, the *Globe* misquoted me terribly," he complained. "They put the worst words in my mouth. I never phoned you about it, but I wish I had."

"Geez, Ken," Megarry replied, "I wondered at the time why you'd make such a statement and I talked it over with the editor involved, but he insisted that you had said it."

"You'll have to take my word for it. I didn't. I'm not that stupid."

Megarry, who persuaded Thomson to invest $65 million in turning the *Globe* into a national newspaper, insists there has been no editorial interference from the Thomson head office, a few blocks away. "It's one thing to own the Barrie *Examiner* and not interfere editorially," he says. "It's another to own the *Globe* in the city where you reside and resist the temptation to put on pressure. But they haven't." On Thomson's sixtieth birthday, Megarry edited a special one-copy issue of the *Globe*, substituted on his doorstep for the real thing, that had a front page with Ken's picture on it and several feature stories about Gonzo. "That morning, Ken did phone me," Megarry recalls, and said, " 'What are you doing, you rascal?'—he frequently refers to me as a rascal—and admitted he had been stunned, because for a split second he thought it really was that day's *Globe*. 'It was a cute thing to do,' he later commented, 'but I hope it didn't cost the company too much money.' "

DURING THE LATE 1970s, Ken Thomson enjoyed a unique problem. With oil prices up to as much as $34 a barrel, his share in the North Sea fields purchased by his father was throwing off annual revenues of $200 million. That's not the kind of sum you keep in a savings account. Tax reasons, plus the wish to get into hard assets, dictated new acquisitions, but the chain had run out of cities, towns and even villages where they could maintain monopolies. Thomson went shopping for a safe, timeless investment for his family.

While on a flight to London, John Tory passed over to Ken an annual report of the Hudson's Bay Company, with the comment, "This is one you should think about." That struck Thomson as a weird coincidence because he *had* been thinking about the Bay, ever since Fred Eaton at a party had mentioned that the HBC was lucky because so much of its profit flowed from non-merchandising sources. "It was like mental telepathy," Thomson recalled of the airplane conversation. At first glance, the Hudson's Bay Company seemed a perfect takeover target. It certainly carried the kind of historic pedigree that would please a British-Canadian lord, it was widely held with no control blocks that would have demanded premium prices and it was a well and conservatively managed enterprise, ideal for the Thomson methodology of acquiring companies that turned decent profits without requiring day-to-day involvement. "It looked to me like a business that in the inflationary environment of that time would do quite well, because the top line was pushed up by price increases while many of the costs, including store leases, were fixed," John Tory recalled. "Also I knew that Simpsons, which they had just taken over, was not well managed, so that a turnaround would have impressive bottom-line results." (There is another theory why Thomson settled on the Bay. He walked Gonzo most often through Craigleigh Gardens, near his Rosedale home, and at night the most visible object from the shrubbery is the ochre neon sign at Yonge and Bloor, announcing "The Bay! The Bay!")

On March 1, 1979, Ken Thomson and John Tory called on Don McGiverin to announce they were bidding $31 a share—36 per cent over market value—for 51 per cent of the Hudson's Bay Company. At the Bay's board meeting two weeks later, Governor George Richardson reported that in a meeting with Thomson the previous Sunday evening he had failed to persuade him to buy less than 51 per cent. The board decided that the premium offered for control was not high enough and that $37 to $40 would have been a more appropriate amount. That consideration was aborted by the sudden entry into the bidding of grocery magnate Galen Weston, offering $40 for the same percentage, though part of it would have been payable in stock. Unlike Thomson, Weston hinted that he intended to fire most of the HBC executives, replacing them with his own.

In typical Establishment fashion, the first telephone call Thomson received after word of his intended takeover leaked out was from Fred Eaton, "I wish you luck. Welcome to the world of merchandising." The second was from Galen Weston, advising him of the competing bid. By April 2, Thomson and Tory had raised their bid to $35 for 60 per cent of the HBC stock. Weston countered with an improved offer ($40 for 60 per cent), but once Thomson came in with an unconditional cash offer of $37 for 75 per cent of the shares—$276 million more than he had originally been willing to pay—the bidding stopped. The Bay board met on April 4 to approve the takeover formally. The Thomson group made only three demands: a pledge that its equity position wouldn't be diluted by the issue of extra treasury shares; two seats on the Bay board for Thomson and Tory; and alteration of the company's banking arrangements so that the two banks on which the newcomers sat as directors—the Toronto-Dominion and the Royal, which had financed the deal—could get some of the business. (There was so little board discussion on these issues that when Governor Richardson pointed out it was Don McGiverin's fifty-fifth, the directors put aside their business and burst into "Happy Birthday.")

There was one strange incident in the takeover. George Richardson, then on the board of the HBC, made a personal profit of more than $15 million by buying—through his own firm, Richardson Securities—1,059,800 shares of HBC stock in twenty-one separate deals between February 6 and 23, 1979, at an average price of $22.50—nearly $15 below the amount for which he traded them in to Thomson six weeks later. "Lucky George," as he quickly became known, defended his amazing good fortune and the Ontario Securities Commission cleared him of any wrongdoing. But he was worried enough about accusations of insider trading that he devoted half his speech as Governor before the 1979 annual meeting to defending his actions.

KEN THOMSON DID little to enjoy his position as the HBC's proprietor, neither becoming its Governor nor taking part in any of its historic rituals. One exception was a summer journey he took to Baffin Island and Hudson Bay with his wife, Marilyn, two of their children, Lynne and Peter, and George Whitman, the company's Vice-President of Public Affairs, a Second World War pilot who had fought in the Battle of Britain and had since earned a cross-Canada reputation as a social animator. They had just finished lunch at Ross Peyton's tiny hotel at Pangnirtung, on Baffin Island, and Whitman was relaxing on a small rise overlooking the town when up puffed Marilyn and said, "George, I want to do some shopping at that co-op you told me about. You got any money? Here I am, married to the richest man in the country, and he won't allow me to have any credit cards or anything like that. Can I borrow a hundred dollars? But don't tell Ken about it."

Whitman peeled off the bills and she skipped off down to the co-op. Just as she disappeared from view, as if on cue, the world's eighth-richest man came up the hill with the same request. "George, I want to go up to the Bay store and buy some fishing tackle. Can you lend me a hundred dollars?" Later that day, as they were fishing, Ken began to eye Whitman's down-filled vest so wistfully that the Bay man finally told him to take off his Eddie Bauer finery and slip it on. "If you like it, it's yours," Whitman offered, expecting to agree with Thomson's refusal. Instead, the press lord held out his hand and said: "Let's shake on it." And that was the last Whitman ever saw of the vest that had been his Linus blanket on many a northern expedition.

Later that day something significant happened, best recorded in Whitman's diary: "We were fishing on the Kulik River and I had gone back to the boat with a double handful of char, when I heard Paul McIlwain, one of our pilots, shouting: 'George! George! Marilyn's hurt bad!' She was down between two river rocks and had a deep cut between her eyes and down her nose. I pulled my shirt and T-shirt off and bound up her head in them. I carried her to the boat where we met Ken and our Inuit guide. We started across the mile and three-quarters of iceberg-studded water to the first-aid station at Pang, Marilyn in the bow, weeping and still in a state of shock. Me on the motor, Ken mid-ships and the old Inuk in front with Marilyn, telling her a story.

"'In the Kulik River, there's a big mother fish,' he was saying, 'but this year the fish was going to die and there would be no more char in the Kulik. But today you put some of your blood in that river and the mother fish is going to live and we'll always have char.' Having used a little applied psychology, the Inuk moved back and stood between Ken and me. He gave me a nudge with his elbow, and pointing at Ken, asked: 'He good man?'

"I didn't reply for about fifteen seconds because to have given a token response to a deeply personal question like that would have been perceived as flippant. So I waited, and then said, 'Yes, he's a very good man.'

"The Inuk, who was one of Pang's elders, turned to Ken, and carefully crafting his thoughts, said: 'You don't go home. You stay. We take boat, we go down Kingnait Fiord. You come. You catch big char, see polar bear, caribou. We live on the land. You stay with us, my wife, my family, George too.'

"Ken was absolutely mesmerized. He tried to mumble something, but nothing came out. He leaned over and whispered to me, 'Does he really mean it?'

"'Of course he means it.'

"'Well, I can go anywhere. I can go anywhere in the world for a holiday.'

"'Yes, but Ken, there are things that money can't buy. You've just been paid the most tremendous compliment that one man can give another. He's offering to share his life with you.'

"Poor Ken, that kind of generous gesture was completely outside his conceptual frame of reference—that some person from another culture would comfort his wife with a beautiful little made-up fairy tale and pay him the highest tribute that a person in a tribal society can extend to someone who comes from away...."

IF THERE IS ONE SANCTUARY where Ken Thomson can find peace it's in the private world of his art objects. Within these hushed precincts he can build his own aesthetic universe, indulging his whims without the budgetary problems that inhibit most collectors. He richly deserves his reputation as the premier collector of *habitant* scenes by Krieghoff (some selling for as high as $275,000), all of them magically revivified by one of England's best restorers. "He knows every picture the artist painted or attempted to paint and is constantly improving his collection," according to the Earl of Westmorland, the director of Sotheby's in London. "He's got a great eye and a passionate love of art," echoes Christina Orobetz, the president of Sotheby's Canadian company.

The best of his Canadiana collection (conservatively estimated as worth $30 million) is now displayed in a 5,000-square-foot gallery on the top floor of Toronto's main Bay store. "I've reached a plateau," says he. "I've got my collection basically together and have reached the point where I can be very selective with gathering my *objets d'art*." They include the only wood carving Michelangelo ever did, stunning boxwood and ivory carvings and some incredible miniatures by Octavio Jenilla. Death is a recurring theme of his collection, which includes any number of realistically rendered skulls—the carving of a sleeping child using a skull as a pillow, the tableau of a starving wolf being strangled by a skeleton, and a pear-wood skull hinged to reveal a miniature Adam and Eve on one side, and the Crucifixion on the other. The most unusual—and most treasured—objects in his collection are the ship models carved by French prisoners in British jails during the Napoleonic era. They did the carvings to keep from going insane but had few tools or materials, so most of the hulls are fashioned out of the bones of their dead, the rigging braided out of their hair.

As with most of his enterprises, Ken Thomson's art collection is not exactly what it seems. It nearly all belongs to Thomson Works of Art Limited, a company owned by his three children so the increase in value of the collection will be exempted from taxes on his death. The Krieghoff paintings offer their owner an extra incentive: every Christmas, Ken lends one or two canvases to Hallmark, which sends him free Christmas cards bearing the imprint of his painting in return. "They give me a thousand cards free and another four hundred wholesale," he admits. (Naturally, the cards are mailed with unsealed flaps to qualify for the lower rates. The Thomson Christmas card list has carefully noted beside each name the year when its recipient will be removed from his mailings. That's due to retirement from business, or as in the case of the author of this book, when he or she displeases him.)

IN RUNNING HIS COMPLEX operation, Thomson enjoys the advantages of proprietorship, so that he can be wrong without triggering any adverse consequences. He also has the supreme luxury of belonging to a dynasty, so that financial results—good and bad—can be spread over generations instead of having to meet quarterly projections. The HBC's stock values didn't climb back to their original purchase price for more than a decade, but there was never a thought of liquidating or seeking other drastic remedies. "We never have to keep looking over our shoulders at people taking over any of our companies," John Tory points out. "Even when we make major acquisitions that have an initially negative impact on our profitability, in the longer term we'll have a broader base on which we're able to grow. It's really that simple."

Not quite. Tory's real function in the Thomson hierarchy is a source of constant conjecture within and without the organization. "I'm a professional and I never worry about my image," says Tory. "As a business person you can have too high a profile and there's no upside to that whatsoever. When we bought the Hudson's Bay Company there was a big fuss, but we didn't say much; when it was down for the count we said even less; and when it recovered we said nothing." Tory refuses to play the Bay Street game. "I don't need the kind of glory others seek," he says.

It's too easy to speculate that John Tory is the brains behind Ken Thomson, because that wouldn't be fair to either of them. Thomson is smarter than that and Tory is not that self-effacing. As president of most of the family holding companies, Tory exercises enormous influence. He acts as a kind of secretary-general of the $11-billion corporate confederacy, prodding, solving, appointing, acquiring, divesting, trouble-shooting—running the damn thing—but never quite making the ultimate decision by himself. He is not exactly a surrogate, because when he speaks no one knows whether it's really with his voice or Ken's. Veterans of the Thomson organization know that it's usually both, and leave it at that.

Tory reads at least two books a year that have nothing to do with business, loves to parse balance sheets, is happy to work sixteen-hour days, plays some golf and tennis, and skis, but when a friend asked him to go sailing, he discovered that John didn't own a suitable short-sleeved shirt. The centre of his life is his family—four super-bright children (John, Jennifer, Jeffrey, Michael) and ten grandchildren. He plays a mean "After You've Gone" on a barrel-house piano and dabbles in bridge, but his most serious hobby is keeping up with his wife, Liz, Toronto's shrewdest and busiest social animator. As well as his Thomson responsibilities he is a director of Sun Life, Rogers Communications, Abitibi-Price, and, for the past twenty years, the Royal Bank of Canada. "If you asked almost anyone on the Royal board who was the most brilliant guy there," says former deputy chairman John Coleman, "they'd say John Tory. He asks the most pertinent questions and can see through a deal most quickly."

Thomson himself doesn't just admire Tory; he worships the man. "If you take the best qualities of the best people in all the different fields of business and roll them into one—that's John Tory," he says. "For him, working is the same pleasure as I get collecting paintings and walking my dog. Above all, he's got a great wife, family and good friends. They have fun together."

That emphasis on family governs Thomson's own life. "He has so much love and affection for the family and Gonzo," says his son David, "we get so much pleasure just seeing him and trying to make him happier." David likes to quote the maxim of Meyer Guggenheim, the Swiss-born American industrialist who maintained a family dynasty by handing each of his sons a stick and asking them to break it. They did. He then gave each a bundle of sticks, which they couldn't break. "Stand alone, and you will be broken," he told them. "Stand together and no one will break you." The Thomson family very much sticks together; they are proud and protective of one another, especially in tragic circumstances.

Just two weeks before Christmas 1990, Gonzo died.

"I've had the loss of dear ones, human beings," Ken lamented, "but I've never experienced anything that shook me more than his death. Gonzo slept with me the last night. I held the little guy in my arms and I thought, I can't really stand this. I left the room and then I thought, no, he really needs me. I've got to be there. I felt him expire. I don't want ever, ever to go through such a thing again ..."

17

WALL STREET—THE FILM

WALL STREET IS LESS a place than a metaphor. As the world's leading financial centre, the seven-block alley of skyscrapers on the seaward tip of Manhattan Island determines the global price of money.

But in recent years it has also determined America's ethical standards or rather, the lack of them.

In his flawed but powerful movie *Wall Street*, Oliver Stone attempts to define Wall Street's gutter ethic that climaxed with the October 19, 1987, crash. He comes so close to succeeding that at times the film verges on being a documentary.

Stone's portrait of moral decay within the upper reaches of American capitalism suspends disbelief without ever becoming preachy, and it is this gritty quality that makes it so compelling.

The 125-minute film is a lightning-paced morality play in which an ambitious but weak young stockbroker named Bud Fox is ensnared by a Boesky-like mogul, Gordon Gekko, who had an ethical bypass at birth and was "on the phone thirty seconds after the *Challenger* blew up, selling NASA-related stocks." The youthful Fox courts the wily Gekko, is quickly seduced into providing illegal inside information, is betrayed, and in the end incriminates his corrupter.

The movie concentrates on mental rather than physical violation, but is as effective as Stone's classic *Platoon*. The dominant theme of that Vietnam film was that the first casualty of war is innocence; the motif here is that every dream has a price tag—and that most people are willing to pay it.

The twin notions converge in Stone's decision to film downtown New York as a battle zone, so that Wall Street's spiritual tundra becomes less of a backdrop than the movie's main theme. People spend their days transfixed by the eerie glow of computer terminals, frantically dialling for dollars as they try to con their equally greedy customers into buying shares in some company that is "in play." The shouting never stops. Like jumped-up cocaine addicts, the big shooters are in it as much for the game as the gain.

Using hand-held cameras and the best of current *cinéma-vérité* techniques, Stone is able to capture not just the action but the killer instinct of the participants. "If you need a friend," one stockbroker tells a complaining colleague, "get a dog." Another dismisses a beautiful and reputedly sexy analyst at a competing firm with the cutting comment, "Having sex with her was like reading *The Wall Street Journal*."

Even nature turns malignant. The New York sunsets and sunrises have the same ominous quality as the sky changes in *Apocalypse Now*. They create a mood of foreboding that can break at any moment into a feeding frenzy.

Under Stone's direction, the camera becomes a predator, probing the film's characters for vulnerabilities of the soul and body. The most devastating aspect of the screenplay, written by Stone and Stanley Weiser, is that insider trading is accurately portrayed not as a crime, but as a natural outcome of the value system that is in play here. "Come on, who really gets hurt?" is the question continually being asked. "It's ridiculous to have laws that regulate the free market, while muggers waste old ladies in the street. We can buy our freedom. There is justice higher than the law."

Although *Wall Street* has seventy-nine speaking parts, at least three of the main characters play considerably below the potential of their roles. Hal Holbrook is ineffectual as a vaguely idealistic broker. Daryl Hannah tries hard to turn herself into a sort of Hertz bimbo (for rent, but not for sale), but ends up portraying only a pouty indifference meant to reinforce her boyfriend's contention that "money is the sex of the 1980s." The worst casting is Charlie Sheen (Martin's boy) as the corruptible stock broker. At twenty-two, he lacks the face and body language to portray pathos, and his upward mobility is about as interesting as an elevator ride.

Apart from Oliver Stone's sensitivity as a director, what turns *Wall Street* into a fine film is the performance of Michael Douglas as Gordon Gekko. Exuding an irresistible field of force, he is a rat-fink poet with a quip for every occasion. "I bought my way in. Now all those schmucks are sucking my kneecaps," he boasts. "Love is a fiction invented by people to keep them from jumping out of windows." "Lunch is for wimps." Such *bons mots* aside, Gekko brings to life the twisted ethics of Wall Street. His creed is simple: "I create nothing. I own."

His best scene occurs during a successful takeover of Teldar Inc., a faltering New Hampshire wood-products company, when he rises from his seat during a shareholders' meeting to answer the incumbent management's charges that he is solely motivated by greed. "The point is," he insists, "that greed is good. Greed is right. Greed works. Greed clarifies, cuts through and captures the essence of the evolutionary spirit. Greed, in all of its forms—greed for life, money, love, knowledge—has marked the upward surge of mankind. And greed, mark my words, will save not only Teldar, but that other malfunctioning corporation called U.S.A."

That tirade may serve as the quintessential explanation for the Wall Street crash. When men and women equate their net worth with their self worth—not just in a movie but in real life—the social contract has been irrevocably corrupted, and the system explodes.

III GOOD MEN IN WICKED TIMES

18

THE WORLD'S RANKING POLITICAL SAINT

I ONLY MET HIM once, but I've never forgotten my few private moments with Václav Havel, the secular saint who presides over the Czech Republic. It was in Ottawa in 1990, when he was on his way to Washington to address a joint session of Congress (to three standing ovations), and he didn't have much time.

But he was glad to meet someone who could speak Czech with him, to be temporarily relieved from having to rely on his interpreter. (She was a tiny Oriental woman he kept tucked under his left shoulder, who was so good at her job that as local well-wishers addressed him in English, she would whisper to Havel in Czech, lip-read his answer and reply almost instantaneously.)

From our brief exchange, I especially recall two fragments. "I've learned never to be surprised by anything," he shrugged, when I asked how it felt for a beleaguered playwright to suddenly find himself a famous president. To my question about the secret of politics, he shot back: "Write your own speeches and express hard truths in a polite way." Then he paused, and added: "Of course ... everyone is replaceable."

I'm not so sure.

Havel is one of those rare conscience-driven politicians we can't afford to lose. He has kept himself removed from the darker tricks of his craft, never impressed by the fumes of fame or frenzy of renown. Havel believes that character is destiny and that it is therefore supremely important to live a highly principled life, even at the risk of being imprisoned for your beliefs.

He sees history as a stage play, with characters performing in front of ever-changing backdrops. A scruffy man of fifty-five with ginger-coloured hair and an orange moustache (one friend joked, "Václav looks as if carrot juice is flowing through his veins"), he revels in his highly developed sense of the absurd. That comes through most clearly in his plays: absurdist creations in mundane settings with universal characters.

Clearly in the tradition of Franz Kafka and Karel Capek, except for his greater emphasis on the precise meaning of language as a perpetrator or destroyer of political systems, Havel started writing when he was thirteen. Most of his works—none were allowed to be staged for sixteen years before the Velvet Revolution of 1989—deal with the complicated issue of human identity. "All my plays are variations on that theme," he once wrote. "The disintegration of man's oneness with himself and the loss of everything that gives human existence a meaningful order, continuity and its unique outline."

At no time in his career did he get a better chance to test the absurdities of politics than the winter of 1989–1990, when he assumed his country's presidency. That meant moving his office to Hradčany Castle, a huge pile of palaces and cathedrals overlooking the Vltava (Moldau) River, which dissects Prague. Just eight months earlier, he had been serving a four-year sentence in a Communist prison a few kilometres away.

The spiritual catalyst of the bloodless revolt that swept the Communists out of power, he was sworn in as the country's first democratic president since 1938. Being a playwright, one of the first things Havel did was to make sure everyone around him wore the appropriate costume. He asked his friend Theodor Pistek (who won an Academy Award for his costumes in the movie *Amadeus*) to design properly pretentious royal blue parade uniforms—complete with toy sabres—for the castle guards. (When they were delivered, Havel promptly tried one on, and yelling, "Let's go scare the cooks!" ran into the castle kitchens, waving his weapon.) Hradčany is so large that Havel sometimes resorts to getting around the place on a scooter, but after the first few weeks in office he agreed not to come to work in jeans and receive visitors wearing a polka-dot bow-tie. (His first press secretary was Michael Zantovsky, whose main claim to fame was as the author of the only study in Czech of the films of Woody Allen.)

While in office, Havel granted amnesty to 30,000 prisoners (three-quarters of Czechoslovakia's jail population), presided over the peaceful withdrawal of Soviet troops, defied public opinion by supporting the reunification of Germany and brought some badly needed enlightenment to a country that had not known democracy for nearly half a century.

But his main contribution was his evocative speeches, written by himself on a manual typewriter. Probably the best was his 1990 New Year's message. "For forty years, on this day, you heard the same thing in different variations from my predecessors: how our country flourishes, how many tons of steel we produced, how happy we all are, how we trust our government and what bright perspectives were unfolding in front of us. I assume you did not nominate me to this office so that I, too, would lie to you. Our country is not flourishing. Entire branches of industry are producing goods that are of no interest to anyone. A country that once could be proud of the educational level of its citizens spends so little on education that it ranks today as seventy-second in the world."

He went on like that for about ten minutes, then came his real point: "Let us teach both ourselves and others that politics does not have to be the art of the possible, especially if this means the art of intrigues, secret agreements and pragmatic manoeuvrings. But that it can also be the art of the impossible, that is the art of making both ourselves and the world better."

"Man," Havel once wrote from jail, "is in fact nailed down— like Christ on the cross—to a grid of paradoxes. He balances between the torment of not knowing his mission and the joy of carrying it out."

Václav Havel did both, and we're all the better for it.

19

VLÁD THE GREAT

THE DWINDLING ROSTER of money men who once endowed Vancouver with its reputation for nurturing a business ethic that ranked somewhere between piracy and alchemy counts few survivors. They're mostly underwater, in court or have gone legit.

Those bonzo capitalists who ruled Canada's Pacific coast during most of the 1980s were men with pawnbrokers' eyes, a circus mentality and U-turn ethics. Their operational code was confined to a simple gospel that he who dies with the most toys wins. If charged with bending Vancouver Stock Exchange rules, they'd shrug and sweetly explain: "My conscience is clear—I never use it."

Their women were sexy, with shampoo-commercial good looks, yet they seemed hard somehow, exuding the grace and mercy of starving lionesses. Dimples clenched, they would pledge eternal love while detaching their guys' balls, wallets or both.

A few of these hillbilly conquistadors are still making the scene. Behind the potted palms at the Wedgewood Hotel, you can catch the occasional glimpse of Nelson Skalbania, looking more than ever like the lead in a travelling company of *Jesus Christ Superstar*, but he now spends more time flipping lawyers than condos. Peter "The Rabbit" Brown continues to cut deals, but he has served as chairman of the board of governors of UBC, for God's sake; Edgar Kaiser, who once did most of B.C.'s imaginative mega-deals, is deep into french fries; Jack Poole is into prime-time leisure; and Sam Belzberg is deep in doo-doo. Peter Thomas hasn't bought a new Ferrari for a whole month (though he visited the factory this summer), while Murray Pezim has been reduced to posing for T&A shots on magazine covers. (Well, T anyway; one dare not think of his A.)

In truth, capitalism on Canada's Pacific shore has become a tame and predictable affair, with guys actually basing decisions on such boring technicalities as balance sheets and auditors' statements, instead of scribbling deals on the backs of napkins at Chardonnays or across the more elegant tablecloths at Il Giardino.

One exception to this decline in personal audacity is a Serbo-Montenegrin immigrant named Vládimir Plavsic, who hit Vancouver's wilder coast forty years ago and has made it big in just about everything he has done—which includes just about everything worth trying.

A Yugoslav by birth and by persuasion, Vlád (as everybody calls him) looks like one of those square, massive pillars that support old country churches in British tourist posters. But there is nothing stony, still or holy about him. Vlád has the temper of a riled-up Anthony Quinn and an ego the size of Grouse Mountain on a clear day.

I first began to realize the dimensions of the man when, having heard that he was a great sailor (one of my own pretensions), I asked him to a house party. We didn't get to talk much, but I found him examining a poster I have in my living room of one of my heroes, Stan Kenton, whose orchestra pioneered progressive jazz.

"That's Stan Kenton," I hesitantly informed my visitor. "He used to lead a band." Vlád looked at me as if I were a total cabbagehead.

"I know who that is, for Christ's sake!" he exploded. "I used to play in Kenton's trumpet section."

For anyone of my generation and musical persuasion, that was like some guy in your living room boasting he was a Beatle or a Rolling Stone. So I snuck into my study to see if there was a Plavsic in my Kenton discography. It was all true, and as I got to know Vlád a little better I discovered that, among other things, he speaks five languages, had been a violinist as well as a trumpet virtuoso at Yugoslavia's Krsmanovic Conservatory, and was for a time world champion in the 400-metre breast-stroke relay. He was a member of the Yugoslavian water-polo team that won two world cups, and played centre on the country's once formidable hockey team. Within two years of taking up sailing in 1969, he earned Canada its first international racing trophies. Some of his offshore records have yet to be equalled or beaten.

Vlád emigrated to Canada in 1951, along with the half-dozen

members of his country's water-polo team who defected at a meet
in Austria. He studied architecture at the University of Toronto
and later switched to UBC. Impatient to get going, he decided to
take on a full-time job and designed Chilco Towers, then the tallest
buildings in Vancouver's West End, while still a student. That, and
the fact that he kept publicly belittling the UBC architecture faculty, got him temporarily expelled. "The trouble," he modestly explains, "was that I knew a hell of a lot more than my professors—
by far."

Vlád has since completed 425 architectural commissions on
three continents—384 as the architect/planner and 41 as the de-
veloper/owner. He has won eighteen major architectural awards.
Some of his local landmarks include the UBC Thunderbird Sta-
dium, the Spanish Banks condominiums, Monk McQueens restau-
rant, Capilano College, the Bridgeport marina and numerous
Shaughnessy townhouses and downtown office buildings.

Probably his best-known international projects were the development of the 500-acre Marina Vallarta on the Mexican Riviera
and the sixty bowling and shopping centres he built across the U.S.
for a rich Philadelphia family. In 1984, he designed a 420-metre-
long pier that was to have been anchored east of the south side of
the downtown SeaBus terminal. It would have cost $16 million and
provided covered parking as well as tie-up docks for the Expo 86 tall
ships and a floating recreation facility, but he could find no backers.

Vlád became interested in sailing in 1969 and with his then-
girlfriend, Cathy Reid, purchased a thirty-foot Dufour Arpage for a
tour of the Mediterranean. In the first race he entered—the half-ton
world championship in 1971 at Portsmouth—he won a bronze
medal, competing against thirty-four of the world's best sailors. He
later won his division in seven Swiftsures and was overall winner in
1987; aboard his self-designed, forty-one-foot sloop *Kanata*, Vlád
won the Victoria–Maui race in 1980 and on corrected time remains
the record holder to this day. As well as *Kanata*, which he still owns,
he designed two production yachts, the Spencer-34 and Ariel-48.
(In his sailing days, Vlád kept in shape by daily running up and
down the stairs to his seventeenth-floor West End apartment.)

Sailing was so much into his blood that Vlád married his second wife, Karyn Babehuk, in a Serbian Orthodox ceremony aboard

Kanata. Sailbags served as the altar, and Karen arrived off the Plavsic residence at Sunset Beach, steering John Newton's first *Pachena* under a billowing spinnaker. The wedding was consecrated beneath a canopy jury-rigged out of a Canadian flag that had flown on Parliament Hill the previous day. The bride went barefoot so she wouldn't slip on the heaving deck.

Vlád has enjoyed a profitable relationship with Asian investors (he is responsible for attracting $240 million worth of Japanese developments into B.C.) and negotiated reciprocal visiting privileges between the Tokyo Tennis Club (yes, he is a champion tennis player, too), where the Emperor plays, and the Vancouver Lawn & Tennis Club. His latest project is to put together the land for a spa and hotel on some property he has acquired at the foot of the main Whistler Express gondola. He vows it will be the ski resort's "only four-star hotel, much more luxurious than the Chateau, which hasn't turned out to be luxurious at all."

Whatever else he achieves (he described himself recently as a "sixty-year-old teenager"), Vlád Plavsic is a badly needed presence in a Vancouver business landscape starved of those wonderful characters of the 1980s.

20

WALLY'S WALTZ

WHILE THE ENTIRE western world is having a nervous breakdown over the Helms-Burton Trading with the Enemy Act, a former Doukhobor from the Kootenays is busy building eleven hotels in Cuba, exploring two significant gold-silver mines on the forbidden island, entertaining Fidel Castro in Canada—and enjoying every minute of it.

Walter Berukoff is one of those rare Canadian entrepreneurs who operates on the principle that taking risks is fun, and that taking big risks is even more fun. He believes that you are what you do, and having tried just about every trade except piracy, he is now very comfortable as a big-time mining executive. His properties in Yellowknife, Nevada, Cuba and Argentina boast proven reserves of more than three million ounces of gold, held through Miramar Mining Corporation and Northern Orion Explorations Limited. On paper the two companies are worth $1 billion; his various enterprises employ 3,000 and his annual revenues top $400 million.

That's a long way from the scrub of a hidebound life when Berukoff started fifty-one years ago. Wally, as everybody calls him because they can't spell Berukoff, simmered up in Salmo, B.C., a tiny Kootenay settlement between Trail and Nelson. "Being a Doukhobor was my main education," he told me during a recent interview. "My family was expelled from Russia, because according to our religion we were pacifists, burned our guns and wouldn't go to war. It was very tough for me growing up, because there was a local breakaway faction called the Sons of Freedom who set their houses on fire, didn't believe in taxes, and whose wives kept taking off their clothes in public as a form of protest. That reflected on all of us in the community. I used to be asked by taunting kids, 'When is your fat mother going to strip?' and stuff like that. I thought very carefully, even at the age of six, what opportunities I wouldn't have because I was Russian. So, I grew up feeling very much like a sec-ond-class citizen—and that's what has made Wally run ever since."

After graduating from the University of British Columbia, he joined a Vancouver brokerage house run by Ward Pitfield, where he set new records. "I was a millionaire twice by the time I was twenty-three," he recalls, "and broke three times by the time I was twenty-four. I figured out how business works, especially how to use leverage, which means borrowing from the banks, something my family had frowned on, almost as a religious belief." He bought a series of farm-implement plants on credit and eventually became the largest independent agricultural machinery manufacturer on the continent.

Berukoff sold out at a profit in 1971 and bought a steel-manufacturing plant in Kelowna, which he still owns. He then spent most of a decade buying about fifty bankrupt businesses from receivers, rebuilding them, and spinning them off. His next stop was the real-estate business, mainly purchasing hotels, shopping centres and warehouses. "I owned a lot of businesses that people didn't even know were mine, because I've always tried to keep a low profile, and still do," he says. "Mainly I worked hard. I tell my kids, life's a trade-off. If you want to have a whole lot of leisure time, don't expect to have a lot of money. For me, it's been Wally Berukoff Inc., from the day I could walk."

Berukoff drives a tough bargain and has earned his reputation as a bottom feeder. He worked his way through college as an under-ground driller and fell in love with the industry. He got into mining when he bought the Golden Eagle Mine, near Reno, Nevada, and in 1993 acquired the Con Mine in Yellowknife, named after Trail's Consolidated Mining & Smelting which had originally been placed into production in 1938. He purchased the property for scrap value; in 1995 it earned $26 million.

The Cuban venture consists of two mines, the Mantua and the Delita, where open-pit operations are being planned. Neither prop-erty has been the subject of U.S. claims. In addition, he recently signed a $800-million contract with a Cuban crown corporation, which will be his 50 per cent partner, to put up eleven new hotels, containing 4,200 rooms. The deal will include new cruise ships, shopping centres, and will, according to Berukoff, earn spectacular returns, even without a single American tourist.

In his dealings with the Cuban government, Berukoff has enjoyed the advantage of a personal friendship with Fidel Castro, who has ruled the island for thirty-seven years. The two men met three years ago at a Canadian embassy reception, and hit it off because they share a common language: Russian. "I've met him many times since, privately and publicly, and after I got more and more involved I kept getting messages from him," says Berukoff. Their most interesting encounter was on Canadian soil.

In December 1995, Berukoff was told that Castro would be returning through Vancouver from a trip to Japan and China, and wanted to meet with him. Neither Ottawa diplomats, airport officials nor anybody else in authority was willing to officially greet Castro, although he was a visiting head of state and deserved special treatment. "Despite the Canadian government telling me to stay out of it because Washington would be very upset, I moved," he recalls. He leased a fleet of the longest stretch limousines in B.C., paid for 300 rooms at the airport Delta to house his entourage, hired a platoon of freelance bodyguards and supplied them with cell phones, and did everything to make *El Commandante* feel welcome, except hire a mariachi band.

The morning after Fidel's arrival, Berukoff sneaked into the hotel, pretending he was part of the security net, and the two men spent a pleasant couple of days together that included a tour of downtown Vancouver and the city's harbour, without anyone knowing about it. "Fidel is very intelligent, highly intuitive, very much a man who sees himself in control, yet pretends he's humble. He outsmarts the Americans because he *knows* exactly what they're doing and how they're going to react to his every move."

How does Castro keep that well informed? "He watches CNN," confides a grinning Wally Berukoff, "and gets the *Wall Street Journal*, just like everybody else."

21

THE GOOD AND THE UGLY

SO MUCH ATTENTION has been focused on General Jean Boyle's self-incriminating confessions before the commission examining the sordid Somalia affair, that a rare and profoundly moving Liberal politician's gesture has not received nearly enough notice.

In his nine days of testimony, Jean Boyle portrayed himself as the innocent dupe of his scheming staff who allowed him to break the spirit and probably the letter of a law of the land (the Access to Information Act). That was how Canada's Chief of Defence Staff chose to side-step the issue of his lapsed accountability, and he did so without exhibiting the slightest twinge of conscience.

In contrast, Monique Bégin, the Montreal sociologist who served as the country's minister of health and welfare for seven of the Trudeau years, voluntarily opted out of the "immunity from prosecution" that Mr. Justice Horace Krever had granted politicians who were in sensitive portfolios during the Red Cross AIDS crisis.

In a letter she sent to the judge last month, Bégin pointed out that as health minister, her responsibilities had included dealing with the advent of HIV infections in Canada. She stressed that while three of her former department's officials had been "named" by the inquiry into the tainted-blood scandal, she had been left off the list. "If you have to lay the blame," she wrote, "I consider it my duty to take my share of the responsibility. The notion of 'ministerial responsibility' is the cornerstone of our executive government. Justice is offended if people at the top are not held responsible for their actions, but employees at less serious levels of the hierarchy are. Public ethics require that those at the top be accountable."

Bégin, who now heads the faculty of Health Sciences at the University of Ottawa, must have known that hers was no symbolic gesture. In France, a similar inquiry resulted in the indictment of President Laurent Fabius and his chief of staff, Louis Schweizer. Yet she felt compelled to place herself in harm's way, because she understands that authority brings with it responsibility, and that individuals in charge cannot escape blame, simply by pleading the guilt of their underlings.

Yet, that's exactly what General Boyle has done. Nothing is my fault, he keeps trumpeting. I'm the very model of an air force general. It was my assistants who made me do it.

This is a shoddy tactic for anyone in high office, but for the man in charge of defending the territorial integrity of this country, it borders on the criminal. In the highly unlikely event that Canada was attacked by hostile forces, how could we place our faith in a commanding officer who passes the buck? ("Whoops, we seem to have lost the Maritimes. Those damn adjutants of mine screwed up again.")

Armies mirror the character of the societies on whose behalf they serve. It is hypothetical but true that our collective survival as Canadians ultimately depends on maintaining sovereignty over our territory. The armed forces are charged with that task, and guarding our turf can't be delegated to a guy who can't run his own office.

Winston Churchill, who served as First Lord of the Admiralty but was an army buff, once explained that armies are not like limited liability companies that can be remodelled, liquidated or inflated from week to week. "An army," he noted, "is a living thing. If it is bullied, it sulks; if it is unhappy, it pines; if it is harried, it gets feverish and if it is sufficiently disturbed, it dwindles in strength."

That has been the effect of Boyle's testimony. According to one internal survey, his confessions have reduced faith among the military in their top leadership to a meagre 17 per cent. That's not surprising. The profession of arms demands a unique contract from its participants: that given the appropriate circumstances, those who sign up will sacrifice their lives in the discharge of their duties. The unwritten clause in that contract demands that in return, those in authority at every level of command, right up to the top, will be accountable for their actions and assume their proper responsibilities.

Every study of military men (and more recently, women) under fire has concluded that they don't primarily risk their lives for their country. They fight for their buddies, defending the psychological bonding that takes place within a regiment, ship or squadron caught up in a common cause.

Under Boyle, that bond has come unglued.

His awkward attempt to hide behind his underlings, coming as it did on top of the revelations that members of our crack regiment had, in their role as peacekeepers, committed unspeakable atrocities against the very people they were sworn to protect, has devalued the vaunted reputation of our armed forces. The images that endure are the home videos of army recruits forced to swallow their own feces and the snapshots of the murdered Shidane Abukar Arone, his head propped by a broom stick, as though he were a trophy elk.

Such horrors don't fade. Neither does the TV image of Somalia inquiry commissioner Robert Rutherford, a former tank commander, asking the defence chief: "When you issue an order, do you expect the forces to obey both the spirit and the letter of the law?" By replying "Yes, sir!" the general cooked his goose.

If the government doesn't have the nerve to fire Jean Boyle, the defence chief must summon up the decency to resign for the good of the country he serves.

But in judging these events, we ought not to forget that politicians like Monique Bégin also decorate the Canadian landscape—and be proud.

22

THE SENATOR WHO
WOULD BE DIFFERENT

MOST SENATORS HAVE abalone-shaped jowls and expend their remaining life-force in irrelevant pursuits, such as a passion for minor French cheeses. But Michael Pitfield is different. Even though he came as close as any public servant to embracing Pierre Trudeau's ideology, the one-time clerk of the Privy Council has been using the Red Chamber as a platform for some highly relevant opinions about the nation's political, economic and social directions.

Pitfield's retroactive presence continues to haunt political Ottawa; John Turner's first act as prime minister was to begin dismantling the Pitfield-inspired decision-making structure, which the new P.M. attacked as being "too elaborate, too complex, too slow and too expensive." The former Privy Council clerk can be forgiven for being a bit sceptical: "We will see what takes its place. There will be the reality of the new system, and there will be the press releases on it. Every prime minister should organize his shop to suit his purposes." He believes the main issue of the election campaign should be the balance of expenditures between social and economic priorities, as well as not so much the degree but the manner of future government intervention.

More immediate considerations aside, Pitfield has few regrets about the initiatives he championed as chief operating officer of the Trudeau administration, especially its concentration on constitutional reform. "I make no apologies for that particular priority, although I regret the confrontations it entailed," he said during a recent interview. "Patriation of the Constitution has removed from the scene an obstacle that had so long prevented any headway at all being made in the maturing of our national institutions. Almost any issue that was brought up required an amending formula, and the provinces were never ready to agree on one unless their needs—never unanimous—were met. That is settled now, a solution about jurisdiction over natural resources is in place, and we can get on with some of our major, national projects." Pitfield's only regret is that the Charter of Rights and Freedoms is open to so many interpretations that the country will be ruined by litigation, with access to the law flowing towards the rich and special-interest groups.

His recent assignment as a senior member of the Canadian delegation to the United Nations has given Pitfield first-hand knowledge of the Reagan administration's chauvinistic world-view, an experience that has turned him into an ardent Canadian nationalist. "I know now that the system of government we have is considerably better than anything we might get by creeping under the American umbrella," he says. "We must cut our own path according to our best national interest as we define it. The sad fact is that there are elements within the American administration that did not welcome Pierre Trudeau's efforts to get other countries to discuss arms control, and they were hinting that our doing so might adversely affect our bilateral relationships." He refuses to provide names but accuses Canadian business leaders of trying to sabotage the Trudeau peace mission because "it was making some people in Washington very unhappy."

It is mainly because of such experiences that Pitfield argues against the free-trade lobby in Canada which pretends that our economic relations with the Americans can be devoid of political dimensions. "Whatever we do in terms of defining our trading relationship with the United States," he maintains, "shouldn't be open to the kind of tail twisting Americans so often use, such as pretending that the administration is on our side but can't dictate to Congress."

On that and other issues Pitfield's views on Ottawa as the centre of the Canadian universe have mellowed considerably.

He concedes that trying to define the Canadian identity was an obsession of his generation but dismisses it as the growing pains of an adolescent reaching for maturity, who finally says to himself: "I am what I am, so let's get on with it. Few realize how very tough the United States can be in the advancement of its interests as a super-power. The Americans know there is no free lunch among nations, even if we don't." What the senator from the Langevin Block advocates is that Canada's private sector return to its 19th-century tradition of merchant adventuring and innovation. "It never ceases to amaze me," he says, "that so few people recognize that business-men are responsible for shaping the whole country's infrastructure. The other thing that absolutely baffles me is that we should, at this precarious stage in our history, be downgrading the priority being given to education."

None of those opinions is particularly radical, but their source is significant. Pitfield, in many ways, is the last of his kind. He went into the public service twenty-five years ago, the way second sons of Anglican vicars in 19th-century England went into the army, or, if they were from Scotland, became Factors with the Hudson's Bay Co. Now, Pitfield is deeply troubled by how far and how fast the power of the bureaucracy has spread and wants to become an hon-est broker between public and private interests, trying to influence the moulders in both places of what passes for Canadian economic policy. "I hope to be a catalyst in that process," he concluded, turn-ing back to the Hyperion computer that processes his thoughts these days. "That may sound presumptuous, but perhaps I can act as a bit of a stimulant so that we stop the rhetoric and start talking about the harsh realities shaping Canada's world."

23

PRAISING RIEL

EVERY ONCE IN A while, almost in spite of itself, Canada's Parliament does something worthwhile. That was the case when the House of Commons granted speedy approval to Constitutional Affairs Minister Joe Clark's motion recognizing Louis Riel's "unique and historic role as a founder of Manitoba."

Clark went on to salute the Métis leader for "deep devotion to his people and his willingness to pay the ultimate price of his life," pointing out that recognition of Riel's crucial role in Canadian history is "an indication that we have matured as a nation."

True enough. When Riel was sentenced to be hanged in Regina in 1885, Sir John A. Macdonald, the Tory prime minister—who was not above playing up to the anti-Catholic voters of Protestant Ontario—told a friend who had requested clemency for the Métis leader: "He shall hang, though every dog in Quebec bark in his favour."

Hang he did, but Riel's strange saga—particularly his refusal to hide behind a justified plea of insanity that might have saved his life—remains Canada's most enduring myth. A messianic rebel in a nation of cloying conformists, Riel remains the perfect Canadian martyr: a well-meaning yet deluded mystic who died prematurely by pretending to be sane.

In his time, Riel inspired hero worship and contempt in almost equal measure, being condemned by English Canadians as a traitor who well deserved to be hanged, while he was worshipped in French Canada as a victim of Anglo-Saxon racial prejudice. The conflict that swirled around him, then and now, is as ancient and as contemporary as Canada itself—the clash between the semi-articulated collective demands of the Métis and the stubbornly held belief in individual rights of English Canadians.

Despite his humiliating defeat and death at the age of forty-one, Riel's defiance salvaged the French-Canadian fact in Canada's North West, and in the process bestowed on the French-speaking Métis a degree of self-confidence and self-assertion they had never possessed. "His name marks a deep furrow in the soil of our young country," editorialized Montreal's *La Minerve* the day after Riel's hanging. "The hand that placed the gallows rope around his neck wounded a whole people."

At the time of Riel's exploits, the Métis around the Red River (the site of modern Winnipeg) had grown restless because their main sources of livelihood—the fur trade and buffalo hunt—were drying up. Possessed by the fierce pride of pioneers—they had, after all, opened up Western Canada—they felt left out of things, recognizing that the newly evolving circumstances would neither restore their past nor validate their future. That was when, led by Riel, they decided to draw on their French and Indian roots to fashion a peculiar world of their own—a new nation, their nation.

Riel captured the local Hudson's Bay Co. post and declared himself President of the Provisional Government of Rupert's Land and the North West, covering most of the Prairies and the North. At the time, his republic was the world's second largest, exceeded in size only by the United States. He chose as his flag Samuel de Champlain's golden *fleur-de-lys* and a green shamrock (to honour the new government's treasurer, a professional Irishman named W.B. O'Donoghue) on a white background. For eight months, he governed his people with enlightened grace—and some considerable ambiguity.

Like some 19th-century Robert Bourassa, he was caught between his French nationalism and loyalty to the idea of a British Canada, never able to let go of either emotion, eventually becoming trapped in a polarization of his own making. While restlessly championing the rights of his people, he was just as insistent on gaining "our rights as British subjects." Riel calmly negotiated the terms for Manitoba's entry into Confederation and told his tiny legislature how proud he was of the people of the North West for "having trust enough in the Crown of England to believe that ultimately they would obtain their rights." Nonetheless, Macdonald soon dispatched an army brigade to bring the rebel to heel.

His greatest error was executing a boisterous Irish Protestant drifter named Thomas Scott, a marginal frontier character who had amply demonstrated his anti-Métis prejudices. Although Scott's only recorded crime was yelling abuse at his Métis captors, he was sentenced to death, and the sole explanation Riel offered at the time was, "We must make Canada respect us." It was that senseless execution which empowered the violent anti-Riel reaction in Orange Ontario.

Even Riel's dress symbolized his split in loyalties. During the time he was president of his puppy republic, Riel received visitors while wearing a Victorian frock coat and hand-sewn moccasins. He drilled a Métis guard of honour to welcome the British troops and planned to preside at the ceremony turning the western territories over to Canada, but was instead chased out of the country.

Macdonald bribed him to stay away, but Riel returned and twice ran successfully for the House of Commons as an Independent from Provencher, though he never took his seat. After a nervous breakdown and a lengthy spell in a mental asylum at Beauport, Quebec, he moved to Montana, but returned in 1884 to lead the last rebellion fought on Canadian soil. This was not the dreamy statesman of his Manitoba period, but a hard-edged religious fanatic proclaiming himself to be the "Prophet of the New World." Riel set up another provisional Métis government in Batoche, a fording place on the South Saskatchewan River forty-four kilometres southwest of Prince Albert. It was there that the Métis nation was defeated by a volunteer Canadian army; Riel was arrested and shipped to Regina for trial. (He was first taken to Winnipeg, but when the authorities discovered that under Manitoba law half the jury could be French-speaking, Riel was transferred to the territories court in Regina, which had no such provision.)

It's very Canadian that Parliament has now bestowed posthumous sainthood on Riel, the tame administrator at Red River, rather than Riel, the untamed rebel at Batoche. But at least we recognized him as one of our founding fathers—an eternal reminder of this country's divided soul.

24

SPARING A THOUGHT
FOR FAIRNESS

AT A PRIVATE OTTAWA dinner party, held to mark the twentieth anniversary of Pierre Trudeau's assumption of power, the former prime minister laid out a political agenda for the 1990s that contained an interesting catchphrase. "For too long," he proclaimed, "we have experimented with the dark side of excellence. For too long this country has suffered from politics that stress economic efficiency instead of social fairness—and it's in that direction our party must make its next policy thrust."

The notion of battling against this "dark side of excellence" has long been lost sight of, as the two Liberal leaders who succeeded Trudeau—John Turner and Jean Chrétien—abandoned their party's traditional political formula.

In the past, the Liberals had championed a loose ideology best described as "sedate populism"—a posture that for generations had allowed the Grits to strike the most marketable balance between élitism and egalitarianism. At the same time, the party lost its internal capacity to formulate new policies, still relying on the outdated resolutions of the 1960 Kingston Conference.

"When we talk about 'the dark side of excellence,'" explains Senator Jack Austin, the intellectual godfather of the idea, "our concern is with the loss of tolerance, the absence of compassion and the downgrading of fairness, as expressed in this neo-conservative age. There has been a hard edge in Brian Mulroney's pursuit of national competitiveness and a subsequent dilution of optimism among Canadians. In contrast, Liberal policy for forty years was based on the politics of optimism through the emphasis on equality of opportunity."

Austin, who was once Trudeau's principal secretary and later became his powerful minister of state for social development, carefully differentiates between the Liberal idea of individual rights, state-guaranteed rights and the collective concepts of the Tories. The Tory approach, he claims, depends on benefits trickling down from a process that inevitably strengthens the already strong. "Under the Mulroney government," he charges, "income disparity began to widen and its changes in the tax system reduced the impact of progressive taxation, putting ever more economic power in fewer and fewer hands.

"Instead, governments must return to the animating idea of fairness," he adds. "A country is not a business and a government should stand for much more than economic efficiency. It's 'the dark side of excellence' that throws people below the fairness line, because those who have already succeeded maintain a vested psychological interest in the lack of success of others in the system."

Austin is not convinced that politics has to be reduced to a popularity contest. "I don't believe," he says, "that to be successful in the 1990s a political leader needs to be personally strident or make more and more spectacular promises to offer even richer rewards for the self-interest of the already comfortable."

Although his approach has won converts in all camps, Austin himself backed Paul Martin instead of Jean Chrétien in the 1990 leadership contest, because he considered him to be the party's most effective consensus builder. He saw Martin as the most dedicated to advancing Canadian sovereignty—and the natural leader of the anti–"dark side of excellence" platform. "Paul," he says, "is realistic about not raising unrealizable expectations among voters. People no longer believe that governments can deliver everything. The age of political magic is over. Hard work, fairness and realism—that's what matters now."

While Austin worries about the size of the federal deficit, he firmly opposes any retreat from universality in social programs. "If we maintain proper standards of fairness, sacrifices as well as benefits will have to be equally distributed," he insists. "The principle of universality was originally based on the idea that there was a charter of economic rights for all Canadians in which each citizen is entitled to basic support. Those who advocate doing away with universality are basically saying that society will confer special benefits on the needy, which hurts people's pride and sense of optimism."

Austin wants to implement the annual guaranteed income system recommended by the Macdonald commission and limit massive federal intervention in the economy to redressing social ills. He would like to see the Federal Business Development Bank turned into a source of equity capital for new Canadian enterprises, instead of financing such marginal and dubious enterprises as strip clubs. He is against government subsidies, unless the economic activity involved is basic to the national purpose.

Austin supports creation of an elected and effective Senate but opposes any move to make provincial representation equal, opting instead for roughly equivalent regional seating, so that the Atlantic provinces, for example, rather than Prince Edward Island alone have the same number of representatives as Ontario. He wants Quebec to possess special upper chamber veto privileges in areas that touch its jurisdictions.

Jack Austin is not the only senior Liberal trying to divine a future direction for his party, but finding a practical way to resolve the problems created by "the dark side of excellence" is his personal obsession, and I say, Amen to that.

25

THE MAN WHO INVENTED
TEAM CANADA

IF THERE'S ONE CANADIAN who personifies this country's future trade prospects with China, it's Jack Austin, the Trudeau-era cabinet minister and former deputy minister of energy, mines and resources who came to prominence as organizer and chief animator of the wildly successful Team Canada trade mission to Beijing and Shanghai.

He has been mining the Chinese territories for years, having first gone to China in the spring of 1971, only six months after Canada officially recognized the Communist regime. At the time, he spent parts of four days in conversation with Chou En-lai, the country's long-time prime minister, and established some valuable contacts. Later appointed president of the Canada-China Business Council, a trade group financed by two hundred Canadian exporters put together by Montreal's Paul Desmarais, Austin is also senior partner in Vancouver's Boughton, Peterson, Yang and Anderson, the first Canadian law firm officially admitted to practise in China.

He is convinced that the success of Team Canada's initial mission has permanently altered the Chinese view of Canadian businessmen. "They believed for a long time that we were ultra-conservative, not willing to make a serious effort," he told me. "They now realize and appreciate that Canadians are willing to do whatever it takes to break into the Chinese market. Such pioneers as Northern Telecom and Power Corp. have shown that doing business in China is a practical and profitable thing to do, providing you know what steps to follow."

As well as including the prime minister, half a dozen federal ministers and nine premiers, the trade odyssey numbered 353 senior Canadian business executives, 108 of them CEOs. They signed agreements worth $8.6 billion of potential business with China, a figure distorted somewhat because at least half the total was accounted for by the pending sale of a CANDU reactor. Still, it was nearly twice as much business as was transacted by a larger German delegation in 1993, and considerably more than the $2 billion in agreements signed by an American group under Commerce Secretary Ron Brown early in 1994.

The problem is to make sure both sides realize it wasn't a one-shot deal. "Participation requires a long and continuous process," warns Austin. "Canadians must make a real effort to comprehend the culture, history, language and aspirations of the Chinese. They have to be prepared to risk time, effort and money to live there for extended periods and offer world-class values in goods and services. The real dilemma now is that we are a Eurocentric country in a Pacific century. Outside North America, we are still preoccupied with exports that cross the Atlantic." He makes the point that although our trade with Asia surpassed European exports back in 1983, Ottawa still maintains more diplomats in either France or England than in China and Japan combined.

The potential prize is immense. World Bank projections show that the China of the 1990s is the fastest-growing economy on earth. In the ten years after 1981, average annual growth of its gross domestic product exceeded 8 per cent and the increase has hit more than 13 per cent a year since. Experts now predict that China's economy will quintuple every twenty-one years. By the end of this decade, China will become one of the four economic superpowers, along with Europe, the United States and Japan. A World Bank study postulates that by 2002, China will surpass the American economy, with a GDP of $13.2 trillion, compared with $13.1 trillion for the United States.

The Chinese economy's most serious problem is inflation, mainly because the money supply is constantly being expanded to bail out inefficient state enterprises. "I believe controls are inevitable," Austin predicts, "because without a pause in inflation, the cycle cannot be broken."

The Chinese are like the Scots: they never do anything by

halves. Under Chairman Mao, China closed its door to the world, and the repression of the Great Cultural Revolution followed. China's passion for economic growth is in part an escape from that terrible time. As one contemporary Beijing essayist has observed: "China is passing through a period of historical amnesia. The passion for the market is as much about rejecting the last forty-five years, as it is about becoming rich."

Meanwhile, Jack Austin is betting that China will find its post-revolutionary soul, and Canada will reap much of the benefit.

26

THE MAVISES' BRAVE CRUSADE

NEW BRUNSWICK IS Irving country.

Kenneth Colin Irving, the family patriarch who founded the dynasty when he established a Model-T Ford dealership at Buctouche in the early 1920s, died in the winter of 1992. His empire was worth an estimated $7 billion at the time and it remained untouched by tax collectors, because Irving had spent the previous twenty years at a luxury villa in Bermuda, the most pleasant of the world's tax havens. He ran the 300-odd companies that he controlled well into his nineties, delegating operational authority to his three sons, Jack, known as "Gassy," Jim "Oily" and Arthur "Greasy," but still made the decisions that counted during the 182 days a year he was allowed to stay in Canada, while maintaining his voluntary mid-Atlantic exile.

The sons, who are now in their sixties, have since been running eastern Canada's largest conglomerate with the harsh ethic they learned at their father's knee: a combination of secrecy and ruthlessness. Their sons, who are now beginning to take over, are cut from the same pattern—they don't smoke, don't drink, don't talk to reporters and work sixteen hours a day, like God intended. The Irvings' penchant for secrecy means that they share corporate information with no one outside the family.

The family's ruthlessness is based on the simplistic but surprisingly effective notion that since they own most of New Brunswick's corporate assets (except those that belong to the McCains) they should also be allowed to run the province and particularly Saint John, where they mainly operate, their way.

Seldom has their brutal exercise of power been more clearly displayed than in the battle they waged with a middle-aged couple, Ross and Willa Mavis, who own a five-room bed and breakfast on the shores of the Bay of Fundy. The Irvings are determined to turn Sheldon Point, an unspoiled, postcard-perfect piece of shoreline near the Mavis home, into a toxic waste dump. The Mavises went to the wall to halt the pollution of the virgin shoreline. It's an uneven contest, and the Irvings will probably win. But at least they'll know they've been in a hell of a fight.

The Irvings own a huge paper mill in downtown Saint John at Reversing Falls which currently discharges its untreated effluent into the St. John River. (This endows the mill with at least one distinction. Unlike other offending industries, it pollutes the water both up and downstream as the tide changes twice daily and the Reversing Falls carry 30 million gallons of the soiled water inland.) When the New Brunswick government recently passed an act requiring the treatment of waste waters, the Irvings decided to pump the offending substance five kilometres west of the city, onto a prime chunk of Fundy shoreline, which happens to be near the Mavises bed and breakfast. There they plan to dig a huge aeration toxic waste lagoon, with most of the wastes eventually pumped in the bay, while the toxic slush and mill ash are buried next to the lagoon.

Willa Mavis is a native of Saint John and a former fashion consultant, who always dreamed of running a bed and breakfast; her husband, Ross, moved East four years ago, after a stint as executive director of the Canadian Community Newspaper Association in Toronto. Before that, he ran a weekly newspaper in Port Hardy, at the northern tip of Vancouver Island. Ross was later in charge of the local United Way campaigns, but his attempts to frustrate the Irvings' plans for the dump site caused him trouble. "Two people have contacted our United Way board president," he told me, "to say that it was improper for me to speak out on the issue. One of them is married to an Irving girl and has hinted that my involvement in the pollution issue might affect the family's corporate contributions to this year's campaign. To the Irvings, living by the golden rule seems to mean, 'he who has the gold sets the rules.'"

Ross Mavis is a thoughtful gummy-bear of a man, not given to violent acts or opinions. But his fourteen-month struggle with the Irvings has given him a tougher edge, made him see first-hand a Canada he never knew existed. "This sort of thing," he says, "might go on here and in other places every day, but this is the first time I've been directly involved in a situation that makes me question whether I live in a democracy. I had no idea how much power the Irvings actually bring to bear on the citizens of New Brunswick. It's almost akin to a Latin American dictatorship, except that the killings go on surreptitiously in our atmosphere, forest lands and waters."

Willa and her neighbours organized a Save Our Shore (SOS) Committee which dreamed up the idea of raising enough money to buy the disputed property from the province and donating it to the University of New Brunswick for a marine biology campus. UNB President Robin Armstrong was delighted with the suggestion, though he never put his reaction in writing. When Willa phoned a professor in charge of the marine biology department, he said, just before he hung up: "I was told you might call me, and that I was not to speak to you." A member of the Irving family sits on the university board. She has been refused an audience by Saint John mayor Elsie Wayne, even though the city discussed the issue three times with the Irvings.

An Irving-financed study cleared the project of causing any blight and they have even opened a nature park on the site. Mainly because of the Mavises' persistence, the province agreed to carry out an environmental impact study, the first ever done on a lagoon. The main barrier stopping the Irvings was to have Sheldon Point rezoned from agricultural to industrial, but they had the necessary votes on city council.

"People say I'm crazy to fight the Irvings," says Willa Mavis, "but I really feel I must. Just because you have money doesn't mean you have respect."

27

ORACLE OF THE COMPUTER AGE

ANY COUNTRY'S MOST valuable asset is the number of original thinkers it nurtures. We've had our share: Marshall McLuhan, John Kenneth Galbraith, Northrop Frye and Harold Innis among them.

The next best thing to fostering such oracles is to import one. Bearing this rare pedigree is Jean-Jacques Servan-Schreiber, a French intellectual who has made himself a one-ring travelling circus on behalf of the computer technology altering our lives.

The grandson of Bismarck's political secretary, he first won acclaim as owner-publisher of the weekly *L'Express*, served as a wartime pilot in the Free French Air Force and wrote the best-selling *The American Challenge*. J-J S-S, as he prefers to be known, has done it all. He has managed a hotel in Brazil, fought in the Algerian revolution, was a confidant of Camus, Sartre, Mauriac and Malraux and negotiated the release of composer Mikis Theodorakis from the Greek junta's jails. He has been a gadfly in French politics, an adviser and challenger of prime ministers, a member of the national assembly and leader of the anti-Gaullist (but non-Communist) Radical Party, always trying to break his country away from the old Napoleonic pattern of centralized authority. The French regard him as something of a class traitor because he came from a rich background but has advocated a welfare system, demanding truly radical solutions to social and economic problems. The Rightists oppose his championing of individual freedom; the leftists attack him for not advocating the overthrow of capitalism.

In a recent afternoon's conversation with Servan-Schreiber, I found what he had to say a mixture of intellectual bravado, romantic impulse and stone-cold truth. There is clarity and urgency in his current crusade to make the world aware of the revolutionary nature of the computer age.

"If we don't utilize the full potential of the personal computer very quickly," he told me, sounding more than slightly de Gaullish, "we'll end up with chaos and war. Nobody can attack frontally what I'm saying because it's obvious. But those who have a vested interest in the present state of affairs will try to ignore it or delay its implementation. That would be tragic. These new machines are powerful enough that they will not only change our working universe but might be able to slow down the inevitability of world war. But there's little time."

For a while he headed the Paris-based World Centre for Personal Computation and Human Resources, which is a mecca for statesmen, economists, philosophers and futurists attempting to comprehend the true impact of computers. Eight French cabinet ministers are on its board; his associations with the renowned Carnegie-Mellon University at Pittsburgh turned Servan-Schreiber into something of an oracle among U.S. industrialists.

"Computer science," he maintains, "is not just a field among others. It is a new language, a fresh way of learning. Only this new technology can help solve our vast unemployment and literacy problems, because only the personal computer can make learning an attractive proposition again. It does away with the classrooms and lectures. You can immediately become active with your own computer, in effect teaching yourself, almost through playing games. Most important of all, the student with a computer is not a passive listener to television or blackboard knowledge. He is not judged by someone else, but by himself."

J-J S-S points out that computers are not just a new method of teaching children but a key to retraining adults. Paradoxically, the very best teachers of the middle-aged are the very young, because they haven't grown up allergic to electronic machines. He admits that the scale of modernization required will mean investments on a huge scale. "But we can't keep wasting our resources by subsidizing obsolete technologies and nonexistent jobs. Computer science is not just one industry among others. What I'm talking about is a basic change in man's universe. Apart from everything else, it will decentralize industry, helping to resolve the problems of overcrowding and pollution."

To document the mesmerizing influence of personal computers, he cites studies that show how their introduction has managed to wean children away from the mind-deadening effects of television.

"What I'm talking about," says J-J S-S, "is the key to man's renaissance in a decadent and disrupted world." As one of the few surviving original thinkers, he has a voice that must be heard.

28

FRANK GIUSTRA'S GREAT QUEST

EVER SINCE THE Big Six banks absorbed the country's major investment houses, the few remaining independents have struggled to
find a new mandate for themselves. Some have become boutique
operations, catering to garlands of wealthy clients; others—like
Bay Street's Gordon Capital—have specialized in block trades,
while a few—such as Midland Walwyn—have stayed alive by relying on their retail networks.

But faced with the undiminished clout of the bank-run institutions that dominate stock trades, most of the remaining independents have moved to occupy niche markets, none more successfully
than Vancouver's Yorkton Securities Inc., which has become the
country's leading financial facilitator of the world's burgeoning
mining industry. Yorkton, which is nominally headquartered in
Toronto, is really run out of its West Coast office which houses the
bulk of its 400 employees. The firm is currently financing the hunt
for "elephant-size" mineral deposits in fifty-eight countries.

Yorkton's chairman, Frank Giustra, is based in Vancouver, but
while he admires the Vancouver Stock Exchange as a source of
venture capital, he has conscientiously stayed away from its seamier
aspects. "The problem," he told me, "is not so much with policing
its operations, as with the way some brokerage companies conduct
themselves. If they didn't allow questionable types of business to be
transacted on the VSE, it wouldn't be there. It's as simple as that."

Giustra is obsessed with ensuring that Yorkton becomes recognized as world leader in analyzing and underwriting mining stocks.
The firm certainly operates in the big leagues, having in a typical
year raised $2 billion for the discovery and exploitation of mines.
"Because most of the big deposits have already been discovered
here," he says, "if you want to bag an elephant you have to visit

elephant country, which means going into one of the emerging economies. The best plays are in the Philippines, southern and western Africa, Southeast Asia and the Andean Cordillera, which stretches from Colombia down to Chile."

Chile has been in the lead to attract foreign investments, partly because of its favourable geology, but equally because of its enlightened tax structure, environmental regulations, foreign investment policies and mining laws. "The Chilean government set the standard," says Giustra. "We all refer to the Chilean Economic Model, and our firm has in fact been instrumental in bringing the representatives of other governments around to their way of thinking."

While Giustra heads Yorkton, the firm is a partnership with none of the seventy-five partners (including Giustra) owning more than 10 per cent of its shares. A good many of those partners are geologists, accountants, economists and corporate finance specialists who spend their professional lives earning for Yorkton what the firm's chairman describes as "our franchise as the brokerage world's best and largest natural resource group." Instead of waiting around for prospectors to arrive with big dreams and small claims, the Yorkton operatives dispatch due-diligence teams to some pretty obscure corners, searching for new mines. "Just once," complains Giustra, "just once, I wish somebody would discover a deposit in Tuscany or the French Riviera. We seem to be always finding minerals in the most bizarre places."

In the hunt for big-game deposits, Yorkton often invests in local infrastructure as an incentive to negotiating permits from indigenous governments. At the money end of the Yorkton operation, the firm now has a loyal following among this continent's leading institutional investors, and an expanding list of European clients who follow its mining plays.

One of the reasons for the firm's success may be that future prospects are seldom exaggerated. "We warn investors that we try to win six out of every ten times we do a deal, and we've been pretty successful at that, but there are no sure bets in this business," says Bob Cross, a former Gordon Capital corporate finance executive who joined Yorkton as president. Ian Lamont, who writes Yorkton's eccentric London newsletter, put the issue more directly, if less elegantly, suggesting that the best way to play stocks was while sitting on a toilet. "Speculating in a market so obviously overvalued is likely to test even the strongest sphincters," he wrote. "To avoid the embarrassment of involuntary evacuation of the bowel or bladder, it is probably safest to conduct stock-market business while one's fundament is seated on a comfortable porcelain throne."

The most obvious sign of Yorkton's success has been the number of competitors trying hard to take away its business. The interlopers don't faze Giustra. "Past fortunes and empires have been built on the back of mining," he says, "And that kind of opportunity exists today. All of a sudden, mining has become like some huge Toys 'R' Us supermarket. There just aren't enough hours in the day to take advantage of all the opportunities."

After seventeen years at York, Giustra left in 1997. He got fed up with some of the questionable goings-on at the firm's Calgary office and decided it was time to head for new pastures. His newly established entertainment conglomerate promises to become a major Canadian creative enterprise—which he is ideally fitted to lead.

29

THE LAST GOVERNOR

THE RIGHT HONOURABLE Christopher Francis Patten surprises.
From the headlines, one expects the last Hong Kong governor to
be a belligerent bulldog of a Britisher, a Bond-like figure braving
the wrath of Asian potentates while sipping Singapore Slings.
Instead, I found the governor of Britain's last major colony to be
something of a "wet." Instead of packing a Walther PPK semi-
automatic, he is armed with historical allusions, has a cowlick and
watches the world through the burning eyes of a poet. He is also
one of the contemporary world's most remarkable politicians, mas-
querading as a bureaucrat. Definitely a fellow to go tiger-hunting
with.

Patten has that rare quality, not uncommon among his fellow
grads of Oxford's Balliol College, of knowing that politics is a
matter of macro-decisions, of measuring luck against ambition and
compassion against expediency. He is a man of conscience who understands that being incautious, as he has had occasion to be in
dealing with Beijing's shock troops, can be a necessary evil.

When I put forward the generalization that while the
Soviet Union seems constantly to be placing economics behind
politics, China has, until the repossession of Hong Kong, reversed
the order—animating the business sector, while leaving ideology to
marinate in its own juices—Patten replies: "You can't separate
politics from economics for very long. In the case of Hong Kong,
the relationship between economic success and its way of life is
intimate, with the latter helping to sustain the former.

"What makes for the success of the city are the economic policies we pursue that have given the framework within which Adam
Smith or Alexis de Tocqueville would have been familiar: the rule
of law and a fairly corruption-free government, plus an impartial

civil service. It has never struck me as being entirely coincidental
that Hong Kong not only has the most open market in Asia, but
one of the freest presses in the region. So it's a very Leninist notion
that you can distinguish between economics and politics."

To the proposition that by harassing him and his garrison,
China may be acting against its own self-interest (since 64 per cent
of the capital flowing into the Communist state originates in Hong
Kong), the governor points out that there is about $27 billion in
Chinese investment in the island colony at the moment; that its
gross domestic product represents 21 per cent of China's; and that
Hong Kong's six million residents have produced one-fifth the
wealth of China's 1.2 billion people. (Since the joint declaration
was signed by London and Beijing in 1984 setting terms for the
leased colony's return to China on July 1, 1997, Hong Kong's GDP
has increased an astounding 97 per cent and the colony is currently
enjoying its thirty-fifth year of uninterrupted growth.) "There is indeed every reason for the Communists not to intervene in Hong
Kong's success," says Patten, "and that's not going to change after
the transfer in 1997. The question mark is whether they understand this. One of the real difficulties we have is that they're so reluctant to be relaxed about Hong Kong, though it in no way represents a threat. Its politics are incredibly moderate and the vast
majority of the people want the transition to be successful—so all
the Chinese have to do is stand back and let it happen."

One of the major problems will be dealing with the 600,000
Hong Kong citizens who have claimed foreign passports, since
China does not recognize dual citizenship. Beijing insists that anyone in this position can exercise "the right of abode" in the post-
1997 city, but must give up their right of consular protection from
their second homeland.

The governor makes the point that it was not he who introduced democracy to Hong Kong, but that this transition has been
evolving for some time. "Just because Asians embrace some of the
values of pluralism doesn't mean that they become less Asian," he
emphasizes. "Japan isn't less Asian just because it's a free and open
society."

Then we come to conscience, to the harsh reality that in handing Hong Kong over to the Chinese, Britain is putting at risk those

refugees who sought sanctuary there from Communism. Surely, I ventured, this is a betrayal of millions of innocents who escaped from the real or imagined terrors of the mainland and have ever since worked hard to stay out of the Communists' grasp.

"The joint declaration is uniquely difficult for both China and Britain," the governor carefully replies. "China is required to comprehend the nature of a free society—because that's what it has guaranteed will survive—and that will certainly be challenging. Britain is challenged because we're used to liberating former colonies by making them democratic and independent. That's never been an option because of the lease in Hong Kong, but it does scratch away at our sensibilities, and makes it particularly important for us to be able to say when we depart that we did everything to bolster the self-confidence of Hong Kong and the values of freedom."

After Patten leaves Hong Kong—according to the rumours— the governor might have a shot at succeeding John Major as leader of Britain's Conservative party. Politics is never simple or predictable, but Patten is an unusual man, not destined for ordinary fates. He has served the Tories for thirty-two years in various senior capacities, and his civility under fire could well turn the Hong Kong post into a political launching pad.

If that were to happen, Chris Patten would be the perfect prime minister: a man eminently comfortable in his skin, who never depends on the kindness of strangers.

IV ABSURDITIES & OTHER DIVERSIONS

30

FEARLESS MIKE

THIS BOOK IS DIFFICULT to pick up once you've put it down. It's almost as dull as its subject: Mike Harcourt, the detached and slightly out-of-tune politician who governed British Columbia from the hopeful autumn of 1991 to the sour winter of 1996.

Yet, not unlike its subject, *Highwire Act* by Daniel Gawthrop is a decent and worthy undertaking, an even-handed profile of the province's departing premier who gave mostly good government to an ungovernable province, even if there were times during his regime when he seemed to achieve the impossible by making Bill Vander Zalm look good.

Being a premier of British Columbia is a bit like presiding over the world's largest and most unruly zoo. There's no way to keep the inmates contented, so you cross your fingers, pretend to be in control and hope you won't be eaten for brunch. Even as the province's top politician, you can seldom gather enough disposable authority to make things stick. Political agendas turn into mush as citizens' coalitions battle authority, each other and every nuance of every new law.

Though they swear that participatory democracy is their mantra of choice, most Pacific Coasters don't really believe in peace, order and good government, preferring—and usually getting—blitzkrieg, disorder and bad government. There was plenty of political havoc in the past five years, yet Harcourt's record in office—especially in retrospect—was admirable. In such areas as forest preservation, park expansion and deficit reduction he did everything he set out to do, and more.

He was a good man in a wicked time, a compromiser in an age that cried out for leadership. His humility and that appealing hang-dog look on TV of an honest but befuddled small-town optometrist, his abhorrence of pretence and his genuine concern for society's underdogs—these were the qualities that made it impossible, even for his enemies, to hate him.

In a revealing aside—one of many which make this book less painful to plough through—Harcourt explains to the author why he didn't try to impose his authority with more gusto: "I looked on my job as running the province well, to give good government. I'm here to govern, not to lead. I'm not involved as a church leader, I'm not involved as a business person for private enterprise—but I believe there's a limit to what I should impose on people."

Harcourt achieved as much as he did by shedding what little personality he had and taking on the momentary colouration of his ever-shifting political environment. Hectoring the B.C. Federation of Labour, he sometimes sounded like a slightly blitzed Che Guevara; addressing the Vancouver Board of Trade, he would slip into the patois of a Good Ol' Boy, lashing out at "the cheats and deadbeats on welfare."

Such quick-change tactics, worthy of one of Darwin's jungle constructs, reminded me of a story about the time Duke Ellington was confronted on a Harlem street corner by a confused fan.

"Hey, man, ain't you the Duke?" the fan demanded.

"Baby," Ellington shot back, "I'm whoever you want me to be."

And that was our Mikey.

What's wrong with *Highwire Act*—and all such pseudo-academic writing for that matter—is that truth is not necessarily the sum of all the ascertainable facts. Gawthrop piles fact upon fact upon fact, quote upon quote, statistic upon statistic, and while his research is excellent and his reporting is largely accurate, the book remains less than the sum of its parts.

The real problem is that Gawthrop, who earned his degree in political science from the University of Victoria and his journalism credentials at King's College in Halifax, writes with all the verve and flash usually reserved for police blotters.

He provides mountain ranges of reportage and very little synthesis. Except for some nasty and well-deserved digs at such NDP apparatchiks as George Ford, Linda Baker, Chris Chilton and Evan Lloyd, who were chosen as Harcourt's personal staff and used their privileged positions to deliberately isolate the premier from reality, the author makes few value judgements.

One exception is this apt description of the Harcourt mystique, or rather the lack of it: "Admirable as it was," he writes, "Mike Harcourt's disdain for the politics of ego often worked against him. Two years into his mandate, the premier was still an elusive figure whose real leadership qualities—setting goals, delegating, chairing conferences, consulting and reconciling opponents—tended to play themselves out in closed-door meetings of cabinet, constitutional negotiations and other political discussions. Not exactly conducive to 10-second sound bites on BCTV."

The most useful chapter of *Highwire Act*—"Trouble in Hub City"—details the gritty goings-on at the Nanaimo Commonwealth Holding Society. That Bingogate, as the bizarre story became known, deserved to become a full-blown scandal is beyond question; that it forced Harcourt's eventual resignation is beyond reason.

Gawthrop reveals a commanding grasp of what happened during the decades that the Nanaimo organization acted as the fundraising arm of the NDP, and worse. All the evidence he has been able to dig up shows that Harcourt acted with haste and anger, launching an investigation of the party's local warlord, Dave Stupich. The only whiff of wrongdoing was the fact that $60,000 in tainted Nanaimo funds had gone to finance the *Democrat*, the NDP's party newspaper, which was promptly repaid. "It's a bullshit issue, as far as I'm concerned," Harcourt insisted, since none of the original misdeeds could be traced back to him.

But by mid-November of 1995, the premier had quit, citing the "baggage" he had inherited from the Nanaimo fiasco as his reason. "When I saw that over a million dollars in personal loans had gone out to Dave Stupich and people around him, I was so angry," he told Gawthrop, and then he said it again. "And I'm still angry."

The premier decided to quit, not because he felt he had done anything wrong, but because the affair had damaged his party so deeply that there was no way he could stay in office and hope to do anything right. And so, forty-eight months and ten days after he was sworn in, Harcourt resigned. Conviction had triumphed over compromise.

Despite its faults, *Highwire Act* is a utilitarian record of a well-meaning politician's stormy stewardship—his achievements, his failures and, above all, his inherent decency. Alone of Canada's ego-driven politicians, Mike Harcourt was not corrupted by power, because he so seldom used it.

31

AH, KIM, WE HARDLY KNEW YE

AH, KIM—WE HARDLY knew ye. And we're not going to know ye any better from this damp squib of a book.

What a story: the self-confessed wood nymph conceived at a timber lookout near Port Alberni becomes the country's first woman (first British Columbian, first yuppie) justice minister, attorney-general, national defence minister and, whammo, prime minister of Canada.

A c.v. to kill for.

Yet her book, *Time and Chance*, surfs instead of dives. We learn little about the real woman who had the chutzpah to grab all that, and survived to write about it. What we do learn is that politics at the top (she was P.M. for 132 days) is just as shoddy as we thought it was. In some ways, Campbell's ingénue approach is useful because the book catches the nuances of promise and betrayal, describes the inner workings of the Mulroney cabinet, and allows the reader to peek into the anatomy of an election campaign, even if it was the worst-run in Canadian history.

Unfortunately, in its middle chapters, this book oozes like overripe Brie. Being a deferential Canadian despite her much-touted irreverence, Campbell uses the awkward device of criticizing her enemies—real and perceived—not by attacking them, but by quoting from her stepdaughter's diary entries that contain her adverse comments. That's a transparent and basically silly device, but it serves to drive home her point that whatever losses her party suffered (a wipeout, in fact) were not her fault.

If indeed the 1993 election was stolen from her by the platoons of Mulroney strategists who ran her campaign, as she charges, there is surprisingly little anger in the book. Too many crooks may have spoiled her wrath. Yet as holder of the nation's highest political office, she must have been responsible for something. Allan Gregg, the pollster she inherited from her predecessor, once told me that the only way for an incumbent P.M. to lose a TV debate was to eat a live rat on stage. Kim managed it without the snack.

She went into the campaign with the highest approval rating of any Canadian political leader in three decades; just six weeks later Campbell was running a poor fourth and facing defeat in her own riding. The most interesting chapters deal with her demise during those critical 42 days.

Instead of her usual off-the-wall charm, she spent most of the campaign delivering school-marmish economic lectures, while promising voters nothing they didn't already have. Probably the most telling moment in her nightmarish election campaign was a stopover in Kelowna, where a cornered and exhausted Campbell let the truth hang out. "I'm working hard to get re-elected," she told a small rally, "because if I get thrown out of office, I'm not sure I can find a job." Delivered in jest, it was the most honest moment of her campaign.

That lack of greater purpose was the ultimate condemnation of Campbell's brand of politics. Any woman or man who seeks to be prime minister of this bedeviled country of ours ought to approach that august office with the courage of her or his convictions, or at least intentions. There must come a moment in the lonely quest to be the big cheese, when passion clambers up to endow policies and issues with something more illuminating than necessity.

For Campbell, that moment never came. She stumbled through the campaign like a Woody Allen in drag, comically inept, blaming others for her pratfalls—even for hotel-room temperatures. One of the fragments of hard evidence she produces to prove that she was being manipulated by Mulroney's former handlers is that they kept the temperature in whatever space she was occupying as cool as he had liked it, but not the toasty temperature she preferred. Death by thermostat. If no executive decisions on radiator heat-levels were forthcoming, neither was there any cogent policy analysis. *Nada*.

Campbell's decision to enter the Tory leadership race in the spring of 1993 seemed to swing on degrees of perceived loneliness. When she was speculating on whether or not to try for the brass ring, her prime concern was what sacrifices in privacy would be required. "I began to wonder if I wanted to subject myself to the loneliness that would come from being in the prime ministerial spotlight," she asked herself. "Weekend parties would be few and far between." So much for constitutional reform, balancing the trade deficit and boosting industrial productivity.

That mood of reaching for power without really knowing why pervades the book. In an aside on page 281 Campbell recalls enjoying the attention of a friendly dog on her campaign travels. "You know, if I win this, I could have a dog," she remarks to one of her assistants. After that, whenever she hesitates in her resolve, members of her entourage whisper "bow-wow" in her ear—and the caravan lumbers on.

What blame for reducing the Conservative party from 157 to 2 seats she doesn't apportion to the Mulroney team is placed squarely on an uncooperative media. Campbell confesses it wasn't until after the election that she discovered that the press was so hostile to her because they had been forced to endure spartan conditions aboard her campaign bus, while those dastardly Liberals plied reporters with free cappuccino. (I do not rise to defend my craft easily, but we can't be bought for cappuccino. Well, maybe rented.)

The American novelist Peter De Vries, describing a character similar to Campbell, wrote: "deep down she's shallow." That's our Kim. Yet occasionally rays of wisdom shine through the book, such as her description of the Trudeau legacy. "Pierre Trudeau had been the unwitting architect of division in this country," she writes. "He had attempted to address the cultural concerns of Quebeckers by giving them what they hadn't asked for—power in Ottawa—in a way that increasingly alienated the West; hence the arrival of Preston Manning and Lucien Bouchard as the leaders of both disaffected constituencies in 1993."

The author's marvellous sense of irreverence seems undiminished. She recalls, for example, being introduced to Nathan Divinsky, her first husband, during her third year at UBC. The good-natured mathematics prof was known to his friends as "Tuzie," because of his inability as a youngster to pronounce his Hebrew nickname, Tula. "My first reaction on hearing this," Campbell recalls, "was to ask: 'Does he have a brother called Threezie?'"

Campbell's fundamental weakness as a politician was that she never took time to serve an apprenticeship at anything except life. She became justice minister only seven years out of law school, counting the brief sixteen months she spent articling at a Vancouver legal factory. (The same leap from graduation to the justice ministry took Pierre Trudeau twenty-five years to complete.) She became a federal Tory only five years before being sworn in as prime minister and had little feel for her party or the perverse idiosyncrasies of Canadian politics.

No matter what her autobiography claims about how she achieved power, it was a fact that the country emerged from the Meech and Charlottetown disasters with only one consensus: no more guys in suits. Since Kim Campbell was clearly not a guy, and as the famous Barbara Woodley photograph proved, held her suits in front of her, Canadians quickly developed a crush on her. That brief affair went sour when the wood nymph turned out to be just another wooden politician, and not a very good one at that.

Reading *Time and Chance*, it's easy to believe that this woman has an unerring instinct for her own jugular.

Kim Campbell portrays herself as charming, irreverent, intelligent, ambitious and decent. She is all of that and more, but in her brief political incarnation she was also tragically out of her depth.

32

CITIZEN HURTIG

THE SAME DAY as this two-kilo memoir hit my desk, a large advertisement appeared in most Canadian newspapers, with the headline: What Mel Hurtig Will Be Wearing Today." The answer, it turned out, was a $1,075 Boss three-piece suit sold by Harry Rosen (the sponsor of the ad), who also donated a $200 shirt and tie to the Hurtig wardrobe.

The juxtaposition was perfect.

Hurtig, as his memoirs amply document, has been our leading nationalist, the articulate and indefatigable champion of Canada's cultural and political independence. But he's no Giuseppe Garibaldi or Che Guevara.

You can't lead a revolution in a Rosen Special.

This long and highly readable book catches the dichotomy at the centre of Hurtig's life. He cares passionately about his country—and believes Canada is in mortal danger of being swallowed up by the American elephant. Yet except for his brief, disastrous 1993 foray, when he led his National Party of Canada into oblivion, he has seldom strayed from the notion that the route to salvation is to stir things up inside the system.

That may have been his fatal flaw. As a potential revolutionary, he was content too long to remain a reformer.

Revolutions are authenticated by radical shifts in national consciousness. Yet Hurtig and his fellow nationalists were satisfied with trying to deal with the symptoms of American imperialism, instead of attacking its causes. How do you effectively hold at bay the U.S. of A., that proud warrior nation that exists in a state of permanent revolution, claiming the world as its playground? And what is the psychological lack in us Canadians that allows us so easily to be conquered?

At Twilight in the Country is an important book because it traces the rise and fall of modern nationalism in this country. Between the late 1960s and the mid-1990s, that great cause was debated, fought over and lost. The most telling parts of Hurtig's book are the dispatches from the trenches of those skirmishes.

An Edmonton furrier's son who became determined early in life that he would make a mark, Hurtig became, in turn, Edmonton's largest bookseller, western Canada's most significant book publisher, a political activist—first as a Trudeau groupie, and later on his own—and a professional speaker.

He excelled in each of these incarnations, making a financial and literary success of his wonderful bookstore, and later publishing many an important best-seller, including the fabulously useful *Canadian Encyclopedia*.

His detailed descriptions of these ventures, particularly the struggle to finance his publishing house, are a clear and present warning about the agonizing difficulties of the commercial side of Canada's book business. His *Junior Encyclopedia of Canada*, which eventually bankrupted his firm, has become a collector's item, and ought to be required reading for every Canadian child.

Hurtig is at his best attacking Brian Mulroney's free trade pact. "This agreement," he writes, "is a massive abandonment of Canadian sovereignty. If implemented, it will be irreversible. We will be saying that once and for all we are giving up on the idea of Canada." The exclusive details Hurtig provides on how the FTA was lobbied and manoeuvred into place by politicians with private agendas on both sides of the border are alone worth the price of the book.

In these 497 pages, Mel Hurtig emerges as a likeable chap and an intellectual patriot, which was once an oxymoron.

That this is no longer true, we owe to Citizen Hurtig.

33

THE NAUGHTY REICHMANNS

LATE IN 1992, when the Reichmann empire was under siege and its elaborate security system had relaxed, I stowed away aboard the luxury launch used to take prospective tenants from Charing Cross, in central London, to Canary Wharf. The turbo-charged motor boat, equipped with blue satin cushions, swept us along the Thames at twenty-five knots, past the Royal Festival Hall, and under Waterloo and London bridges.

Then the shore view quickly deteriorated. For six dreary kilometres we motored by moss-covered piers, derelict barges and rotten pilings that seemed to be precariously held together by their occupied rat holes.

Suddenly, rising out of the river mist, there was Canary Wharf, the $3.5-billion office complex erected by Paul Reichmann as his intended corporate headquarters of the new European Community.

Its fifty-five-storey tower, fashioned out of premium marble imported from thirty countries, together with its commodious outbuildings that housed 4.5 million square feet of office space, set lavish new standards in luxury. Touring the place as a pretend prospective tenant, I nodded appreciatively when the rental guide explained that the flow in the outdoor water fountain we'd just passed was governed by sensors, so that its arc would be reduced in high winds and bystanders wouldn't get splashed. But I lost it, when she confided that the row of Crimean linden trees lining the entrance had been cultivated at a German nursery for thirty-five years, where they had their roots trimmed semi-annually, and went on to point out that the project's main structure was so precisely aligned that on a clear day you could see St. Paul's Cathedral.

The whole thing seemed as incongruous as coming across the Taj Mahal on Baffin Island, or Xanadu in Scarborough.

As I stumbled around the site, blinded by all those stainless-steel fittings and brass ornaments, I remember thinking that this canary would never fly. This wasn't office space. This apparition was a monument to Paul Reichmann, who may have had money and guts to burn, but ought to have realized that when you go bungee jumping—especially on a scale as grand as this—it's a good idea to tie one end of the cord to your ankles.

I was reminded of that day on the Isle of Dogs (as the navigation charts aptly describe the outcrop of land which supports the Reichmann extravaganza) while reading Anthony Bianco's wonderful new book on the family. The 510-page volume, *The Reichmanns: Family, Faith, Fortune, and the Empire of Olympia & York*, is a great achievement in business journalism, immaculately documented and evocatively realized. It is far more realistic a monument to the rise and fall of the bizarre clan it portrays than Canary will ever be.

Bianco recognizes the British project as the perfect symbol for Paul Reichmann's simultaneous and apparently equal devotions to greed and religion. "In straddling the disparate worlds of casino capitalism and Jewish fundamentalism," he emphasizes, "the Reichmanns performed one of the most singular balancing acts of the century."

Taking off from Reichmann's declaration at the Canary Wharf ground-breaking ceremony that the only question was whether its success would happen immediately or later, Bianco observes: "He seemed to have come to believe in his project with the same absolute faith with which he had always believed in God. In secular terms, Reichmann's flaw was hubris in the classical mode. For a devoutly religious Jew to assert his certain success was tantamount to blasphemy, since only God could have known the project's outcome. Indeed, in the view of some of Reichmann's co-religionists, Canary Wharf per se was ambitious beyond the bounds of Orthodox norms of modesty. "I don't believe God wants anyone to be as big as the Reichmanns were becoming," said one Orthodox leader who had generally been admiring of the family.

This paradoxical theme of the Reichmanns' obssession with their faith and their fortune dominates the book, as it did the lives of the mysterious Hungarian brothers who arrived here from Tangiers in the mid-1950s, and blossomed in the real estate trade as rapidly as flowers opening in one of Disney's speeded-up time-lapse cartoons.

In a taut narrative of the brass-knuckle chess the Reichmann family played with their bankers, tenants and creditors, Bianco traces the yellow-brick road its members followed from the Old World to the New, from one generation to the next, from obscurity to wealth—never deviating from their contradictory paths: "Vaulting ambition, on the one hand, and rock-ribbed piety, on the other."

Some fortunes become so big and abstract that instead of belonging to anyone, people belong to them. This was clearly the case with the Reichmanns. They were for a time the world's greatest developers, buying or building 40 million square feet of prime office in thirty-five North American downtowns. Those glossy American magazines that make a habit of listing the world's richest families ranked them just behind the inevitable Arab sheiks and the pre-alimony British royals. *Fortune* once estimated their net worth at $14.7 billion. Cash. (Bianco sticks with a mere $10 billion.)

A senior writer at *Business Week*, Bianco benefited from the cooperation of most of the Reichmanns, including five interviews with Paul that lasted six hours each. He has maintained his objectivity, and the book, which weighs in at just under five pounds, is not a heavy read. The author is at his best as a guide to the intricacies of Orthodox Judaism. His riveting descriptions of how Renée, the amazing matriarch of the Reichmanns' current generation, successfully embarked on daring rescues of east European Jews trapped by the Nazis ranks as a seldom equalled adventure in courage and compassion.

The Reichmanns' legend was created and fuelled by their penchant for secrecy. The defining comment on their clandestine behaviour and fiscal clout was the *cri de coeur* of the senior Bay Street analyst Ira Gluskin, who wailed, "I'm overwhelmed by the bastards!" ruefully adding: "Why won't they ever see me?"

Though Bianco didn't get a peek at their balance sheets, he traces how the brothers were able to keep their earnings and business methods confidential, thus maintaining the mystique that they were not only rich, but invulnerable. The money men who backed them didn't get a hint of how overextended they had become until it was too late.

Some of the Reichmanns' best friends, it turns out, were WASP bankers. Led by Canada's Big Five (except the Toronto-Dominion), ninety-one of the world's biggest banks showered the Reichmanns with virtually unlimited credit without ever demanding a glance at their books. The bankers quite plainly went bonkers in their bunkers. "No banker was more culpable," Bianco reveals, "than Don Fullerton (then chairman of the Commerce) for, as Olympia & York's lead bank, CIBC had effectively sanctioned the company's exemption from standard disclosure requirements."

Among the many highlights of Bianco's intriguing chronology of the family's downfall is a detailed analysis of how they broke their own code of ethics in the final hectic months of Olympia & York's attempts to avoid outright bankruptcy. "In the end," he concludes, "Paul Reichmann's ambition would ruinously exceed his talent, vast though it was. Nor would all the family always live up to the exalted moral code it espoused and came to epitomize."

The empire collapsed under its own weight because the Reichmanns had run it like a Mom & Pop convenience store, with family members making all the decisions—often based on nothing more than their hunches, formed within the protected and rarefied world in which they lived and worked.

Devastated by the avalanche of spending required to keep Canary Wharf afloat, their balance sheets eventually suffered losses that even the Reichmanns couldn't sustain. The minute Olympia & York was forced to undress in public, it became clear that the empire had no clothes.

V SCARING THE HORSES

34

THE GOSPEL ACCORDING TO PAUL

WHILE THE EARS and eyes of the nation are glued to Kim Campbell's every pronouncement and gesture, Paul Martin, Jr., the putative heir to Jean Chrétien's tarnished crown, is touring the country, selling the Liberal party's vision of a new Canada.

Whether or not Martin's ideas are ever translated into action is as important as their source and substance. His concepts boast the double advantage of being both practical and stimulating. Along with party research director Chaviva Hosek, a former Ontario cabinet minister, Martin has homed in on two or three of the country's most agonizing dilemmas and come up with sensible options. "Any new government," he told me, "will be facing two constraints: that this country is bankrupt and that the nation state has evolved into a new kind of entity which has suffered a substantial loss of sovereignty." Explained Martin, who was once a senior executive with Paul Desmarais's Power Corp. in Montreal and later took over the presidency and majority ownership of Canada Steamship Lines Inc. before entering politics in 1988: "Central governments such as Canada's have become too small to deal with the big, global problems, yet they remain too large and distant to deal with problems of local concern. So the challenge is to redefine the role of the central government as an institution that can do a limited number of things well, instead of continuing to pretend it can do everything for everybody."

For Martin, the most urgent priority in actualizing the cultural shift required to modernize Canada is to defrost the mind-set in which this country has been caught for a couple of decades. "The real problem started in 1973 during the OPEC crisis, when Pierre Trudeau tried to isolate us by claiming we could withdraw into ourselves and operate on oil prices lower than the rest of the world,"

Martin claims. "From then on, we stopped evolving. When Brian Mulroney took over, he had a tremendous mandate at just the right time, but didn't understand what he was supposed to do. By the time he did, during his second term, he had lost four crucial years and it was too late. You can't force change on a country without leading the cultural shift that would make it acceptable."

Martin sees that cultural shift being triggered by the creation of an innovative economy which, in turn, would require much more funding and facilities for industrial research and development. "But even if we doubled the research budget tomorrow," he says, "it would go down a sinkhole, because we can't absorb it. We don't know how to gather it, diffuse it or market it." Instead, he advocates that Ottawa get out of regional equalization programs and stop handing out grants to industry. He wants to use the savings to increase federal research expenditures, but with an important proviso. "We would focus R and D funds only in areas where Canada has a competitive advantage, because there just isn't any use trying to do something that's not world class," he contends. "I believe that a quarter of federal funds should go into environmental technologies flowing out of all those areas that have to do with natural resources, because we've got a comparative edge there. Another 25 per cent should go into medical research and the other 50 per cent into whatever areas current markets dictate, whether it's cold-water engineering or some of the remarkable submarine research being carried out in British Columbia."

Martin can visualize doubling Ottawa's current research budget, which he says totals between $2 billion and $3 billion annually, over the next decade. University labs and other research institutions would compete for these funds, and private-sector companies would only have access to the results if they had invested matching amounts at the beginning of the research project. Martin concedes that Canadian industry might have trouble financing such initiatives, but he believes that it could undertake joint ventures with foreign multinationals.

On the key issue of debt reduction, Martin's formula is a lot less imaginative. He supports Chrétien's semantic advocacy of doing away with the GST—only to have it replaced by another tax producing precisely the same painful consequences. Martin is convinced that huge amounts of public-sector expenditures could be saved by rationalizing the three levels of government to eliminate duplication. That's true enough, but no one has yet devised a way of forcing any level of Canadian government to give up a sliver of jurisdiction without the sort of quid pro quo constitutional negotiations involved in the ill-fated Meech Lake and Charlottetown accords. And only a transparently certifiable politician bent on self-annihilation would dare revive that process.

One of Martin's most intriguing policy pledges is that if the Liberals form the government, they will take on the banks. They've been granted tremendous benefits from their monopoly position," he says, "and they are not living up to their responsibilities." Declared Martin: "I would tell them, 'If you don't begin to exercise your mandates in a responsible way, we'll remove the restrictions on foreign banks operating here and make the market totally competitive.' The Big Six Canadian banks must start financing innovation, putting out some risk capital into small and medium-sized businesses, instead of pouring most of their credit into real-estate boondoggles." Martin also insists that once the banks have helped business clients develop products or services, they should stick with them in export markets, instead of leaving them gasping for credit lines at the Canadian border.

JUST BEFORE PAUL Martin, Sr., the veteran Liberal social reformer, died in September 1992, he told Paul Jr. at one of their final family gatherings, "I was the father of Canada's social revolution; you will create the country's *economic* revolution."

That's exactly what happened. The Liberals' second budget was a watershed document because it broke the back of the defeatist psychology, subscribed to by the half-dozen finance ministers who served in the Trudeau and Mulroney cabinets. They believed—or were convinced into believing—that if their budgets contained anything but marginal reductions of obvious extravagances, their government's political base would be threatened. That was why they never dared make the kind of deep cuts required before the Canadian economy could regain some semblance of reality.

Martin broke that psychological barrier, partly because he had no choice—the international money traders were in ambush, waiting to turn Canadian dollars into pesos. More significantly, Martin believes that only by detonating the kind of cultural turn-about triggered by his cuts can he save the country.

His second budget was a Magna Carta of the way Canadian society, especially the role of government, will evolve from now on. The cultural shift that Martin prescribed will force Canadians to finally accept the fact that universality is dead and that Santa Claus "don't live here any more." Universality was a wonderfully Canadian idea—the notion that everyone was entitled to every-thing, so that those who really needed financial help would bear no stigma. During most of the first four decades after the Second World War, Ottawa's social net kept growing until it now accounts for most of the financial burden expanding our national debt.

What Martin realized was that there was no polite, painless way to wean people away from expecting governments to provide every conceivable service from womb to tomb. This year's budget is the first instalment in a long winding road back to fiscal sanity.

Martin is only beginning his run. Having earned his spurs inter-nationally with this budget and having established the fact with his cabinet colleagues that Canadian voters are smart enough to under-stand the debt crisis and why we must worm our way out of it, he will now concentrate on trying to rationalize this country's three levels of government. Part of that exercise will involve deeper social-program cuts in the two budgets following this one. That is why Lloyd Axworthy's review was halted. In fact, Axworthy refused to sign off the budget's welfare-threatening provisions until the very last minutes before its presentation date had to be announced.

As more and more people study the details of the Martin bud-get they are beginning to realize that this is a truly remarkable doc-ument, not merely the annual accounting of Ottawa's revenues and expenditures. It is the blueprint for a social revolution that will eventually change the way we live and work. The first senior Ottawa bureaucrat to understand that was Tony Manera, the CBC president who resigned in protest. "This will change the definition of public broadcasting in Canada," he warned, understandably stunned by the $360-million cut the Mother Corp. was being asked to absorb over the next three years.

Apart from his courage in standing up for his principles, what

Manera realized was that the CBC would soon exist only in a brutally different and much-reduced environment. That's what revolutions are all about: they change value systems and nothing is the same ever again. That's what will happen to every institution that has even a whisper of federal funding in it. Canada's fundamental problem is that over the past few decades, our social objectives became divorced from increased productivity. That was why the culture of entitlement—the notion that we are owed a living by politicians just because we voted for them—broke down. For years now, we have consumed more than we have earned, and we must now pay back the debts we incurred by earning more than we consume, with governments using the difference to pay back the country's negative loan balances.

Martin's budget will cause much human suffering. But without it or some comparable document, we would not have made it through.

Now, we have a chance.

CANADA'S TWO GREAT political issues—Quebec independence and national debt—feed off each other: the more Ottawa cuts spending to reduce the deficit, the more trouble Lucien Bouchard can make for the federalists among Quebec voters. And the more shrill the separatists become in their demands, the higher move our interest rates, thus increasing the national debt.

The man caught in the middle of this agonizing dilemma is Paul Martin, who as federal finance minister has to consider the nuance of his every public word, in case a casual remark sets off a run on the already precariously poised Canadian dollar. During the couple of hours I spent privately with him recently, I found him surprisingly relaxed about his job and his country, confident that both will continue to flourish. "First of all," he told me, "I start with the basic premise that Quebeckers want to stay in Canada. I say this as a Quebecker. I've lived over half my life in Quebec and in the past six months have spoken in every nook and cranny of the province. They absolutely want to stay in, but they don't want to be pandered to. They want a country that works, which is why Jacques Parizeau's statements have been so damaging to him. On the one hand, he says, 'Don't anybody try the politics of fear in this thing.' Then, he immediately tries the politics of fear himself. That hurts him. The ease with which Parizeau is able to insert his foot in his mouth will sow the seeds of his defeat. Fortunately, he also has the habit of saying what he really thinks, which is enough to scare the hell out of anybody."

Still, Martin remains optimistic about the country's economic future. "Given the fundamentals of the country, within a year we're going to be looking very, very good," he predicts. "The European and Japanese economies are beginning to pick up, as is Latin America's, while Asia will continue its spectacular growth and the United States economy will attain its full potential. And here we'll be with our large, unused capacity. I really believe there's an opportunity here for a repeat of our post–Second World War boom. I've lived through a lot of business cycles, but I've never seen such underlying strength as today. All those businesses out there are lean and mean as hell, and their markets are growing."

What happens will depend largely on Martin's own ability to eliminate the deficit and start dealing with our national debt. He admits that he has been less than successful in communicating exactly how this can be done, because his government's 3 per cent deficit reduction target is not nearly radical enough. "That's only an interim objective," he insists. "The ultimate goal is to eliminate the deficit, but we must have realistic yardsticks by which we measure progress. The alternative is to do what the Tories did, which was to set unrealistic targets and then not meet them. Instead, I've set out precisely what it will be—a $39-billion deficit this year; $32 billion next year and $25 billion the year after that. Then, the year before the next election, we'll set new targets and the voters will be able to judge us on what we've done."

Meanwhile, Martin is getting a little tired of business supporters who tell him to accelerate deficit cuts, but argue that their industry should benefit from special exemptions. The country's long-term economic solution, he maintains, must involve real productivity gains. "The break year was 1973," he says. "That's when the productivity of all Western economies started to drop, unemployment started to rise, debt began to multiply—nowhere worse than in Canada.

"Brian Mulroney's most serious mistake was that after 1985 he didn't try to do anything with the deficit but allowed monetary policy to take over. The great battle John Crow waged should have been fought first on the fiscal side, by cutting government expenditures. We've got to rethink the role of the state, refocus it, make both government and the economy more productive."

Martin intends to recast the financial architecture of the country. "People rightly feel they're entitled to a job," he says. "Our problem is that we've forgotten that. What we've got is a society that says people are entitled to the alternative of a job. Apart from its human dimensions, the effect of getting people back to work on the deficit would simply be overwhelming."

He dismisses the threat of the International Monetary Fund moving into Canada, but insists he will not use devaluation of the currency to help resolve the debt problem. (That may be a theoretical proposition, since the Canadian dollar dropped to 72 cents from 89 cents in 1991 without the government's help.) "Devaluation always backfires," he says. "All it does is create a fool's paradise where you hide facing up to your real problems. Maintaining the integrity of a country's currency is essential, especially when you borrow as much money abroad as we do."

Although he lost to Jean Chrétien for the party leadership and many Liberals still think he should have won, Martin has not stopped aching to fulfil his father's quest. Paul Martin, Sr. ran unsuccessfully twice for the Liberal crown. Chrétien lifted the curse of finance ministers never being elected prime minister. Previously, only three men, John Turner, Sir Charles Tupper and R.B. Bennett, managed to occupy both offices, though only Bennett was elected to the top job.

Paul Martin recently moved into an Ottawa condominium that was once the ground floor of Sir Charles Tupper's original home.

It may be an omen.

35

THE ENGINEERING
OF PUBLIC CONSENT

THE CHRÉTIEN GOVERNMENT'S chief asset is the Hon. Paul Martin, the only cabinet member who has kept the faith by keeping his word. Against all odds, the finance minister has reduced spending by at least $15 billion, and will easily meet his target of wiping out the deficit by the end of the decade.

Martin is in a class of his own.

In their attempt to win public approval, other politicians resort to rhetorical flourishes, self-inflated authority, distortion of the facts, flattery, threats or even cheaper tricks. Martin prefers to be the *agent provocateur* of Canadian politics. (The term originally described the radicals salted throughout Paris crowds to fuel disturbances or riots during the French Revolution.) In Martin's case, he has successfully mobilized Canadian opinion to support one of the most painful cost-cutting exercises ever attempted by a democratic government in peacetime.

He has succeeded because he understands the engineering of public consent. Martin has been wise enough to follow the iron law of Canadian politics. It states that to get your way on any contentious issue, you don't have to be loved by the voters, but you sure as hell must be respected. (That sentiment sums up the difference between the still-revered Pierre Trudeau, who gave the country the finger and earned sixteen years in power, and the still-hated Brian Mulroney, who tried to endear himself to the people, and was terminally snubbed instead.)

Martin knew two things when he reluctantly agreed to be conscripted for the finance portfolio in 1993 by Jean Chrétien, then the freshly minted prime minister. The first was that Chrétien, who had so recently beaten him for the Liberal party's leadership, had pushed him into the kamikaze finance slot for one reason only: to permanently rid himself of an ambitious and capable rival. The second was that neither the Liberal party nor Canada would prosper, unless his crusade to eliminate the deficit succeeded.

In his battle to balance Ottawa's books, Martin never wavered. Faced with an inherited deficit of $46 billion, Martin treated the national accounts with the same intensity that a great climber gives a mountain face. By 1998, the deficit will fall below a respectable $10 billion.

Then will come the second phase of his strategy. Having established his credibility, Martin plans to demonstrate that cost-cutting isn't his only skill. "You can cut your way to deficit elimination," he told me, "but you can't cut your way to economic growth. The best way to handle the national debt is to get enough economic growth going so that the debt-ratio shrinks as a percentage of what we produce.

"Canadians are looking for some person or some institution to articulate which direction this country should go," he contends, "and the reason they're defying authority is that they've discovered authority isn't delivering for them any more. The problem is that politicians consistently promise things they can't deliver. Governments must emphasize the things that are essential for a good standard of living, or simply a decent life."

That will prove to be easier said than done. In the past three years, Martin's cost-cutting has reduced social safety net spending by 40 per cent, transferring many programs to the provinces, which can't afford to continue them. "The provinces represented 20 per cent of our spending and we had to deal with it," Martin insists. "The premiers consistently tell us to cut in our backyard first. We did that, and besides, we don't have a backyard that's separate from the provinces—there isn't any other Canada out there where we can cut."

Martin has made his choice. He knows having achieved the impossible dream of balancing the federal budget, and done so with the blessing of Canadian opinion, he has not only boosted Canada's international viability, but emerged as the natural contender for the P.M.'s crown.

36

THE LONELINESS OF THE LONG-DISTANCE RUNNER

WHEN I FIRST SAW Jean Charest, in the spring of 1993, he was lamely mouthing his prepared speech to the Tory leadership convention. It was one of his bad hair days. Too smooth by half, he sounded like one of those cocktail-bar piano warblers, substituting technique for soul. His leadership campaign had been an exercise in circumspection, bound by the high catechism of Tory orthodoxy. He seemed not so much too young to lead Canada's Progressive Conservative party as too untested.

Seventeen months later, when I met him again on one of his speaking trips to Vancouver, he was a different man. The weed-garden mop of hair was still there, and he still seemed younger than his thirty-six years, but there was also evidence of self-determination and inner strength. Being one of two survivors from the Tory massacre of 1993 has done much to concentrate his mind and harden his spine.

The political movement Charest leads, the one that founded this country and ruled it for 51 of the 127 years since Confederation, has no power, no platform and no money. The party went into Kim Campbell's 1993 campaign with a surplus of $5.6 million and emerged from the slaughter with a deficit of $5.2 million. That means their two seats cost them more than $5 million each. The Conservatives have been deprived of official recognition in the Commons, and Charest has only a minimum backup staff—a dozen people, including clerks and secretaries—to help him kick-start the Tories back to life.

What he does have is charm to burn, an agenda and, above all, the surefire conviction that history is on his side.

He could be right.

Charest has enjoyed a charmed political life. Having won his first election in 1984, he was immediately named assistant deputy speaker of the Commons and, two years later, elevated to cabinet at age twenty-eight, appropriately as minister of state for youth. Within the next seven years, he rose to become deputy prime minister and, shortly afterwards, Conservative leader. Now, he has everything except a party.

In the coming election campaign, Charest believes the issue will be Jean Chrétien and his inactive government. He is angry and determined, accused the Chrétien administration of being "the most unprincipled, cynical and opportunistic this country has ever seen."

Politics, he emphasizes, must be about Canada's future as we step into a new century, and this is where Charest, as the only leader young enough to straddle the millennium, is heating up the rhetoric. "We cross our own rivers and it's one thing just to continue selfishly along and think about our own future, but we have an obligation to build a bridge to those following us—and that's what the next election will be about.

"One of the quotes in my policy document is that by the year 2026, almost one in four Canadians will be sixty-five and over," he points out. "I stopped myself when I read that and calculated how old I'd be in 2026, and discovered I'll be sixty-eight. When you combine that with the fact that there will be a lot fewer younger people paying and supporting all the things that we've come to expect, you begin to realize that it really is in our interest to build bridges to the next generation. I don't see the Chrétien government even being aware of the issue."

CHAREST WAS THE ONLY politician who advanced his status during the 1995 Referendum. Freed from the ridicule that attends his minuscule caucus of one in the Commons and tied into a national unity cause that has always been his mission, he emerged as an attractive national figure with an unlimited future.

A minor figure during the Mulroney years, Charest rose to prominence with his handling of the parliamentary committee that examined the Meech Lake Accord, just before its collapse in June of 1990. The job gave him a chance to observe raw politics at the summit, and his friendship with Lucien Bouchard (who once acted as his mentor) taught him a harsh lesson about how little loyalty counts at those perilous heights. He went into the PC leadership campaign three years later, a last-minute candidate enlisted not to make Kim Campbell's coronation too obvious, and very nearly won. But it was the 1993 election campaign that really turned his head around. Aware that Charest's appeal was far more potent than hers, Prime Minister Campbell refused to allow him to campaign nationally. He withstood the Bloc Québécois tide in his home province, and despite attractive offers from the private sector, decided to hang in. "The main reason I chose to stay," he says, "was because I anticipated the Referendum, and it didn't make a lot of sense after what I'd been through to leave and not to be on the ice when that happened."

His role in the Referendum was deliberately ambiguous, because the Liberals stage-managing the No campaign didn't want to give him the kind of exposure that would allow him to outshine their own leaders. But Jean Chrétien opted out of the day-to-day combat, and Daniel Johnson didn't have the charisma. That left Charest at centre stage and he made the most of it.

"No amount of manipulation can hide the real and dramatic consequences of a Yes vote," he was telling voters across Quebec. "Whatever kind of candy coating they put on, it still comes out tasting like the traditional Jacques Parizeau sticky bun. The separatists will never be able to disguise the real risks of independence.... Parizeau and Bouchard, for whom overlap and duplication are a cardinal sin, have promised to rehire all the federal servants working in Quebec. They are guaranteeing us access to an economic market from which we have just separated!"

Unlike most of the federalists, he didn't rely on facts and figures to make his case. "People pay no attention to figures, no matter who puts them on the table," he says. "I had to emphasize to Quebeckers the strong link they have in their hearts for Canada, which I am convinced is there, and has always been there." The most moving part of his presentation occurred when he stopped himself, reached into his pocket and brought out his blue Canadian passport. "If you vote Yes," he intoned, holding the document in front of him, as if it were a chalice, "you're putting your passport on the table, giving your passport to Lucien Bouchard—in exchange for what ...?"

CERTAINLY, AS FAR AS Jean Charest is concerned, there isn't a chance in hell that Preston Manning can realize his dream of taking over the Progressive Conservative Party of Canada, as so many Tories and Reformers have suggested.

"The party I lead is not for sale, rent or hire for someone else's gain," Charest told me. "Under my leadership, the Conservatives will not abandon their history, heritage and commitment to balanced and comprehensive national policies."

Reform could claim some impressive gains in the 1993 campaign, but what it could not claim was to be a sponsor of policies that are either national or balanced. By its nature and its genesis, it is a protest movement, the voice of frustrated westerners who want—and deserve—adequate recognition in the corridors of federal power. Preston Manning has been able to enlist many well-meaning adherents, but he has also attracted and never really rejected some of the looniest fruitcakes ever to emerge from the political swamps.

"You can't put the two together," Charest emphasizes. "People are very badly misreading the situation when they talk about uniting the Canadian right. Progressive Conservatives have a totally different tradition. Nation-building is part of the core and the fibre of the party, whether it's in social issues or unity issues, while Reform under Manning has stood quite clearly on the other side, having built political capital on the things that divide us. It's not as though they expressed their destructive philosophy at one point and abandoned those ideas, they've confirmed and reconfirmed it before, during and after the Referendum."

He regards it as a sweet irony that this so-called grass-roots party had to distribute a memo to their members scripting precisely what they ought to say when trying to woo away renegade Tories: "Preston must think his MPs are dumb, if he has to tell them what words to use. On the other hand, he must know them a lot better than we do."

The assumption that loyal Conservatives would jump ship to bolster a party that no matter how hard it tries to camouflage its hidden agenda wants Quebec out of Confederation, doesn't match with much of an understanding of Canadian politics. The Tories believe in free enterprise, self-interest and the right to own property, just as Reform does. But unlike Preston and his true believers, Conservatives don't consider individual liberty to be an infinite concept unconnected to the wider interests of Canadian society. "Unlike Reform, I believe in the creative role of a national government, and that a national political party must seek to balance the aspirations of the language and cultural majorities and minorities and articulate a truly national interest," Charest insists.

It's the difference between Reform's distrustful view of government as essentially a destructive force and the PC vision of government as fallible and badly in need of change, but in its potential, still the highest expression of the collective will of the people. "To assume that we could ever become part of the flash-and-burn extreme right that's found now in some quarters of American conservatism is just silly," Charest complains.

There's never been much illusion about the Tories, under any of their recent leaders, espousing a consistent philosophy or being able to enact into law whatever idealism they may feel. But their pragmatic determination to ensure equity in the distribution of collective and individual benefits is vastly different from the Reform view of governing, which holds that everyone must be left to their own devices, at the mercy of life's unpredictable calamities.

Like most mainstream Tories who care about their country, Charest is highly cynical of the ideological shindig being staged in Calgary by that yappy puppy David Frum. "Frum's conference is a perfect illustration of people who don't care about their country," he says. "It's very clinical and has no relation to what's really happening. They act as though the Referendum had never taken place and pretend that the national unity issue will not reappear on the screen again, and that there won't have to be political leaders who can deal with it."

Although Charest was the only politician to emerge from the Quebec Referendum with his honour intact, he stresses that this is only one of the many issues that must be tackled. "As a political party, as opposed to a movement," he contends, "we're committed to espousing a broad range of issues and offering the country a cohesive vision of our future."

Charest will have a tough time maintaining his proud stand as a political general without an army. The fact that his party made a dismal showing in last month's six by-elections can't be easily dismissed. Only a good showing in the next election can provide the critical mass of followers—and MPs—that will allow the Progressive Conservatives to claim the rightful place that their long and distinguished history has earned for them.

Canada's Tories date all the way back to the Family Compact of pioneer Canada and the rebellions of 1837. Conservatives were then, as they are now, emotional loyalists, which was the common factor in uniting under one banner the fanatically crown-worshipping Orangemen of Ontario with the *Ultramontanes* of Quebec—a marriage between those who were more loyal than the King of England and those who were more Catholic than the Pope. Sir John A. Macdonald was able to unite these factions behind his moderately nationalistic Tories to establish what he carefully called the Liberal-Conservative party which brought about Confederation in 1867.

THE CONSERVATIVES' LONG history has been an unrelenting search for the reincarnation of a chieftain as successful in smoothing out internal differences as Macdonald; in the process, they went through nineteen leaders, compared to the Liberals' nine, and changed their party name five times.

What the Tories needed just as badly as another Macdonald was another Sir George Etienne Cartier, the Montreal lawyer whose diplomatic skills enlisted Quebec behind the idea of founding a "self-governing colony." The hunt for someone acceptable to Quebec voters grew so absurd that in 1938 the Tories chose as their leader a Lakehead physician named Robert James Manion, whose chief claim to glory was that he had a French-Canadian wife. The most successful Tory campaigner since Macdonald was the party's first Quebec leader, Brian Mulroney, who won two majorities back to back.

Although they were originally far right of the political centre and a voice if not of Big Business generally, at least of Bay Street and the secondary manufacturing industries of central Ontario, the Tories took a tiny step to the middle in 1942 when a rump of 150

Conservatives met at Port Hope, Ontario, and came out for the welfare measures which until then had been considered rank socialist heresy. The party chose a prairie Progressive and former Manitoba premier, John Bracken, as their leader. After running a disastrous election campaign, Bracken was forced out, though he managed to change the party's monicker to its current Progressive Conservative oxymoron. In his farewell address to the 1948 convention that chose his successor, Bracken defined the ideology that has driven the party ever since. "To the left," he intoned, "lies the hidden slope of communism; to the right, a short and bitter descent to oblivion. On the other hand, this party can follow the straight path to reasoned progress."

Unlike Reform, the Tories have ever since not allowed themselves to be captured by ambitious ideologues hunting for a political roost.

By giving in and abandoning his historical roots, Jean Charest could quickly become the conscience of a Reform-Tory merger.

But it would never work.

37

PRESTO'S CONTRADICTORY VISION

PRESTON MANNING'S APPROACH impresses his followers for one big reason. Canadians have lost confidence not only in politicians, but in representative democracy itself. The Reform party appears to offer an alternative: a system of direct representation in which elected MPs act as their constituencies' delegates, reflecting their specific views rather than those of their party, or even of themselves.

But that approach won't work because a country of this size and complexity, which also happens to be bankrupt, cannot be governed without its central authorities making tough, often unpopular decisions. Manning's utopian approach to government is superficially attractive and totally impractical.

More serious and much more dangerous is his policy that Quebec must give up its distinctions, which is reminiscent of Clyde Wells's obdurate stand during the Meech Lake debate. Presto's vision of the New Canada is blunt and brutal: either Quebec stays on precisely the same terms as every other province, or it must leave. That's what he means when he keeps repeating: "The Old Canada is dying. We need a New Canada!"

In fact, of course, the Old Canada isn't just dying. It's dead. But the Reform party's New Canada without Quebec is no Canada at all. Yet a Canada without Quebec is where Manning's policies clearly lead, though he insists that he doesn't want the country to break up. He is against official bilingualism and multiculturalism, pretending that this country remains dominated by WASPs like himself. Current demographics disprove that, but it's bound to be a popular stand with the White Anglo-Saxon Protestants who don't realize they've become a shrinking minority.

Manning preaches that the Pearson-Trudeau-Mulroney approach

"has produced a house divided against itself." He is at his most eloquent pursuing that theme. "We do not want to live, nor do we want our children to live, in a house divided against itself," he emphasizes, "particularly one divided along racial and linguistic lines. We do not want to, nor do we intend to, leave this house ourselves—even though we have spent most of our constitutional eves on the back porch. Either all Canadians, including the people of Quebec, make a clear commitment to Canada as one nation, or Quebec and the rest of Canada should explore a better, but more separate, relationship between the two."

I recently spent an afternoon with Manning. Unlike most contemporary politicians, he is acutely aware of Prairie history, champions a genuine ideology, is smart, sophisticated and very much in tune with what's happening in his part of the country. Yet he must know that to tell Quebeckers, in their current mood, that they're welcome to stay in Canada as long as they have the same sanctions, and powers, as Prince Edward Islanders, is to invite them to leave. No Quebec politician or citizen can support this narrow view, which amounts to cultural genocide.

His policy explains why Manning has no intention of nominating Quebec candidates, and why his party has caught fire across western Canada. For those Canadians who resent Quebec's special place in Confederation, or have felt that French Canada's aspirations have received too much attention and too many federal dollars, the Reform party represents a legitimate alternative to express their anti-Quebec feelings.

It would be wrong and much too simplistic to accuse Manning himself of being anti-French. Neither was John Diefenbaker, the last western leader to seriously advocate a One Canada policy. Because he had been a victim of discrimination himself, Diefenbaker's dream was to foster a single nationality that would wipe away any stigma that could be attached to a person's ancestry. That was a worthy political goal, articulated in his support for "unhyphenated Canadianism," but it took no account of Quebec's special place and history.

By rejecting that basic demand, Manning has become English Canada's champion of sovereignty-association and is effectively encouraging Quebec's separatists to make the break. "Quebec is the only province that can crack the Canadian Constitution wide open," he emphasizes. "It's our hope in the West that Quebec does crack it open. We have some fundamental changes to propose as well, and our list will be quite different from Quebec's."

As architect of the Reform party's determination to capture a majority of the seats in the House of Commons, by rejecting Quebec's aspirations, Manning has launched himself on a risky political venture. Should he succeed, Quebec would separate and that would leave Ontario—with its ninety-nine seats—predominant in the New Canada he advocates. He would then have to face the anger of his western followers who started the Reform movement, only to find that it helped consolidate Ontario as the country's power centre.

Canadian politics has become so volatile that anything can happen. But Reform, which not so long ago was a fringe movement that no one outside Alberta's Oil Patch took seriously, has become a significant political force. Only Preston Manning can determine whether its success will help win proper Ottawa representation for western Canada—or tear the country apart.

38

THE CLYDE WELLS
OF THE NINETIES

EXCEPT FOR LUCIEN Bouchard's diplomatically timed trip to the bathroom—which, come to think of it, may go down in Canada's constitutional history as one of its few inspired moments—the recent first ministers' conference served one useful purpose. It introduced the rest of the country to its newest and potentially most disruptive political operator: Glen Clark, British Columbia's street-smart premier, who has chutzpah to burn and threatens to become the Clyde Wells of the late 1990s.

During the decade he spent as premier of Newfoundland, Wells's pursuit of his personal agenda aborted Ottawa's attempts to reach accommodation with Quebec. An island with less than 3 per cent of the country's population thus set the national agenda, or at least prevented Canada and most of the other provinces from realizing theirs.

Clark is bent on blowing up national initiatives by lobbing similar hand grenades at Ottawa—unless the feds take account of *his* priorities first. In these confrontations, the Pacific-coast politician will exercise far more leverage than his Atlantic predecessor ever did. Unlike Wells, whose ideas flowed from an overdeveloped sense of his own divinity, Clark's initiatives are rooted deep in the attitudes of his province. He rules over the nation's most dynamic regional economy, is as self-confident as any Canadian politician since Pierre Trudeau and owes Ottawa nothing.

The NDP premier's remarkable domestic policy clout reflects the fact that his anti-Ottawa posture faithfully reflects the thinking of the overwhelming majority of the province's voters—including the 61 per cent who didn't support him in the 1996 election. It has already been forgotten that in the only national vote on reaching an accommodation with Quebec—the 1992 Referendum—B.C. led the polls against the Charlottetown Accord, with a decisive 68 per cent of ballots cast on the No side.

British Columbians are patriotic Canadians but they define the country their own way. Anyone who lives east of Toronto's CN Tower can't begin to comprehend how alien the notion of Quebec as a "distinct society" feels on Canada's Pacific coast. British Columbians don't have much sense of history and have never considered themselves to be a founding people. But they know exactly what they are: rebels with a cause who live in an autonomous state of mind and don't know what they'll be when they grow up—because they never intend to. They feel B.C. society is just as distinct as Quebec's. More than that, they're convinced that every one of the province's four million citizens represents a majority of one—and act accordingly.

At a recent first ministers' conference, Clark accused the federal government of being "arrogant, intransigent and stupid," exercising his well-known aptitude for understatement. He was the only premier who joined Quebec's separatist leader in opposing a national securities commission, a national tax-collection agency and national social policies, warning that he will boycott Team Canada's next effort to boost Canadian exports.

Clark's outburst was triggered by the Chrétien government's refusal to consider handing over management of the crucial Pacific salmon fisheries to provincial administration, later rescinded. But B.C.'s complaints run much deeper, touching the very core of Jean Chrétien's national unity initiatives. "We can't allow our agenda to be dominated by appeasement to the separatist government of Quebec," the B.C. premier insists, heretically maintaining that if he were to learn another language, it would be Mandarin, not French.

Clark and his ministers regularly trot out legitimate complaints about how the feds mistreat B.C. But those who occupy Ottawa's command posts pay not the slightest attention. The Canadian navy's multi-billion-dollar contracts for frigates and other warships were given exclusively to yards in Quebec and New Brunswick, killing the B.C. shipbuilding industry. Ottawa finances half of Quebec's welfare costs, but only a third of B.C.'s. The province's taxpayers send $1.1 billion to Canada's poorer regions through equalization payments, and feel justified in wanting something back.

The excuse for Ottawa's lack of action is that the Pacific economy is healthy enough to carry the extra load. Still, job creation may be Clark's biggest problem because the private sector has become increasingly nervous about the NDP's threats of imposing a wealth tax and Clark's refusal to rank lowering the provincial debt as his prime objective.

In the weeks and months ahead, Glen Clark will become a reluctant architect of 21st-century Canada—mostly through the impact of his vetoes. Yet his anti-Ottawa crusade is rooted firmly in British Columbia's political traditions. Amor de Cosmos, one of the province's first premiers, whose real name was John Smith, set the pattern with his battle cry: "I would not object to a little revolution now and again in British Columbia, if we are treated unfairly," he declared, "for I am one of those who believe that political hatreds attest to the vitality of a state."

Expect vitality galore from the Pacific coast in the run-up to the millennium. Glen Clark may yet achieve the impossible and make Clyde Wells look like a great statesman.

39

JEAN CHRÉTIEN'S
WINNING FORMULA

BENJAMIN DISRAELI, THE wisest and most cunning of British states-men, once observed that a good politician has to know both himself and his times.

That aphorism goes a long way towards explaining Jean Chrétien's undiminished popularity immediately after his election in 1993. The Liberal leader demonstrated an uncanny ability to read the times.

Except for killing the military helicopter purchase and the Pearson International Airport expansion, Chrétien did virtually nothing during his first two years in office. Yet according to a survey by Insight Canada Research, public approval of his performance was running at 75 per cent. That was the highest rating ever recorded by a Canadian prime minister, and the popularity of his Liberal government was only a few percentage points behind his own. According to Insight's Michael Marzolini, Chrétien's extraordinary ratings were based on "value-alignment"—his ability to personify the values Canadians want in their prime minister: integrity and humility, respect for the law, the determination to govern without being in people's faces all the time, and the determination to run the country quietly, without disturbing the horses.

Historian David Bercuson, dean of the University of Calgary's faculty of graduate studies, whose fascinating books and articles mostly warn about Canada's imminent disintegration, concluded that Chrétien "has so far proven to be the most popular and capable Canadian prime minister of the past 25 years."

Chrétien knows that politics is unpredictable and that his popularity is bound to sag, but he also knows that for the moment he can smugly bask in the comfortable pew of having no rivals. He can relax and follow the Napoleonic dictum that no leader should ever interfere with an enemy while he is in the process of destroying himself. The 1993 campaign decimated the Tories and the NDP, producing those twin movements of regional rage and discontent— the Bloc Québécois and the Reform party—that seem to be relentlessly playing out their journeys to eventual oblivion.

What made Chrétien all but untouchable is that ordinary Canadians believe he is one of their own, instead of one of those blow-dried élitists who run the country according to their smug, self-serving agendas. Most people see Chrétien as a guy who feels very comfortable in his own skin, a politician who, without fuss or fanfare, is trying to make the best of the difficult political circumstances in which he finds himself. After a quarter of a century of the confrontational styles of Pierre Trudeau and Brian Mulroney, the overwhelming Canadian response to politicos who want to enrol them in yet one more nation-saving crusade is: "Don't go away mad, just go away." Chrétien is responding to that passive anger by refusing to be drawn into constitutional wars, playing to the balconies of public opinion by doing very little, and saying less.

Since there has been no action out of Ottawa—as opposed to position papers that are consuming Canadian forests at an alarming rate—it's impossible to ascribe any ideological stance to Chrétien's version of Liberalism. He seems to define the political centre not so much as a firm philosophical position as that welcome point in the ideological spectrum where he is being attacked from both the left and the right. His beliefs were probably best summed up by Senator Jack Austin, who recently organized Chrétien's successful selling jaunt to China: "Neither the public nor the private sector should dominate the other. The Liberal commitment is to govern in a way that achieves a harmonious balance between the two. Liberals believe that encouraging self-initiative and self-responsibility requires society to create a realistic set of costs for those who take those initiatives and accept those responsibilities. It is not a law of the jungle, where the winner takes all."

Chrétien read the political winds wisely enough to win the 1993 election, and the only one he lost—to John Turner for the 1984 Liberal leadership—was fortunate, because Brian Mulroney would have beaten him at the polls that year in any event.

His policies and principles can be summed up in two words: whatever works.

40

THE CHRÉTIEN MYSTERY

EVEN THOUGH JEAN Chrétien keeps assuring anyone who will listen that he wants an early election, the Liberal leader remains a mystery.

Chrétien became a member of Canada's House of Commons when John Kennedy was still in the White House and Harold Macmillan was prime minister of England. That was nine presidents and five prime ministers ago.

There's something vaguely reassuring about his Shawinigan-on-the-rocks accent, his Gallic charm and that crooked smile lighting up a face that looks as if someone had been practising taxidermy on it.

But whatever reassurance that image produces must be tempered by a reminder of Chrétien's political shortcomings. He rose through the ranks of the Liberal party by being well briefed, fast on his feet, aggressive and tart, hiding behind his *habitant* mannerisms whenever the going got tough. Tracing his performance in the nine portfolios he has occupied, it quickly becomes clear that most of his policy initiatives have consisted of mildly groping towards orthodox solutions.

He has yet to have an original thought.

That wouldn't matter much, because few of our political leaders indulge in such luxuries, but his real problem is that he has never been a leader. That requires very special qualities that seem foreign to his personality and outlook.

Being a nice guy just isn't enough.

The plain fact is that the Liberal party has yet to recover from Pierre Trudeau, who dominated its every move for sixteen years. His presence on the national and international scenes was so compelling that no one has since been able to match his intellectual legacy. On the other hand, Trudeau left the party with a clean slate: no policies, no field organization, no money and a Quebec power base that within months would switch its allegiance to Tory blue.

The Liberal party under John Turner was no better off, being a dispirited residue of survivors from the political wars, innocent of policy, philosophy or any other purpose except to replace Brian Mulroney's Conservatives in power.

Trying to guess exactly where Chrétien stands on any issue depends on which day you ask him. The fabric of his political commitment is like a veil, translucent but not transparent, serving to protect the inner man, rather than expose him and his ideas to wider constituencies. His convictions (except that Tories are evil and Grits are saints) seem negotiable, so that he gives the impression of profound detachment, moving through many worlds, without fully belonging to any but his own.

He runs his party as an instrument of accommodation of ideas that swings like a miscued pendulum between Sheila Copps on the left and John Manley on the right, with Paul Martin bravely holding up the centre. This notion of brokerage politics may have worked once, but now it has an old-fashioned odour about it. No longer is it politically desirable to judge policies and propositions solely by their consequences.

The country is crying out for leadership. We suffer from horrendous economic and social problems, but beyond specific issues is the loss of faith in the system. Lacking the unity of purpose that allows a people to think together on fundamental issues, Canadians have become citizens of a country that no longer believes in itself.

That's the challenge facing the Liberals at a time they've tied their destiny to a leader who seems a generation or two out of tune with the real world. What the Liberal party needs is a young Walter Gordon, a revolutionary proponent of change and reform, not afraid to stub his toes on genuinely fresh ideas. Not since Gordon served as minister of finance in the early Pearson years during the mid-1960s, have the Liberals had the advantage of leading their own crusade, instead of following someone else's.

41

THE INNOCENCE
OF BRIAN MULRONEY

IN AN AGE WHEN O.J. Simpson remains a regular on L.A. golf courses, Dorothy Joudrey is back hosting Calgary house parties after pumping six shots into her estranged husband, and Alan Eagleson appears on the CBC's Royal Canadian Air Farce to joke about the many indictments outstanding against him—the quality of justice is obviously strained.

But at least that dubious trio enjoyed the advantage of facing the accusations against them from that most basic tenet of justice in civilized society: the presumption of innocence until proven guilty.

That was not the case with Brian Mulroney. In trying to defend their actions, the minister of justice and the commissioner of the RCMP just kept digging themselves deeper into the legal quicksand that has from the start characterized the bribery charges surrounding the 1988 purchase of thirty-four Airbus jets by Air Canada. What these two befuddled worthies contend is that while they are sorry they lied in the letter they sent to the Swiss government—in which they portrayed the former prime minister as being guilty of "criminal activity" in attempting to "defraud" his own government—they're in no way absolving the ex-P.M. from having committed such crimes.

That's about as close to subverting the justice system as the Canadian government has ever come. It means that any one of us can be condemned of any crime, without the recourse of the Crown having to prove its case. Under existing Canadian law (Section 487 of the Criminal Code), police and Crown prosecutors must establish "reasonable grounds" for issuing a warrant. That fundamental safeguard was ignored in Ottawa's proceedings against Mulroney.

It's obvious that Ottawa's motive in pursuing this curious case had less to do with its facts than its politics. Tearing apart Mulroney's record in office is fair ball; denying him justice is not.

Not being a Liberal has yet to be declared a crime in Canada—though the Chrétien government seems to be working on it.

Another perverse aspect of this whole mess is that even though Ottawa has now accepted the responsibility for having fumbled badly in its handling of the case, no one will accept any blame or even admit a smidgen of accountability for what happened. The RCMP had no qualms about dragging Mulroney's name through the mud, but is now shielding from view the behaviour of its investigator who broke the force's own rules by leaking the contents of its Swiss letter to an unidentified "third party." His actions will only be reviewed by a powerless internal panel.

It gets worse. According to Roger Tasse, a former deputy minister of justice and now one of Mulroney's defence lawyers, the RCMP offered to withdraw its offending letter, if Mulroney opened his bank accounts for RCMP perusal. That smacks of blackmail. Mulroney's people have also revealed that never in the course of its investigation did the RCMP contact Mulroney or ask to hear his version of the Airbus incident.

That doesn't mean that the former prime minister necessarily has truth on his side, while his accusers don't. But in the fifteen months that the Mounties have been investigating the situation, it surely would have been relevant to at least listen to an alternate version of events that led the force to the assumed "guilty" verdict in its Swiss memorandum—sent before it seriously started its investigations. Under Canada's system of justice, an accused has the inalienable right to confront his or her accusers and answer their evidence. That was denied Mulroney.

This is a deadly serious issue. The RCMP has made mistakes and obviously is incapable of guarding a building, even if it happens to contain a sleeping prime minister. But the force has throughout Canadian history earned a justified reputation of acting fairly in its pursuit of criminals. The Mulroney case will not destroy that hard-won reputation. But it will weaken it at a time when the credibility of all our institutions is under siege. The RCMP is too essential in the Canadian pattern of justice to allow itself these kinds of lapses.

One of the pieces of evidence lost in the turmoil of this goofy case are the public statements of Pierre Jeanniot, currently director-general of the International Air Transport Association, who was CEO of Air Canada from 1984 to 1990, when the decision to buy the $1.8-billion Airbus fleet was made. He has outlined in great detail how Canada's national airline chose the European planes, squarely on the basis of its own technical committee's recom-mendations. He has also emphatically noted that no lobbyist approached him to try and influence the deal.

The Canadian request was obviously a fishing expedition launched at the initial stage, not the end or even the middle of the judicial investigation of Mulroney, whose international reputation got crunched in the process.

Mulroney is convinced that the justice department's serious errors of judgement in handling his case has created a gross injustice that can only be alleviated if he is totally and publicly absolved. One of Mulroney's former chiefs of staff, Stanley Hartt, emphasized that the case threatens the most important freedom we have. "Leaving aside the fact that the person involved is a former prime minister," he says, "the main issue in this case is the casual disregard of the rights of the accused. The British system of justice which we have in this country is the fairest there is, because you're presumed innocent till proven guilty, the Crown has the burden of proof beyond any reasonable doubt, and you have the right to confront your accusers in an open court and answer their evidence. None of that's happened in this case, which has seen the justice department being careless about their use of evidence and casual about the presumption of innocence. This should send shivers up and down our spines, worrying that because of this case, the state can now destroy us without having the burden of proof in their possession that our system demands."

And so it should.

In retrospect, the Mounties must have realized early on that they didn't have adequate evidence to pursue this case. Last May, they requested but were denied an eight-month extension on the trial date, presumably hoping to gather facts to justify the criminal indictment they had already couriered to Switzerland. It never happened.

Why don't Mulroney's accusers admit that during the past fifteen months of relentless investigation, including the hard-won access they gained to Swiss bank accounts, they have turned up nothing to justify their hunt? If they had, their apology would never have been issued. Justice Minister Allan Rock and RCMP Commissioner Philip Murray ought to call another press conference and admit that they were wrong, not only about the "tone" of their Swiss letter, but about its contents.

The only way to reduce the damage inflicted by the unjustified persecution of Brian Mulroney is to end it.

VI QUEBEC ON A HOT TIN ROOF

STANDING BY IS NOT ENOUGH

THERE WAS A TIME, not so long ago, when Hugh MacLennan's adoption of Rainer Rilke's romantic epiphany about "two solitudes" adequately described the benevolent disinterest that characterized French-English relations in this country.

Yet now, when Quebec seems close to realizing its dream of nationhood and the disintegration of Canada looms as a distinct possibility, we seem to have lapsed from solitude into lassitude. Except for professional constitutional gunslingers and the odd Canadian patriot (a breed as rare as witch doctors in modern African documentaries), few English Canadians seem to care what happens to their country or to Quebec.

We stand in danger of becoming the only nation in world history to break up out of sheer boredom.

The situation reminds me of a dialogue fragment in one of Arthur Koestler's early novels, in which an exasperated citizen innocent of wrongdoing is being interrogated by a relentless KGB agent.

"I accuse this man," intones the prosecutor wearily, "of complicity in murder and crimes of the present, past and future."

"But I never killed a fly," pleads the astonished defendant.

"Ah, but the flies you didn't kill," replies the triumphant official, "brought pestilence to the whole province."

Similarly, the possibility exists that what we're NOT doing could cost us our country.

It's because of this very real quandary that I believe standing by is not enough, that we must rally our thoughts and actions in defence of Canada. It won't be easy. There have been too many false alarms—after all, Confederation was supposed to have caved in when René Lévesque won the 1976 provincial election; a decade later, the sun was never supposed to rise again if Meech Lake failed; and two years after that, hell was going to freeze over if Canadians voted to reject the Charlottetown Accord.

While there's no way of knowing whether the results of the next Referendum will be different, on each of those previous occasions there were passionate voices raised to make the case for a continued partnership. Now, there is mostly silence. If none of us speaks out, *we* deserve to be charged with treason—like that misguided innocent in the Koestler trial—not Lucien Bouchard, who is dedicated to fighting for *his* country—Quebec.

Separatism in Quebec remains a minority cause, but its adherents are buoyed by a vibrant form of politics and a sure sense of place. Since most English Canadians have no personal framework within which to fit or even understand that kind of impulse for self-determination, they tend to interpret each of the Parti or Bloc Québécois's policy declamations as the hot breath of revolution.

That does not make for useful dialogue. It is essential we get to like or at least tolerate one another again. More important, we must discover what value we can place on staying together, how useful we can be to each other within a continuing Canadian alliance.

For starters, that means English Canada must give up the silly notion that the status quo remains a viable option. It is not, and we mustn't keep pretending that not discussing alternatives makes it so.

At the same time, moderate Quebeckers must begin to realize that their historical notion of Canada as a marriage of convenience between two distinct societies is dead—if it was ever alive. When Toronto, which is the capital of non-French Canada, is populated by less than 40 per cent of what used to be called WASPs, you know there's a new country out there and that those porridge-eating, pale-skinned conciliators with Scottish names and mid-Atlantic accents aren't in charge any more. That doesn't make English Canada any less interesting or less worthwhile—on the contrary—but it does mean that there's a new reality in play, which most Quebeckers have so far ignored.

What they've not taken into account is that English Canada's new coalition has roots, just as strong, if not as deep, in its society as French Canadians have in theirs.

Monsieur Bouchard is a shrewd ambassador for his cause, but

some of his ideas are strictly Looney Tunes. Lucien's basic tactical and strategic error is to believe that Canadians outside Quebec will accept the splitting asunder of their country with cool equanimity.

It's not going to happen.

In this modern age, you don't need too many people at the barricades to make the point to the world (especially the international currency traders) that Quebec's future as an independent state will not be financed by a Canada suddenly deprived of its history and geography. Canadians love their country as much as Bouchard longs for his would-be republic. Quebec independence will not be achieved without a horrendously traumatic period of adjustment. The most likely victims of that transition—at least in terms of lower living standards—will be citizens of Quebec, the very people who imagine that sovereignty will resolve the very issues it will create.

The Parti Québécois keeps reiterating its curious position of coming out simultaneously for virginity and motherhood. "Let's keep things as they are," Jacques Parizeau used to snort through his moustache. As well as affirming that Quebec would retain the Canadian dollar as its currency ("to maintain the economic status quo between Quebec and Canada"), Parizeau suggested that such potentially controversial issues as division of the national debt (and presumably the status of the First Nations within a newly independent Quebec) should be left until "after the political situation has calmed." In other words, Quebec will claim its independence from a supine Canada led by a spineless Ottawa that allows the most tricky negotiating points to be set over for discussion to some ill-defined future.

I think not.

The last time separation in Quebec became such an ugly issue was under the late René Lévesque, who in 1980 called—and lost—a referendum on sovereignty-association. That hybrid term signified anything anybody wanted it to mean, even in a country like Canada, which once oxymoronically billed itself as "a self-governing colony." The only historic precedent to sovereignty-association was the madcap constitution of the Austro-Hungarian empire. The late Eugene Forsey, a lapsed socialist who was appointed to the Senate by Pierre Trudeau and who knew more about the Canadian constitution than anyone else (including his Senate sponsor), once described sovereignty-association as "a horse that won't start, let alone run. You can no more negotiate sovereignty-association than you can negotiate sour sugar, dry water, boiling ice or stationary motion."

The substance of Forsey's argument hasn't changed, even though the PQ position often smells like its updated version. The Bouchard scenario of embarking on this pure and beautiful mission of shedding the Canada that has held Quebec in its constitutional chains for 130 years—yet wanting to keep all the good things about their tormentor—makes no more sense now than it did in 1980.

We're either one nation or two. Period.

In this context, it's one of the supreme ironies of the Quebec *indépendantiste* movement that its leaders intend to finance the breakup of Canada using Canadian dollars. That—as the country-and-western ditty has it—is like being your own grandpaw.

In his many speeches and interviews, Lucien Bouchard keeps stressing that "Canada will have the same reasons as Quebec for maintaining the present rules relating to the free circulation of people, goods, services and capital. Good sense will prevail during these discussions. Already holding a quarter of the Canadian supply, a sovereign Quebec will support the maintenance of a monetary union as an important guarantee of economic stability."

It ain't necessarily so. No province of any state anywhere that has split away from its mother country has been able to maintain use of the stronger currency of its original nationality. Not a single one of the many republics that once made up the U.S.S.R. uses the ruble as their official currency, even though they all want it. It, for example, is nothing less than political fraud for Bouchard to pretend, as he does, that if Quebec separates it can keep everything it has now, as well as gain the benefits of political independence.

Bouchard has been very specific on the point. "We already have 24 per cent of the Canadian currency circulating, and we'll keep it," he tells anyone who will listen. "That's our money and we'll use it. Nobody would want to see Quebeckers dumping $24 billion on the market—it would be a terrible blow to the currency."

Even if English Canadians were mutton-headed enough to consider sharing their currency with the newly created political entity that had destroyed their country, it is quite simply impossible for two major sovereign states to have a single currency. Several countries (mainly Panama and Liberia) use the American dollar as official tender, but their balance of payments positions are so dismal that no functioning monetary union actually exists. Similarly, the nine former French colonies that combined their monetary destinies by forming the West African Monetary Union have since had to impose severe foreign exchange controls to prevent capital flights. The world's only functioning monetary union is the partnership between Belgium and Luxembourg, but the tiny grand-duchy's population is only 4 per cent of Belgium's, and since it regularly runs budget surpluses, the postage-stamp country has felt little policy restraint.

The great experiment in forging a monetary union has, of course, been the attempt to establish use of a common currency within the European Union. Paradoxically, those negotiations prove why Quebec and Canada couldn't follow that example. Monetary union is forcing member countries to move towards a high degree of political integration. The Maastricht Treaty of December 1991, which set down the matrix for monetary union, also made it very clear that this would mean loss of not only monetary but fiscal autonomy for its dozen member states. If the partners implement the dramatic pact, the end result will be a political, economic and sociological European union not that different from Canadian Confederation. That's what Canada has now, so it hardly seems worthwhile for Quebec to separate while insisting on a common currency. The ultimate consequence of maintaining a joint dollar would mean evolving into a new Canada that operated much like the old one. Why bother?

Not only do Canada's provinces and territories form a functioning (if far from perfect) economic partnership but existing trade-flow statistics show that Quebec sells more of its products to the rest of Canada than it does to the balance of the world. Canadians left behind in a split-apart country would not likely place much emphasis on perpetuating that access. At the same time, the new Bouchard republic would not necessarily gain access to the North American Free Trade area—especially since Canada holds veto power over the admission of new members.

"Simply put," stated a Royal Bank study published in 1992,

"there is no realistic possibility of two truly sovereign states sharing the same currency while exercising independent control over the monetary, fiscal and other economic policies that underpin that currency. A nation's currency is one of the most basic expressions of its existence. If two countries share the same monetary, fiscal and other essential government policies, then neither country is truly independent."

Because both territories would be severely weakened by separation, the resultant dramatic jump in interest rates—with all the damage that would inflict on consumer and corporate buying patterns—would significantly weaken two already fragile economies. There would, at least in the initial stages, not be sufficient funds flowing into the country to pay the annual $55 billion or more in interest on Canada's national debt, no matter how it's divided. That would set off a high-risk foreign-exchange crisis that would inevitably attract the International Monetary Fund's emergency measures squad. Pension funds would be among the hardest hit, but every aspect of Canadian and Quebec life would suffer. Living standards would drop at least 15 per cent, personal incomes would plummet by about $10,140 per family and unemployment would rise to 15 per cent or more.

Canada would become Newfoundland writ large.

Sensing the loss of opportunity, at least a million Canadians would emigrate to the United States. As is always the case in such an economically inspired exodus, we would lose our best and brightest.

So far, the leaders of the PQ have not been able to demonstrate a single advantage of nationhood to the *people*—as opposed to the politicians—of Quebec.

Not only will a sovereign Quebec keep the Canadian dollar and Canadian passports, Bouchard has promised, but the newly independent republic will belong to the Commonwealth, will join NATO and NAFTA. The Bouchard logic would have us believe that transition to independence would be so smooth that hardly anyone would notice.

None of Bouchard's calming homilies ring true.

If Quebec were to become independent, everything would change. The Canada we know and love would vanish as a viable state. Our geography, outrageous to begin with but held together by its coast-to-coast reach, would be split. The gaping hole where Quebec once flourished would tear the country into many pieces. Because the means used by Quebec to leave Confederation would have to be made available to the other provinces, British Columbia and Alberta, together or apart, would soon follow, becoming either Pacific Rim principalities or northern extensions of the new Cascadia already forming on the Pacific coast.

The main problem for those of us who care about this country is that the federalist side lacks leaders. Ottawa's tactics are either dumb or naive; certainly they're grossly inadequate. Jean Chrétien's hands-off policy reminds me of a Robin Williams sketch in which he parodies Britain's traditionally unarmed constables. Faced by an escaping bank robber, the policeman shouts, "Stop!" Nothing happens. The thief keeps running. "If you don't halt immediately," comes the warning from the law, "I'll shout 'STOP!' again!"

"For Quebec to separate from Canada would be completely illegal and unconstitutional," Chrétien keeps repeating, like some mountain dweller's mantra. He's right, of course, but the world works according to different rules. It's not easy to find a country that in recent times has separated from its former motherland by strictly legal and constitutional means. Countries get born through revolutions or some charismatic leader declaring to the world community: "Hey, guess what? We've just become a country! Let's party."

Canada's optimists have always comforted themselves with the notion that this country takes a lot of killing.

That questionable aphorism is about to be tested.

43

SIX DEGREES OF SEPARATION

THE SINGLE CONSTANT in Canada's evolution over the past four decades is that Quebec has set the national agenda. The electoral fate of the half-dozen prime ministers bold enough to pretend they were governing this country has swung on the reaction and support they received from French Canada.

The nationalistic sandstorm that has overwhelmed the province followed in the wake of the Quiet Revolution, launched in 1960 by Jean Lesage, the dapper Quebec City lawyer who became the reluctant reformer of a society that had lapsed into collective slumber. What Lesage achieved was an essential separation of church and state: the Roman Catholic clergy that had dominated Quebec since the Conquest was hived into the spiritual realm, while politicians took over the educational, health and welfare functions.

Lesage acted more like a king than a premier. He recruited a personal staff of twenty-eight (including a *chef de protocol* complete with morning coat) and had his appointment schedule mimeographed two weeks in advance. Three Montreal dailies once solemnly reported how the prime minister had been bitten by a mosquito on the middle finger of his right hand. Although he was condemned as a radical at home, Lesage was a closet federalist. He established a secret hot-line to Gordon Robertson, then Ottawa's clerk of the Privy Council, so the two men could discuss federal Quebec appointments and initiatives before they were announced.

During one of our interviews, when I asked Lesage whether he considered himself a Quebecker or Canadian first, his jaw worked, his face flushed, and then he burst out: "Hell, I'm a Canadian. That's my nationality." One comment from that long-ago meeting still haunts me. "If Confederation fails," he told me, "it will not be because Quebec separates, but because the way to keep Quebec in Confederation hasn't been found."

That, of course, has been the quest of Canadian politicians ever since, and in the end it defeated Lesage himself, because he tried to become a statesman before it was time for him to cease being an agitator. It was among Lesage's entourage that I first met one of his middle-rank assistants, a stout chap called Jacques Parizeau. When I walked into his office, he was doubled over at his desk in a fit of belly-pumping laughter about Lesage's pretensions. He explained that the premier had just ordered him to write a speech for a rally he had that night at Levis, across the river, "specifically designed to impress Harold Wilson." (Wilson was then prime minister of the United Kingdom and Lesage required British parliamentary approval to abolish the Quebec legislature's upper chamber.)

After leaving Parizeau free to struggle over his impossible assignment, I discussed the day's events with the resident bar fly at the Chateau Frontenac's La Place de la Fontaine, an out-of-office politico by the name of Daniel Johnson. Nobody took the Union Nationale opposition leader very seriously at the time and young Liberals who caught a glimpse of his brooding, dark-suited presence would nudge one another and quip: "There goes Danny Boy."

When he became premier, Johnson answered my inevitable Quebecker-or-Canadian question slightly more toughly than Lesage, whom he defeated in 1966. "If I have to choose, I would choose Quebec first, because that's my duty. With a name like Johnson I could have educated my children in English, but I'm thinking of the guy in my county whose name is Laframboise ... Some politicians in the past have been ready to save Confederation, even at the expense of Quebec. I want to develop Quebec, even at the expense of Confederation. But I'm no fanatic."

And he never was, despite his fierce political war cry demanding Equality or Independence. He would go to a meeting of Toronto bond dealers, and tell them, "Quebec won't separate if we can live in Canada as a group." Then, on his return to Quebec he would boldly declare: "Unless Quebec can live in Canada as a group, we'll separate!" Journalists would subtract one statement from the other, come up with zero, and Johnson would promptly attack the press for misinterpreting his position. Johnson was a charmer, mainly because he didn't take himself very seriously, but I've never forgotten a couple of his wiser comments. "Where the French-Canadian nation finds its freedom," he said, "there too will be its homeland." When I asked him to define his political ideology, he gave me the only honest answer to that silly question I've ever received. "You know," he said, "in politics it's very dangerous to have a philosophy. In a democracy you should settle the problems that exist, instead of setting out to prove your philosophical ideals."

When I went back to Quebec City a few years later to interview Jean-Jacques Bertrand, the Union Nationale premier who succeeded Johnson, I found a moderate devoid of ideas, whose main concern seemed to be how his $450-million bond issue would be received by Wall Street. When I asked my inevitable question, he replied: "Well, I'm a Quebecker first in matters of provincial jurisdiction and a Canadian first in other areas." (No wonder he was defeated six months later.)

Bertrand's successor, Robert Bourassa, was the ultimate pragmatist, seeking Quebec's salvation through economic prosperity. When I asked him about the measure of his Canadianism, he didn't answer directly. "I've been told," he confided, "that I represent Quebec's last chance, and to some extent it's true. If I fail in my relations with Ottawa, people will say Bourassa was well prepared and rational, and Trudeau is also well prepared and rational. If these two guys can't make the system work, it's impossible. And they could be right."

They were.

44

QUEBEC ON A HOT TIN ROOF

A VISIT TO QUEBEC in this sweltering, pre-Referendum summer reveals a province in search of itself. Most citizens seem more preoccupied with plastering themselves with sun screen than bothering to follow the twisting subtleties of the independence debate.

But as the fateful day of the Referendum approaches, it's becoming clear that as much as Premier Jacques Parizeau might prefer it, the vote will not be decided on the basis of the passionate slogans. Instead, it will—as always—be the economics of the situation that sway the ballots.

The harsh fact is that more than 800,000 Quebeckers currently live full-time on welfare—including 18 per cent of Montreal's population—costing the province $300 million per month. That's a huge and politically volatile group which, it could be argued, would have nothing to lose by voting for separation. That mentality seems to fit in with the fact that nearly half of them have refused to participate in any retraining programs.

Another unpredictable factor is the province's youth, once the fountainhead of the sovereignty movement. Survey after survey shows that, certainly at the university level, students are much more interested in the Internet and much more worried about getting jobs than being politically radical.

It sometimes seems as if the Quebec independence movement were pure theatre in which the lead actors take the stage to perform for one another. The audience has meanwhile grabbed a life. Yves Fortier, the eminent counsel who served as Canada's chief delegate to the United Nations and is one of the province's most astute political observers, told me that while he's not complacent, he feels quite confident about the Referendum's outcome. "I recognize that much can happen between now and the vote," he said, "but barring any unforeseen events I believe that the great common sense Quebec voters have amply demonstrated in past referenda and at election times will reassert itself again."

Fortier points out that if independence ever did take place, it would trigger a major financial crisis not just in Quebec but in Canada as a whole, because Ottawa might be stuck having to repay 100 per cent of its outstanding loans, while having lost a quarter of its tax base. "Also," he adds, "Quebec would eventually have to devise its own currency, which would be horrendously disruptive."

It's not weighty topics such as this that preoccupy most Quebeckers. The big news in Quebec these days—and it's treated as news instead of the rumour status it deserves—is that Jacques Parizeau has started to seriously drink again, which could have grave political consequences. Drunk or sober, he realizes that this will be his final shot at the Quebec presidency. Some of his recent decisions have had the mark of a desperate man taking desperate measures. The best example was his decision to hand a subsidy of $60 million to the perpetually bankrupt MIL Davie Shipyard, because its one hundred employees threatened to vote against sovereignty if he didn't keep their industry alive. Even if he never becomes Quebec's head of state, Parizeau has thus assured himself a place in history, or at least an entry in the *Guinness Book of Records*. It's doubtful if any politician anywhere has paid a bribe of as much as $600,000 per vote.

Most of the bad news about the Referendum focuses on the leadership of its No forces by Daniel Johnson of the Liberals. Well-meaning as he may be, he brings little political savvy and no inspiration to his task. During a recent news conference, he insisted that he would not detail his party's plans for Quebec, because to do so might deflect the focus from the Parti Québécois's sovereignty campaign. That sounds suspiciously like the rejoinder that turned Kim Campbell from a prime minister into a radio talk-show host. (Remember her immortal words during the 1993 election about how campaigns were the worst possible time to "get involved in serious issues"?) It's just not enough for Johnson to become the champion of the status quo. People seldom vote for what they already have.

One alternative might be to accept Claude Ryan's suggestion that Ottawa, instead of sitting on its hands, grant Quebec a veto over all future constitutional changes, before the Referendum is held. That sounds like a huge concession, except that, as the Meech and Charlottetown negotiations proved, no constitutional revisions are possible without unanimity among the provinces—and that's almost the same as granting Quebec the veto power it wants. The point is that the federal government must at least give the appearance that it cares about the Referendum outcome, which it so far has failed to do.

At the moment, the only legal way for Quebec to achieve separation would be to pass a constitutional amendment that would require unanimous support not only from the Commons and the Senate but the legislatures of all ten provinces. For Quebec to simply declare itself independent would, at the very least, allow Ottawa to support the territorial claims of the natives of northern Quebec. As Prof. Patrick Monahan pointed out recently in a C.D. Howe Institute study on this issue: "That would produce a period of legal uncertainty and the possibility of civil unrest. It would also result in a massive sell-off and devaluation of Canadian securities, a drop in the value of the Canadian dollar, and a significant increase in interest rates."

But on these long summer days, it's just too damn hot to dwell on such improbabilities.

45

THE GREAT LOBSTER REVOLT

JACQUES PARIZEAU'S MOST charming habit as a politician has always been his proclivity for having one of his feet firmly planted in his mouth. Recently, he had them both jammed in his jaw, when he compared Quebeckers after a Yes Referendum vote to lobsters in a pot.

Whether the pot was a trap at sea, as he maintains, or a kitchen boiler, as some of the diplomats who heard his speech reported, makes no difference to the metaphor. All that matters now is whether the lobsters will behave like typical Canadians—and typical lobsters—and drag whichever animals try to climb out of the pot, back in with them, to stick around and get boiled—or if they'll try to do something novel about their predicament.

That won't be easy.

All of the worry and attention about the coming Referendum has so far been focused on what's been happening in Quebec, but the Referendum itself—the dilemma that makes it necessary—reflects equally what's going on in the rest of the country. What has happened, as far as Canadians outside Quebec are concerned, is the death of the notion—so dear to French Canada's nationalists—of this country being the home of two founding nations. For that idea to remain valid required not only Quebec to have a distinct society, but the rest of Canada as well.

Instead, Canada has turned into a multinational country, not by government edict or sociological hocus-pocus, but as a fact visible to anyone walking down just about any Canadian street. When I first arrived here, from Europe in 1940, we felt immersed—or more accurately, drowned—in a WASP-dominated world. Toronto was bicultural then, British and Irish; except for the bankers who were Scottish.

That's why I never subscribed to the benevolent notion of this country as a "cultural mosaic," which was supposed to differentiate

Canada from the American Melting Pot. That wasn't the Canadian way. The nation's ethnic infrastructure had been set in place during the first decade of this century, when a million immigrants chose the western plains to make their last, best life. It had been a perfect arrangement: the WASPs got in on the kill of the construction and manufacturing booms in the heartland, while the honkies (all of whom tended to be grouped as "those damn Ukarainians") had patronizingly been allowed to maintain their culture—just so long as they kept it to themselves—breaking the soil, doing the dirty jobs and folk dancing on Dominion Days.

That point of view was most brutally articulated by Bryce Mackasey, then a Trudeau cabinet minister, as recently as 1978. "Where?" he demanded during a by-election speech defending the country's immigration policy. "Where would we be without the Italians, the Czechoslovaks and the Portuguese, the Greeks and Lebanese? Who would do the dirty work, and dig the subways, mine the mines, sweep the floors … ?"

Sheer numbers muted such prejudice. Now, no ethnic or linguistic flavour dominates the present-day Canadian Stew. Every five years or so during the past two decades nearly a million immigrants from Asia, Africa and other non-white continents have arrived on Canada's shores. The fact that the members of Canada's founding societies are no longer in the ascendancy means that a new and radically different country has been created.

The politically correct notion of Canada as the home of two nations has outlived reality. Only diehard constitutional reformers still maintain that one society (Quebec) is distinct while the others, by default, are indistinct, or somehow interchangeable.

To politicians outside Quebec, such a "two nations" theory had always been a sociological phenomenon which meant not very much except that it gave legitimacy to their constitutional initiatives; to Quebec nationalists, it meant everything. To have your own language and culture recognized meant being a proud people instead of a marginal tribe with curious ethnological affinities. "Quebec sovereignty is not about resentment against English Canada," Lucien Bouchard keeps insisting, "it's about two nations which need to go their own way politically to give themselves the kind of society they both need and deserve."

It was a wonderful dream—that Canada, with two founding nations and two founding genders, was calmly evolving towards the

21st century. It was a wonderful dream, but it no longer reflects what Canada has become. "Nobody any longer can dwell inside a zoological garden in which you preserve yourself as a species unaffected by changes in ecology," I was told by Dr. Vivian Rakoff, chairman of the University of Toronto's department of psychiatry. "And the world's ecology is changing drastically. Like it or not, we're all blood brothers now."

Equality of treatment, which became the great cause of the 1990s, is plainly incompatible with any form of officially sanctioned privilege based on language, ethnicity or length of tenure. The time has come to acknowledge that liberalism and tribalism are terminally incompatible.

Collapse of the legitimacy of the two-nation theory outside Quebec has moved debate on Canada's future to new ground.

Deprived of its founding myth, by the mid-1990s Canada had become a land with a common past but no common history. Resolution of this troublesome new factor is at the heart of every Quebec Referendum: if Canada has abandoned its historical *raison d'être* for being one country, should it become two?

FOR WELL OVER THREE decades, ever since the Quiet Revolution of the 1960s, Quebec and the rest of Canada had been dealing with one another in a series of confrontations and eruptions of unequal intervals and unpredictable intensities, seeking but never finding the ultimate compromise. Each hopeful agreement produced its own problems, without alleviating the tension between French dreams and English impatience. Federal politicians of goodwill sacrificed their larynxes, careers and budgets trying to find an answer to the eternal puzzle: what does Quebec want?

For most of the decade, Quebec's case was put forth by Robert Bourassa who represented his seven million citizens with maximum clout and minimum risk. For nearly a generation, his moods, ideology and operational code had set the tone and content of Quebec politics. Being neither a convinced federalist nor a dedicated separatist, he was mistrusted by both sides—thus retaining the ideal Canadian political posture. He would ultimately almost always come down on the side of Canada, but he also understood that Quebec could achieve the most by theatrically pushing any given situation past its logical limits.

Unlike most Quebec premiers, he was not at all interested in rekindling the hazy dreams of glory snuffed out on the Plains of Abraham. He believed in very little that didn't have a bottom line; his political catechism was based on computer spreadsheets. That was the essence of his "profitable federalism" approach. He saw the federal-provincial tug-of-war as a chance to push the population into an equal technological partnership with the rest of Canada. In the process, Bourassa often stated unequivocally that Quebec must be a nation without becoming a state, but he never explained the difference.

Such tactics aside, he was truly the 20th-century incarnation of Alexis de Tocqueville's dictum that "it behooves moderate men to ensure the success of a moderate republic." The basic assumption in the endless negotiations with Robert Bourassa was that no matter how Quebec and the rest of the country settled things, neither group would be free of the other, that after more than a century of fairly calm partnership between French and English, Canadians could find a way to muddle through.

Quebec nationalists, bound to their revolutionary creed as dutifully as their fathers had once been indentured to Rome, remain convinced they can advance their claims effectively only outside Confederation, or so loosely tied to the rest of the country that the link would be almost meaningless. Inflammatory rhetoric aside, Quebec's position could be reduced roughly to the Francophone conviction that when communities are integrated, individuals are assimilated—so that only political independence (or the next thing to it) could guarantee the long-term survival of Quebec's language and distinctive way of life.

The problem is how to grant Quebec control over its destiny without wrecking Canada in the process—how to acknowledge the symbolic existence of two "nations," and still have one country.

The solution remains elusive, inevitably being reduced to a formula that sounds suspiciously like the nightclub patter of Montreal comic Yvon Deschamps, who gets laughs by innocently asking, hands spread in puzzlement: "Why do the English think we're inconsistent? All we want is an independent Quebec within a strong and united Canada!"

Right on.

46

REFERENDUM BLUES

WHEN BRIAN MULRONEY called the 1992 Referendum, it was there for the Yes side to lose.

And it did.

The biggest miscalculation by the Charlottetown Accord's architects was that the Referendum's outcome would swing on the substance of its provisions. They thought this would guarantee a winning streak, since to them, after half a decade of negotiation, it seemed like a miraculous achievement. Instead, the constitution became more of a symbol than a document, and the No forces were able to tap into the underground rivers of prejudice, racism and loathing of Mulroney that polluted the debate—and determined its results.

Anti-Quebec feelings in western Canada were stronger than anyone suspected, but it was mostly expressed in codes, such as referring to the Grand Chief of the First Nations as Ovid Wednesday. A staff columnist in the *Victoria Times-Colonist* vented his indignation for the Accord with the thundering revelation that Brian Mulroney had once "smuggled *French* bull semen into Canada."

At a more serious level, the Yes camp faced the insurmountable problem of having to win right across the board, while the naysayers could kill the deal with one dissenting province. The Yes strategists never were able to play their trump card: to convince Canadians that a No vote would significantly enhance the forces of Quebec separatism, leading to the country's breakup. Instead, by the end of the campaign, 66 per cent of voters felt convinced their ballots were merely passing judgement on a constitution—and that the outcome would only marginally affect Quebec's—and Canada's—future.

The Yes side was never able to demonstrate that the Accord delivered the proper balance between individual and collective rights, and that the courts could be counted on to protect both. On the contrary, Charlottetown's "distinctive society" clause for Quebec and the self-government provisions for aboriginals made it appear that Canada was developing into a multi-national state, with more than one class of citizenship. This was particularly true of Quebec's guarantee of having a perpetual 25 per cent of the Commons seats. Nobody bothered to point out that this was not a demand championed by French Canada, but a compromise proposed by Saskatchewan's Roy Romanow, and accepted by Quebec in lieu of giving up some real power in the restructured Senate.

On top of all that was the timetable. We don't like to be rushed; we hate deadlines. Yet the Charlottetown agreement was so fragile, its ratification could not be delayed. As it was, two of its architects—Alberta premier Don Getty and Yukon premier Tony Penikett—disappeared from power during the Referendum, and two others—Manitoba's Gary Filmon and Nova Scotia's Donald Cameron—were hanging on to office with one-seat margins.

The most disappointing result was rejection of the Accord by the Indians. No group was granted more of its demands. It looked as if we would actually bring the way we treat our aboriginals into the 20th century. Ovide Mercredi's brilliant diplomacy was rejected mainly by the Indians' more reactionary leaders who were afraid that application of the Charter of Rights and Freedoms would politicize the women in their bands, making them too militant to handle. The definitive comment came from Ron George, president of the Native Council of Canada: "My grandfather's generation paid the price of dispossession. My generation has been schooled in the art of negotiation. With a No vote, the next generation will be left with only one choice—resistance."

The strangest intervention on the No side was the militant opposition of Judy Rebick and her National Action Committee on the Status of Women. As Ed Broadbent, the former NDP leader, kept repeatedly pointing out, the existing constitution plus the Charter already provide more rights for women than any other constitution on earth. On top of that, Section 28 of the new document gave an absolute guarantee (overruling even the dreaded notwithstanding clause) that every right in the Charter would apply equally to men and women.

As salesmen, the provincial premiers proved to be a bust. Don Getty collected his marbles and went home. B.C.'s Mike Harcourt took so many political pratfalls in the campaign's first ten days that his major positive contribution turned out to be the fact that he took off for a business mission to Los Angeles for most of the campaign. Moe Sihota, his constitutional affairs minister, did his best to torpedo the deal by recounting in great detail how the premiers had ganged up on Quebec and stopped Robert Bourassa in his tracks.

For his part, Bourassa must have looked around at his cadre of advisers and wondered why he needed enemies. From the release of the taped cellular-phone conversation between Diane Wilhelmy and André Tremblay to an *Actualité* article's briefing notes—at every turn the Quebec premier was condemned by his own officials for having caved in. Significantly, none of the critics were at the bargaining table, where Bourassa more than held his own, but one could hardly blame Justice Minister Gil Remillard, a stout federalist, for complaining: "Every morning when I wake up, I don't know what's going to happen next."

The most important influence in swaying the vote against the Charlottetown Accord was the massive intervention by Pierre Trudeau. He dismissed Quebec's gains and aspirations as "blackmail," and condemned the whole constitutional process—even though it was his patriation of the British North America Act without Quebec's support in 1981 that made it necessary. What Trudeau achieved was something that no French-hating redneck ever thought possible. He made opposition to Quebec's demands politically correct.

And so at the end of the long and agonizing Referendum, Canada has become something of a beached whale—large, immobile and beginning to stink a little.

British economist Kenneth Boulding once observed that "Canada has no cultural unity, no linguistic unity, no religious unity, no economic unity and no geographic unity. All it has is unity."

Now, we've lost that too.

47

FLASHPOINT

THE 1995 QUEBEC REFERENDUM, indecisive as it was, left no doubt about it: the status quo was dead.

It will be tragic to dismiss the razor-thin majority of the federalist forces as a call to do nothing. It's true that we have avoided the agony of a Yes victory, but that doesn't mean we will not suffer the pain of having to drastically alter a system that caused nearly half the citizens of the nation's second-most populous province to reject their country.

The surge of separatist power was based not so much on Lucien Bouchard's call for Revolution as on Jean Chrétien's inability to make staying in Canada inspiring. By defending nothing more noble than leaving things as they were, the prime minister won by default, despite the federalists' strategic errors and policy misapprehensions.

When the campaign began, it was there for the federalists to mess up, and they certainly did. That they squeaked into first place was due mainly to the emotional impact of ordinary Canadians disobeying Chrétien's instructions to stay out of the Referendum battle, and showing ordinary Quebeckers that they cared and didn't want them to leave.

At the same time, nearly half of Quebec's voters endorsed a separatist platform that remains the gospel of the government in charge of Quebec's affairs at least until 1999. By turning over his leadership of the Yes forces to Lucien Bouchard in mid-campaign, Jacques Parizeau amply demonstrated that he will stop at nothing (even self-immolation) to make his dream come true.

To pretend for a moment that Quebec opted to preserve things as they are would be to dangerously misread the vote. Despite the efforts to make French Canada feel at home in the rest of the country, Quebeckers have at least temporarily rejected the argument that French culture can be protected by an English-Canadian government—even if it's led by a Québécois. They seem determined to nurture their own way of life, convinced that the hope for constitutional change is, if not dead, at least dormant.

The No campaign's low point occurred on October 24, when Clyde Wells, whose 1990 decision to kill the Meech Lake Accord by not allowing his own legislature to vote on the deal, came out for no reason at all against "ever" granting Quebec the distinctiveness it was seeking. The substance of his intervention was stupid; its timing could have been tragic. He made it clear that any effort by the Ottawa government to satisfy Quebec's constitutional aspirations will fail, because they will never gain unanimous support.

The political lesson that has emerged from this Referendum is valuable. The same collective of "ordinary Canadians" that helped defeat the Meech and Charlottetown accords, that dethroned Kim Campbell and Lyn McLeod, that humbled the Rogers Cable executives who didn't realize what was really going on with their customers—everything that the Establishment's gurus supported—turned out to be irrelevant or indefensible. The complacency that set in among Ottawa's No team almost lost us our country.

We cannot bet the farm with these clowns in charge, ever again. What marks a democracy is that leaders must be accountable. Jean Chrétien has one more chance to prove that he can actually do something, instead of merely occupying an office that has a sign "Prime Minister of Canada" on its door.

I hope he grabs it.

48

"I TOLD YOU I LOVE YOU— NOW GET OUT!"

As ENTRAILS OF THE failed national Referendum vote continue to be examined, one major long-term effect is becoming clear: out of that emotion-laden debate came a hardening of English Canada's attitudes towards Quebec.

Certainly in the western provinces, the rules of the game have changed. The mood of the people, as far as one can determine their feelings about Quebec, seems to be very close to the attitude championed by Preston Manning: indifference bordering on hostility. Even those who in the past have supported the province's aspirations and did their best to support national unity now say flat-out that they will not allow Quebec to decide Canada's future.

The mood is harsh and uncompromising, reminiscent of the old Chicago blues song, "I told you I love you—now get out!" The unwritten message from the West is that Quebec should make up its own mind whether it wants to remain in Canada on terms that will not be very different from those offered other provinces, and then either go along with those restrictions, or leave and begin to negotiate its terms of separation.

That tough, take-it-or-leave-it reaction is far removed from the two-founding-nations theory that has up to now coloured French-English negotiations. What the voters, at least in western Canada, seem to have decided is that every Canadian should have exactly the same legal and constitutional rights as every other Canadian. Whatever goodwill there was for granting Quebeckers—and aboriginals—special status seems to have vanished with the fall leaves.

The real meaning of the Referendum was the assertion by the

majority of Canadians that they no longer trust elected politicians to be their surrogates in the exercise of power.

The current Quebec dilemma dates back to Brian Mulroney's strategy in the 1984 election that brought him to office. He had grown up in a province which then seemed permanently in the grip of the federal Liberal machine that had maintained the party in power for an uninterrupted eleven years, and except for John Diefenbaker's five-year fling, for twenty-five years before that. Mulroney's dream was to replace that coalition with a new one, dominated by his Progressive Conservatives.

He believed the only way to build such a "permanent" majority in Quebec was to negotiate an alliance with the province's nationalists, while at the same time trying to tame their more radical impulses by aligning their aspirations with the goals of his brand of federalism.

In retrospect, he didn't have to deal with the nationalists, then still in thrall to René Lévesque, because the Liberal machine in Quebec had seen its best days and was tired and corrupt after so many years in power. The era of natural majorities, even in Quebec, was over and Mulroney didn't need the ultra-nationalists he had collected to his cause—Lucien Bouchard, Marcel Masse and others—because they had nowhere else to go politically anyway. He could probably have attracted most Francophone federalist Liberals to his colours at the time, because they were hungry for leadership—and disillusioned with Trudeau's intellectual Jesuitry.

If Mulroney had chosen to strike a bargain with these pragmatists instead of the nationalists, he would have had a much easier time managing the strains between his Quebec and western caucuses, and been able to enjoy more manoeuvring room as prime minister. The crunch came not on Referendum day, but in the winter of 1988, when Robert Bourassa, then himself trying to stem the tides of revived Quebec nationalism, introduced Bill 178, the dreadful language bill which eliminated English on the province's outdoor signs. John Meisel, the Queen's University political scientist, rightly referred to these restrictions as "a scandalous denial of individual rights and an affront to English Canada" and blamed the measure for the failure of the Meech Lake Accord.

Conrad Black took this line of reasoning to its logical conclusion.

"In the last fifteen years," he declared, "Quebec has become of all important Canadian jurisdictions the most officially hostile to bilingualism. Quebec has chosen to remain a sullen victim and officially to oppress its own minorities more thoroughly than French Canadians have been oppressed."

According to Black, Bourassa's invocation of the notwithstanding clause to put through his language bill lost the game for anyone trying to promote a community of interest between French and English Canada. He insisted that when Brian Mulroney stood up in parliament and defended the Quebec legislation, "he made a Faustian bargain" with Quebec and unwittingly killed Meech Lake. "Either we have a free country or we do not. If Quebec's version of federalism is to suppress and render invisible the language of 70 per cent of Canadians and 95 per cent of North Americans, while expecting English Canadians to continue to pay billions of dollars of real or disguised equalization transfers to Quebec, it won't work. That version can't work and no one should try to make it work."

Black is convinced that the best way to keep Quebec in Confederation is for English Canada to act tough and to make certain its leaders—and voters—understand how high the price of separation would be. He believes that once Quebeckers understand that the terms of secession would include permission for every county in Quebec to vote on whether or not it wanted to remain in Canada, that significant parts of the province's northern areas (including the sources of much of Hydro Quebec's power) would revert to Canada, and that the province as a country would have to assume its full share of the national debt, while also having to renegotiate a free trade agreement with the U.S.—once all of these conditions were met, enthusiasm for independence would decline precipitously.

That kind of hardening of attitudes reflects a new reality that will colour future constitutional bargaining. The two-nations concept has been shown to be an unworkable and undesirable historic irrelevancy.

LUCIEN BOUCHARD'S
FAUSTIAN DEAL

EVERY TIME I SEE Lucien Bouchard in person or watch him on television, I have the same two reactions. The first is to imagine that the Parti Québécois leader is constantly being trailed by a chorus of trombone players sounding ominous chords as he stalks the land. This is how trombones are used in Verdi operas when the untrustworthy villain—inevitably a bass-baritone intent on defiling the heroine's lily-whites—appears on stage. (She, of course, fails to heed the trombone warning, and at least temporarily falls for the oily charms of the black-eyed baritone.)

My other reaction to the slick Monsieur Bouchard is to feel like the victim in James Thurber's celebrated *New Yorker* cartoon which depicts two men duelling with swords. One cuts the other's head off but his stroke is so adept and so subtle that his opponent doesn't realize what's happened. He insists that he's feeling fine and that they should carry on with the fight, until the victorious duelling partner casually remarks: "Try sneezing."

If I haven't sneezed yet it's because I'm afraid to try. Bouchard has been so successful in desensitizing Canadians to the possibilities of Quebec separation, that this country seems to be marching to its own destruction with the false bravado of the headless guy in the Thurber cartoon.

It's all discouragingly Canadian somehow and entirely typical that the revolutionary whose aim is to destroy our 130-year-old democracy should be not some hollow-eyed revolutionary in a back-street basement, but a middle-class lawyer in a navy-blue pin-stripe.

But after watching and listening to Bouchard during his visit to

Vancouver recently, it seems to me that if we allow Canada to break up it will be more our fault than his.

The day Bouchard spent on the West Coast happened to coincide with Nelson Mandela's electoral victory in South Africa. The contrast was chilling. At the foot of the dark continent, blacks and whites had peacefully resolved their horrendous differences, paid for in blood by both sides since the Union of South Africa was born eighty-seven years ago. To have overcome apartheid while remaining united is an extraordinary achievement, particularly since that policy's original objective was to hive blacks and whites into separate territories. Now they are united in one nation, ready to take on the world.

Yet, here was Bouchard in Vancouver seriously insisting that life within the Canadian context was no longer tenable for Quebeckers because of the 1990 rejection of the Meech Lake Accord.

Spare us.

How many Meech Lakes add up to one Sharpeville? It's a historical fact that few, if any, national minorities have been treated more generously than Quebeckers. Their shaky allegiance to Confederation has been repeatedly rewarded with high-ranking jobs, regional transfer payments and most other measurable ways.

The Faustian deal offered by Bouchard, if we let him have his way, is not "peace in our time" but a war of nerves (or worse) designed to advance his political career as president of a new country called Quebec. For him, political discourse merely amounts to a bully pulpit from which to lob demands and abuse at English Canada.

Art Grant, the Vancouver lawyer who organized the Bouchard visit, maintained throughout that Bouchard was proposing that we handle the country's breakup "with traditional Canadian decency and compromise," emphasizing that "if Canada and Quebec decide to part ways, then I hope we do it peacefully and with our historic common sense." The answer to such nice-nellyism is to proclaim loudly and clearly: to hell with common sense, one-sided decency and compromise.

You don't win a country that way and you shouldn't lose one either.

What we're discussing here is not the winner in a high-school

debate—or even who'll pick up what pieces after the country has
been split—but whether or not Canada has a future. Instead of playing by Roberts Rules of Order, let's tackle Bouchard on his own
terms. Let's leave no doubt in his mind that our will to survive as
one nation is at least as strong as his intention to turn himself into
the first head of a socialist republic straddling the St. Lawrence
Seaway.

It's time that Bouchard and his followers realized not all Canadians outside Quebec swoon at the sight of the Queen, behave like
perfect (if constipated) ladies and gentlemen and don't give a damn
about their country.

Typical of the attitude we should avoid at all costs is the un-
caring approach of such Bay Street bottom liners as Norman
Bengough, president of Goodman & Co., which manages fifteen
mutual funds. "The Canadian dollar could strengthen were Quebec
to secede," he declared recently, sounding his patriotic best. He
told *The Toronto Star* that he wouldn't be broken-hearted if the
country broke up, providing Quebec assumed its fair share of the
national debt and floated its own currency.

Contrast that to the ardent cry of McGill University constitutional professor of law Stephen Scott, who has suggested that Quebec's separation would entail "the gravest crimes known to our law,
the gravest threats to our social order, and the gravest outrages
upon the rights of each Canadian citizen individually and of all as
a group."

The most bizarre intervention in the Quebec debate came from
U.S. Senator Edward Kennedy who has praised Quebec for following its own path. I only hope that if there ever is a conference on
Quebec involving Kennedy and Quebec's separatists, Teddy gets to
drive Monsieur Bouchard home.

50

WHY BOUCHARD
IS ANTI-SEMANTIC

QUITE A FEW YEARS ago, when the federal Social Credit Party (predecessor of today's Reform movement) had thirty seats in the House of Commons, its leader was a fundamentalist preacher-missionary named Robert Norman Thompson.

An amiable lightweight, his main contribution to parliamentary debate was his wonderful misuse of clichés. "The Americans," he once declared during a foreign-affairs debate, "are our best friends—whether we like it or not." On another occasion, he set the record straight by declaring that "two rights don't make a wrong," and later startled a Tory cabinet minister, who was defending his record, with the admonition: "You've buttered your bread, now you must lie in it."

Thompson was one of the last believers in former Alberta premier Bill Aberhart's brand of fundamentalist politics that flirted with the anti-semitic notions of international Zionist conspiracies run by unidentified cliques of "Jewish bankers." Thompson himself didn't subscribe to such garbage, but he was a true believer in Social Credit's voodoo economic theories, which spilled out of him in an unanswerable gush that left most of his listeners glassy-eyed and terminally baffled.

My own conclusion, after interviewing him at length one spring afternoon back in 1967, was that while Thompson was not anti-semitic, he certainly was anti-semantic.

The point of recalling the Social Credit leader's dilemma with attempting to balance what he said with what he meant is that Canadians have recently been treated to Robert Thompson's contemporary reincarnation, in the person of Lucien Bouchard.

Being anti-semantic has always been one of the Quebec premier's problems—not because he doesn't understand the ideas he's expressing but because his loyalties are limited to each political moment. Even if he is not for sale, he can be rented. His words, like his loyalties, serve his ambitions, so that their intent is defined according to his personal agenda that has nothing to do with dictionaries.

Like Thompson before him, Bouchard has some serious linguistic hangups. While he didn't really get serious about learning English until he became a federal Tory cabinet minister in 1988, he now speaks the language almost faultlessly, having become nearly as adept at toying with its subtleties as Pierre Trudeau, who was the most brilliantly bilingual politician in Canadian history. Still, Bouchard has a serious problem with the word "real." According to *Gage's Canadian Dictionary*, "real" signifies "existing as a fact—not imagined or made up." But Bouchard seems to believe that something becomes "real" only in terms of the emotions and meaning he chooses to attach to it.

On the day he was sworn in as premier of Quebec, for example, Bouchard attacked Stephane Dion, the then freshly minted minister of inter-governmental affairs, for suggesting that Quebec might be divisible. No way, he countered: "We are a people; we are a nation." Canada, on the other hand, he went on, of course was divisible, because "it is not a *real* country."

Although he later semi-apologized for this touch of lunacy, Bouchard's original comment revealed his inability or unwillingness to recognize any truth but his own. This is a man capable of anything. He inhabits a world where only what fuels his own view of the world carries the stamp of reality.

While chairing a Quebec City summit meeting with sixty members of the province's various élites, he dismissed their fears about his repeatedly stated intention of making Quebec independent as being "more psychological than *real*." That was a particularly strange interpretation of his own words, since at the same meeting he set out his operational code as Quebec's premier: "I say it loud and clear. Don't count on me to squander the historic opportunity which will allow the Quebec people to finally assume their destiny."

Although the Quebec City conclave ended triumphantly for Bouchard, because both business and labour agreed on a deficit-cutting timetable, those participants who don't support the separatist option quickly realized the premier's threat to hold another referendum remains as real as ever. And it scared the hell out of them. Reality deals in facts not fantasies, and the business leaders who attended the conference and objected to Bouchard's assurances that the effects of his determination to separate from Canada wouldn't be "real" had some telling statistics on their side of the argument. Quebec's economic growth, which stumbled along at a sluggish 1.8 per cent last year, is running at less than half the national average, down dramatically from the 3.9 per cent that the province achieved in 1994—when attaining independence was little more than Jacques Parizeau's wet dream.

There were many significant statements made during the Bouchard-sponsored conference, but in terms of making the case for Quebec to remain in Canada, one of the simplest and most persuasive arguments came from Jean Monty, CEO of Nortel, speaking to the Montreal Canadian Club last week. "The fact is," he said, "that Quebec is too small to fulfil the dreams and aspirations of Quebeckers. Just as Newfoundland is too small for Newfoundlanders, Alberta too small for Albertans and British Columbia too small for British Columbians. A Canadian platform is what we all need."

51

PUTTING LUCIEN IN A MINI-VAN

FOR WHAT SEEMS like an eternity now, those Canadians who live under the harsh designation ROC have been wondering what it is precisely that Quebec really wants. The resolution to that question—and to whether French Canada's desired destiny can be accommodated inside the country's existing borders—will shape Canadian politics in 1997, as it has every year since Lord Durham wrote his report, back in 1839.

But there may be some interesting differences this year. For one thing, the root cause of separatism may finally be revealed for exactly what it is: a struggle for power. Period.

The Parti Québécois's genesis and ideology are supposed to be rooted in the notion that the only sure way to protect the French language is for the province to break away from Canada. In the months ahead, it will become increasingly clear that what's threatening use of the French language in the province is not some dark plot hatched by the desperado survivors of the Meech Lake gang in Ottawa, or even Rafe Mair, the outspoken Vancouver open-line radio host.

The threat to the universal use of French—not just in Quebec, but in France, and every other members of the *Francophonie*—is the undeniable fact that English has become *the* international language of diplomacy, finance, commerce, science, higher education and, most important of all, of computers. And that's before the full impact of the Internet, which operates largely in English, is felt on Quebec society. As commerce increases in cyberspace, being part of those transactions will become essential.

English is also the universal tongue of popular culture the world over. To young people everywhere, speaking English is the key to being "cool." This is the generation that will take charge in the next millennium. Nothing can stop them from speaking the language of most of the singers and movie stars who shape their consciousness.

Nor does the nationalist revolution in French Canada have much to do with *les Québécois* being subjugated by *les maudits Anglais*, as the militants so often claim. No minority in world history has been treated with less condescension and more generosity. One example: for all but twelve of the last forty-eight years, the prime minister of Canada has been a Quebecker who placed the welfare of his home province at the top of his priority list. If Jean Chrétien is re-elected the total will be twelve out of fifty-two years—which hardly seems like the enslavement of a voiceless minority.

Despite this and many other examples of Quebec's ascendancy in federal affairs, its nationalist politicians have in the recent past been pushing back the frontiers of credibility, stuck on the idea that they are an oppressed minority. Just before the 1994 election, for instance, Bernard Landry, then deputy leader of the PQ, told the Paris magazine *L'Express* that Quebec was the western world's last colony. "Our population," he lamented, "has endured a cataclysm comparable to the Chernobyl nuclear catastrophe."

Now, Monsieur Landry, who has since risen to be Quebec's deputy premier and minister of finance, has come to the rescue again, finally defining what Quebec really wants.

It's limousines.

At a press conference, just after announcing that his premier would participate in Team Canada's visit to Southeast Asia, the finance minister added a significant footnote. Lucien Bouchard would not agree to travel in a mini-van, like the other provincial premiers accompanying the trade crusade. "The perverse symbolism that the prime minister of Canada is in a limousine and the others in mini-vans," the province's second-ranking politician declared, "would be harmful for the government of Quebec."

Now, there's an obvious head-slapper. How *could* we have been so silly, fiddling around with constitutional amendments, distinct society clauses and all that complicated stuff? Why didn't all the Meechkins and other well-meaning supporters of good old *bonne-entente* just take up a collection and rent Lucien a stretch-limo?

After all those decades of soul-searching, is that what the struggle for Quebec independence has come down to? Is that all there is? Are we expected to sacrifice the geographical and political integrity of this beloved country, so that if and when Lucien Bouchard becomes president of a newly independent Quebec, he can lounge in the back of a tug-size black Cadillac (the *fleur-de-lys* proudly fluttering from its fenders) and be chauffeured to the United Nations? (There, presumably, to address his fellow heads of state—who, predictably, scurry for coffee breaks, as the potentate of the new Quebec launches a rant about how Canadians had tried to humiliate his people by forcing him into a mini-van.)

Any revolution reduced to protecting its symbols is no revolution at all.

It all has to do with legitimacy. A good case can be made that Bouchard has spent nearly all his time since he became premier reaching for such symbols of political legitimacy as a balanced budget, a working relationship with the province's business community and even agreeing to be part of a federal trade-promotion crusade.

None of that has altered his objectives. Though seeking legitimacy from the very country he is pledged to dismantle can have its problems, Bouchard has never allowed such details to deflect him from his course.

What we must stop doing is granting his separatist cause the legitimacy it doesn't deserve. Unfortunately, the prime minister has being doing precisely that by stressing in nearly every public appearance that Quebec will be allowed to separate if it votes an unambiguous yes to an unambiguous referendum question.

This is not what the Canadian constitution states, may or may not be the Supreme Court's view of the subject, and it certainly isn't mine.

Instead of inviting Quebec to leave, let's give it good reasons to stay.

VII EXITS

52

FOND FAREWELL TO ROB DAVIES

ALL MORTALS ARE replaceable runs the modern mantra, betraying the ethic of programmed obsolescence that has come to dominate our culture. But there are exceptions, and one of them, Robertson Davies, died recently, leaving a gap in the Canadian conscience which can never be filled.

A society can afford to lose only so many voices of civility before it feels cut loose from its spiritual moorings. In the past decade that list of departed Canadian beacons of enlightenment has included Morley Callaghan, Marian Engel, Barbara Frum, Northrop Frye, Margaret Laurence, Bruce Hutchison, Roger Lemelin, Arthur Lower, Hugh MacLennan and Sandy Ross. Perhaps the greatest of them was Davies.

"Rob," as he was known to his friends, cast himself as an inheriter of 19th-century thought and sentiment and the most reluctant of patriots, finding Canada hard to endure yet impossible to flee. "God how I have tried to love this country," one of the characters in his play *Fortune My Foe* exclaims. "I have given all I have to Canada—my love, my hate, and now my bitter indifference. But this raw, frostbitten place has worn me out and its raw, frostbitten people have numbed my heart."

In less lofty language, he once explained to me that while he had many chances to live elsewhere, he just couldn't bring himself to leave. "I belong here," he told me. "To divorce yourself from your roots is spiritual suicide. I just am a Canadian. It's not a thing you can escape from. It's like having blue eyes."

Well, not quite. The life Davies chose for himself hardly qualified him as one of your McKenzie Brothers, run-of-the-brew Canadians. After graduating from Upper Canada College and Oxford's Balliol College, he eventually created an intellectual haven for himself as founding Master of the University of Toronto's Massey College. Inside its elegant, very un-Canadian walls he moved among his Fellows in their gowned splendour, looking quite magnificent in his necromancer's beard, living in the Master's Lodge, presiding at High Table, sniffing snuff out of Aram's horn, sipping claret, and responding with supreme indifference to charges that the institution he headed was snobbish, sexist, anachronistic and maybe even a little absurd. The place reflected perfectly his view of life and his genius for civilized eccentricity that was captured so brilliantly in his novels.

All the while he presided over Massey College, stressing tradition over practicality, the Master was playing a splendid joke on his detractors. In 1970, after writing twenty-one novels, plays and works of theatrical criticism that brought him mild approval at home and virtually no notice abroad, Davies published *Fifth Business* to universal international acclaim. Saul Bellow and John Fowles, then the English-speaking world's best fiction writers, were loud in their praises, as was *The New York Times*, and just about every other review. Davies had finally found his place at the pinnacle of literary acclaim, where he'd always dwelt in spirit. That success was repeated with *The Manticore* that followed and his ten subsequent novels.

I spent much of an afternoon chatting with Davies while he presided over Massey College, later attending one of his High Table dinners. Despite his theatrical appearance and deliberately dated manner, Davies hated nothing worse than what he called "young fogies"—those pretenders who look young and everlastingly harp on the fact that they *are* young, but think and act with a degree of caution that would be excessive in their grandfathers. "They are the curse of the world," he thundered, "their very conservatism is second-hand, and they don't know what they are conserving."

While he had great respect for his craft, Davies categorized himself as a storyteller. "I think of an author as somebody who goes into the marketplace and puts down his rug and says, 'I will tell you a story,' and then passes the hat. And when he's taken up his collection, he tells his story, and just before the denouement he passes the hat again. If it's worth anything, fine. If not, he ceases to be an author."

In our conversation he kept coming back to why he felt so alienated yet obsessed with being Canadian. "Canada demands a great deal from people," he pronounced, each syllable emphasized, like a preacher mouthing a benediction, "and is not, as some countries are, quick to offer in return a pleasant atmosphere or easy kind of life. I mean, France demands an awful lot from her people too, but France also offers gifts in the way of a genial, pleasant sort of life and many amenities. Canada is not really a place where you are encouraged to have large spiritual adventures." And he lamented: "A lot of people complain that my novels aren't about Canada. I think they are, because I see Canada as a country torn between a very northern, rather extraordinary, mystical spirit which it fears and its desire to present itself to the world as a Scotch banker. This makes for tension, and tension is the very stuff of art, plays, novels, the whole lot."

Like his novels, Davies's conversation was peppered with the supernatural. "I am very interested in the condition of sainthood," he told me, presumably including his own. "It is just as interesting as evil. Most saints have been unbearable nuisances in life. Some were reformers, some were sages, some were visionaries, but all were intensely alive, and thus a rebuke to people who were not. So many got martyred because nobody could stand them. Society hates exceptional people, because such people make them feel inferior."

Robertson Davies was, if not a saint, certainly a genius, and most assuredly a sage and a visionary. It was to his credit and to our gain that he was also such a magnificent storyteller.

53

GORGEOUS GEORGE

GEORGE HARRIS HEES, dead at eighty-five, was the last Canadian politician who treated his chosen occupation as a fun gig.

And it *was* fun for this unusual hunk of a man (210 lb., 6 ft. 3 in.), who gave energy and verve to every day, as if each were his final one on earth. He was a big man in every way: his smile the radiance of a searchlight, his large frame planted on the ground with a permanent backward lean, as if he were holding the world on a leash. (The fact that his face was always flushed with the glow of good health wasn't an accident; he deliberately bought shirts with too-tight collars, so that his flushed face seemed to be enthusiastically bursting out of his clothes.)

"Gorgeous George," as his detractors called him, brought gusto to the business of government, a delight in power and in self that few can sustain past the age of twenty. He was master of the Big Hello, loved partying and physical contact in all forms, giving Ottawa's more cerebral functionaries the distinct impression that he might, at any moment, get down on the rug and wrestle them in a burst of boyish enthusiasm.

From the time he went into politics, Hees was plagued by charges that he was a mental lightweight, a perpetual playboy, an amiable goon. These accusations were more than offset by his zest for life and his determination to succeed at everything he did. Those who thought they knew Hees well (and that included anybody who had ever shared an elevator with George—so pervasive was his charm) were constantly being surprised by his performance.

He served as an outstanding minister of transport and minister of trade and commerce in the Diefenbaker governments and distinguished himself in the veterans' affairs department in the Mulroney administration. His secret was that he was the best-prepared minister on any issue that touched his portfolios. While his cabinet colleagues took most embarrassing questions as "notice," Hees's many years in opposition taught him which topics would most likely be raised, and he was always ready. "I just happen to have brought my music with me," he would guffaw, as he batted down yet another potentially explosive query. He was also the first Canadian politician who learned how to exploit television news. He would ask inquiring reporters how long a clip they wanted, then promptly answer their question with a, say, ninety-second statement that had a beginning, middle and end, so closely reasoned that it was virtually uncuttable.

Part of his natural ebullience came from having been born into a rich Toronto house-furnishings manufacturing family, who financed his education at Trinity College, a private boys' school in Port Hope, Ontario. He compensated for his failure at high-school football with a grim private training schedule that eventually made him a star linebacker with the Toronto Argonauts team that won the 1938 Grey Cup. He then tested himself further by taking up boxing. After being flattened by Canadian heavyweight champion Bill Maich in a brutal round at Maple Leaf Gardens in 1933, he went on eventually to beat the boxing champion of the British Army. Ever afterwards he compared politics to boxing. "If you take your eyes off your opponent's gloves for one moment, he'll knock you out—and it's the same thing in politics," he once told me.

He had a good war, ending up as Brigade Major of the Fifth Canadian Infantry Brigade, but grew so disgusted with the Canadian government's handling of overseas troop shortages that he ran as an opposition Conservative in 1945. Having been wounded in the elbow at Antwerp, he campaigned with his arm tucked into a sling under his army walking coat, its empty left sleeve undulating with the passion of his rhetoric. He lost, but was elected five years later, and remained in the Commons, with one brief interruption, for the next thirty-eight years.

He never did things by halves. In 1958, when as minister of transport he was supposed to turn the sod for Edmonton's new airport, instead of digging some puny ceremonial shovel full of dirt, Hees taught himself how to run a bulldozer, and while local dignitaries watched, efficiently ploughed up the first twenty feet of excavation. He seldom missed his daily swim (twenty lengths without a pause) in the Chateau Laurier pool and made up to a hundred phone calls a day, beginning with a hearty "How-you-doin', it's George HEES!" and ending with a cheerful "Right-ee-O Boy!"—regardless of the sex of the caller.

Hees ran a poor fourth at the 1967 Tory leadership convention that chose Robert Stanfield. His candidacy was hurt by word of his relationship with Gerda Munsinger, the German prostitute who had cavorted with several cabinet ministers. (There was a story going round Parliament Hill that Hees, having been shown an explicit photograph of Gerda in the buff, was asked if it really looked like her. He inspected the shot for a long moment before musing: "I'm not sure—her eyes aren't quite right....")

After he decided not to contest the 1988 election, Hees was called in by Mulroney who, wishing to reward him for his long service, appointed him "Ambassador-at-Large," charged with travelling the Third World to see if our aid funds were being efficiently spent. Hees was happy, but pointed out that he preferred to travel with his wife, "Mibs," the former Mabel Dunlop, whom he had married in 1934. The P.M. agreed, and the order-in-council appointing Hees to his new job was the only one in Canadian history that specifically ordered an ambassador to travel "accompanied by his wife."

Hees was about as far from being a political philosopher as you can get. Speaking at an Ottawa West Tory gathering during the 1962 election campaign, he explained his theory on how political candidates ought to be chosen. "When we were boys," he confided, "we used to stand on the corner and watch the girls go by. Some girls had IT, and some didn't. Now, we could tell just like *that* which ones had IT, and which ones didn't. And that's how you pick candidates—they've got to have IT."

George Hees had IT in spades.

54

EATON'S: FALL OF AN ICON

ONLY TWENTY-FIVE YEARS ago, Eaton's still ruled Canadian retailing. Its stores set our national style; the family lived like kings, occupying private castles and even erecting its own church. Eaton's was the country's fourth largest private employer, ranking right behind the two railways and Bell. The company's sixty-two stores moved goods worth $25 million a week (half of all merchandise sales), while their catalogues enjoyed annual circulations of 18 million copies.

Founded by Timothy in 1869, four generations of Eatons extended the company's reach across the country, and through mail-order offices into every hamlet. They turned the store's sales pitch—"Goods Satisfactory or Money Refunded"—into a phrase as familiar as the first line of the national anthem.

Although the family's idea of staging elaborate Santa Claus parades in Canadian downtowns was copied by rival department stores, the kids knew which Father Christmas to trust. "Eaton's Santa was the real one," recalled Rick Rabin, of Gander, who once lined the parade route. "You can't fool kids about anything as important as that."

Befitting their aristocratic behaviour, the family had its share of eccentrics. Sir John Craig Eaton (son of the founder) and his wife, the former Florence McCrea of Omemee, Ontario, lived like monarchs in a seventy-room Norman castle they built at King, just north of Toronto. They travelled the country in a private railway car, spending most summers at a villa (originally built for Queen Elizabeth of Romania) in Florence. Lady Eaton made the headlines only once. In a 1927 interview with *The Toronto Daily Star*, she praised the Italian dictator Benito Mussolini because there were "fewer beggars hanging around the cathedrals."

Her son Timothy Craig spent most of his life playing with model trains. His prize possession was a one-eighth-size model of the locomotive that had pulled Sir Winston Churchill's funeral train. One of the family's many secrets is the tale of the mistress of one famous Eaton who, when asked what would make her happy, brazenly declared that she wanted "one of everything" in the family's Montreal store. The merchandise kept pouring into her Côte-des-Neiges apartment (that featured a bedroom lined entirely in mink), until a load of bicycle tires was delivered and there was no room to stack them. That was when she called a halt to the charade. In 1909 the family built its own church, Timothy Eaton Memorial, in mid-town Toronto, which quickly became the Establishment place of worship.

Unlike most family dynasties, which fall apart as succession duties dilute their holdings, the Eatons discovered a way of passing on their fortune virtually intact. Their secret was "estate freezing," a process that allowed the hiving-off of assets into a holding company (Eaton's of Canada), which controlled all the common stock. It was placed under the control of succeeding generations after payment of a relatively modest gift tax.

John David Eaton, father of the four brothers whose flawed stewardship has reduced the once-proud firm to near-pauper status, headed the firm from 1942 to 1969, and like his predecessors prided himself in never going to the market for new investment capital. That maintained the family's obsession with keeping balance sheets secret, but it also kept the stores from having the funds required to modernize.

The current generation took over in the early 1970s and under Fred's leadership, the company initially prospered, with net profits totalling an impressive $60 million by 1979. That represented a huge turnaround. It was only when the brothers grew bored with the business and hired a daisy chain of surrogate managers that things began to fall apart. Part of the trouble was that while Fred emerged as the natural leader, none of the brothers had clearly been designated to carry the family's corporate torch.

Fred himself left to spend four years as Canada's high commissioner in London, and when he returned, stayed on as chairman of T. Eaton (the operating company), but his heart was no longer in retailing. He began to transfer the family fortune from yesterday's business (department stores) to tomorrow's technology—by taking over (with brother George) the Baton Broadcasting System, and eventually the CTV network.

Of the brothers, only George has been spending much of his time minding the store. John Craig devotes most of his energy to good works and such internal public-relations gestures as handing out twenty-five- and forty-year pins. Thor concentrates on his racing stables. Only two of the brothers' children—John David and Fred Jr.—work in the stores.

I dropped in to see Fred Eaton on December 20, 1996. It was the Christmas rush and he was following family tradition by walking around the stores, wishing employees a happy holiday. When I asked about the retailing revolution that was devastating his industry, he shrugged: "Our company was accused of being the Wal-Mart of its age when Timothy was running it, because it was so different from anything that had come before. There is room for all kinds of operations, the more traditional, fashion-conscious retailers like us, and the big box discounters like Costco and Wal-Mart."

As I was leaving and we stood in his office admiring a model of the *Brave Wolf*, the pleasure yacht Fred had used while in England, I mentioned the rumours that had been swirling around the company for the past decade. Was Eaton's in big trouble?

"No, no," he shot back. "Why would you think that? There are always stories about us, that we're being sold or something. Nothing to it."

Two months later Eaton's was seeking court protection, the first step towards either bankruptcy or sale to an American mega-retailer.

Family dynasties that aren't properly nurtured perish.

Even the Eatons.

55

ALWAYS A REFORMER,
NEVER A REVOLUTIONARY

THROUGH A SERIES of circumstances that no longer matter, I happen to be the first journalist to interview Robert Bourassa in 1970, when at a yeasty thirty-six he was elected Quebec's twenty-sixth premier.

His Quebec City office was crowded with supplicants of all shapes and desires that day—political functionaries with thin moustaches and large ambitions, already hunching their shoulders against the burdens of office they expected to bear. Bourassa, who had become a politician only four years earlier, looked even more cerebral than usual in the office he would eventually occupy for fifteen years.

Although he had just turfed out of office the once-powerful Union Nationale party (and as it turned out, drove them permanently into exile), the new premier seemed unimpressed with himself, just sitting there doing his grainy thing, playing Monsieur Cool.

"During the election campaign," he told me, with all the emotion of a CBC announcer reading commodity prices, "I didn't have time to destroy the Parti Québécois. I challenged them to say what they would do to solve unemployment, and René Lévesque just kept repeating that the independence of Quebec would mean economic prosperity. This is an intellectual fraud. Separatism has at its base economic grievances, which, if I make a good showing, will be resolved in the next five years."

They weren't, of course, but Bourassa kept the faith, and during the 1980 referendum fought on behalf of the federalist cause, "inch by inch, village by village, Rotary by Rotary."

His recent death of cancer, after a long illness, robbed Quebec of a worthy and skilful leader who achieved more for his province than any previous premier. A reformer who never became a revolutionary, he moved carefully, latching onto the political expediency at the heart of each of the many crises that marked his time in government.

Whole forests were consumed to provide the newsprint for endless think-pieces speculating whether Bourassa was a Quebecker first or a Canadian first. He was, of course, neither, being firmly a Bourassa Liberal first, with all other categories ranking a distant second. Still, the unity nerds in Ottawa never stopped believing that he would become the dedicated federalist they wanted him to be, while his nationalistic followers in Quebec swore that he was really an *indépendantiste*, about to leap out of the closet. They had some reason to believe that was the case, especially after the Quebec premier passed two anti–English language bills and in 1992 committed his province to stage a referendum on sovereignty that, had it been held, might have climaxed in Quebec's unilateral declaration of independence. As it was, the manoeuvre was pre-empted by the national referendum that defeated the Charlottetown Accord.

A disappointment to ideological purists on both sides, Bourassa was condemned for being an opportunist, when all he ever wanted was to gain more political goodies for his province. At this, he was a master. He earned a black belt in the dubious art of maximizing equalization payments to his province, while pleading dire straits at the same time—and he never let up.

What neither his critics nor his supporters understood was that to Bourassa pragmatism was not so much a comfortable political position, as his personal religion. His idea of long-term planning was next day's lunch. He never viewed the political process as a progression from one point to the next, but as a kaleidoscope of possibilities, constantly in flux.

Except when he went back on his word and repudiated the constitutional patriation amendments that he helped draft at the 1971 meeting of first ministers in Victoria, Bourassa seldom closed himself off from further negotiations. He set the outer limits of

Quebec's constitutional demands in 1990 and stuck to his moderate position during the Meech and Charlottetown accord debacles.

Although Pierre Trudeau put him down as a "hot-dog eater," Bourassa was not only a consummate politician, but he earned his intellectual credentials, having honed his talents during the decade he spent at the universities of Montreal, Oxford and Harvard. Between his two terms of office, he studied and lectured at Yale and Johns Hopkins University's Center of Advanced International Studies. At one time, his theoretical ideal for Canada was based on the European Community's loose style of partnership.

Bourassa's relations with Pierre Trudeau and Jean Chrétien remained cool, but his friendship with Brian Mulroney was profoundly felt by both men. Beaten at about the same time—Bourassa by Lévesque at the polls in 1976, and Mulroney in his first try for the Tory leadership—they huddled together in the Mount Royal Club, plotting their comebacks.

Back in office—Mulroney in 1984 and Bourassa a year later—their partnership bloomed. They seldom made an important move without briefing one another. But for the stubborn opposition of then Newfoundland premier Clyde Wells and Elijah Harper's success in stopping Manitoba's approval, the Meech Lake Accord might have passed. That was meant to be the Mulroney-Bourassa monument, and had the agreement passed, Lucien Bouchard might not be in the powerful position he is today.

Ironically, my interview with Robert Bourassa, on that long-ago 1970 morning, ended with the off-hand comment that his failure might doom Canada. "I've been told," he said, "that I represent Quebec's last chance, and to some extent, I suppose it's true...."

Maybe. But I hope not.

56

ARTHUR CHILD'S LAST FLIGHT

THE DEATH OF Arthur Child, the recently retired chairman of Burns Foods Ltd. in Calgary, robs the province of its most fascinating character. The most important non-oil businessman in Alberta, he was a proud workaholic whose potted corporate biography boasted that he has "no social or sports interests whatsoever. His time is spent at his office, his home, or travelling on business."

It was true that Child invested most of himself in his work and that he turned the once insolvent Burns Foods into a $2-billion corporation that became Alberta's largest private employer. And it was true that Child deliberately maintained no public profile outside his company, but he also led a fascinating private life, worth describing now that he has passed away, at eighty-six.

He was a skilful flyer, performing impressive aerobatics in his own vintage Tiger Moth and captained his thirty-ton motor yacht, *Cybele III*, on some hair-raising voyages off British Columbia's west coast. The self-designed vessel was typical of Child, toughly built but functional, its white-carpeted engine room as neat and innocent of bric-a-brac as the desk in his Calgary office. (It was also typical of Child that when he purchased his boat, he also bought the company that made it, Canoe Cove Manufacturing Ltd., just to keep tabs on getting first-class work.)

He was a learned man, having graduated from Queen's in Commerce, read French literature at Laval, taught himself French, German, Spanish and Russian, as well as writing a Ph.D. thesis for the Harvard Business School. He wrote three books and personally saved the Canadian Authors' Association from financial collapse. He owned the largest private collection of military history in the country and during the Cold War was regularly flown to the Pentagon for secret briefings.

An unpretentious gent with a wry sense of humour and a romantic's soul, he was kind to strangers and ruthless with competitors. His only vanity was to wear a red toupee that fitted his head so awkwardly he must have known it was a bad joke. He came daily to his office until six months before he died, and was already well into his eighties when he experienced one of his greatest thrills.

A visiting American fighter jet pilot had heard about his flying skills and allowed Child to pilot his supersonic jet fighter. When he started to lecture the octogenarian on how the ejection seat worked, Child gently interrupted: "I won't need that. At my age, if I get into trouble, I'll just ride her down ... "

57

SALUTE TO THE BEACHCOMBER

Spoken in tribute, at his funeral, November 26, 1995.

If the eyes are the window of the soul,
Bruno Gerussi was possessed by a magnificent soul.
Those eyes—which dominated his presence—
were beacons of mischief, of compassion,
of wisdom, of an animal instinct for survival
—and sometimes a reflection of
an inner pain so intense, no one knew its name.

He was an actor.
Most actors trade on their personalities.
Bruno never did that.
For him, personality was secondary.
It was character that mattered.

And it was his character that marked him,
that made him such a valuable human being,
such a great friend—and incidentally,
such a great actor.

It is not easy to define the man.
I cannot pretend to have been close to him.

But what came through was not just his decency,
not just the dedication to his craft
and devotion to his loved ones.

What made Bruno unique

was a quality seldom granted
mortals—especially Canadians.

What set him apart was this:
That when he believed in you
—you believed in yourself.

That was the essence of what was sometimes
mistakenly categorized as his charm.
He was of course the ultimate charmer,
but he was much more than that.

When he believed in you—
you believed in yourself.
That was his secret.

So we are here today
less to mourn his death
than to celebrate his life.

He was indeed a man for all seasons
and he knew them all,
especially spring and fall.

There is a gypsy saying that
we are all kings when we die.
Bruno's epitaph is no less majestic.

In some ways, Canada was the death of him.
Yet he gave so much of himself
—occasionally like Don Quixote,
urging us to jettison
"the melancholy burden of sanity."

More often to inspire us
with the elegance of his spirit,
and his unfailing generosity.

He gave so much of himself
that we sometimes forgot
he had talent to burn.

His greatest performance was his life.

"I write with an axe," declared the Quebec
polemicist Jean-Paul Desbiens.
There was a touch of Bruno Gerussi
in that thought.

He will be missed.

So goodbye, Nick,
farewell, Romeo,
See ya, Tom,

And Bruno—God Bless.

58

THE GENTLE TYCOON
WHO WALKED ALONE

PETER FREDERICK BRONFMAN, the most sensitive and most secretive member of one of history's great business dynasties, is dead.

The Edper Group of companies that he founded and built up during the last quarter of his life turned into an astonishingly diverse and successful $18-billion empire, employing 64,000. Its top executives spent much of last week trumpeting their late chairman's "corporate statesmanship" and "selfless leadership." Peter would not have had much patience with such sentiments. "I happen," he once told me, "to have a very low threshold for bullshit."

What he meant was not so much to denigrate his corporate successes, as to affirm his own priorities. He spent most of life becoming his own man, allowing the roaring boy deep inside to take command and cut loose from the constraints of his upbringing.

To be a Bronfman is never easy. "I grew up in a castle on a hill [Upper Belvedere Avenue in Montreal's posh Westmount district], and I wasn't really aware of what was going on. I had no friends and no real relationship with my parents," he would recall. "I had a nurse for five years when I was very young, and when we happened to meet in Ireland much later, when I was twenty-eight, we just fell into one another's arms, and hugged and hugged."

Sam Bronfman, the dynasty's father and Peter's uncle, could make boys out of men, and with Peter he almost succeeded. Allan Bronfman, Peter's father, always hoped that he and his brother, Edward, would be granted a major role in running the Seagram empire. But just after Peter graduated from Yale, Sam made it very clear that there was to be no place for the two boys. Command of the giant distillery was ceded directly and exclusively to Sam's two sons, Charles and Edgar. Allan's reduced nest egg of Seagram stock was enough to provide his sons with seed money to start their own, initially tiny conglomerate. But Peter never got over the slight.

The business empire he built along with his brother, which at different times has included such well-known firms as Labatts, London Life, Brascan, Noranda and Royal LePage, took up most of his working time, but his heart and spirit were never in it. He became something of a recluse, attending only the occasional, compulsory corporate cocktail party. He would stand at the back of the room, hunched over in a penitent position, sipping his flat ginger ale, silently praying for relief.

Peter liked nothing better than to put on his raincoat, and walk alone through the fluorescent desolation of big-city streets, investigating the radiant miscellanies along the way. He also wrote poetry, none of which was published, though he did produce a slim, mimeographed volume for his friends in 1969. His generous nature—quiet philanthropy was his favourite activity—seldom surfaced publicly. Neither did he allow himself to show any emotion except around the kitchen table of his home, which was his favourite roosting spot.

The business venture he enjoyed the most was ownership of the Canadiens hockey team and the Montreal Forum from 1971 to 1978. Bob Wilson, one of the radio commentators who worked out of the press gondola at the time, later recalled that Peter would frequently sit beside him. When the reporter asked the landlord why, Peter explained that he could relax during games only by sitting next to somebody with an open microphone—so that way he couldn't yell when he felt like it. His respect for the players knew no boundaries. Only a few months before he died, he flew to Montreal for a private visit with the former Canadiens star Floyd Curry, suffering from Alzheimer's. The Habs won four Stanley Cups during the seven years he owned the team. After he sold it to Molson's and bought the Toronto Blue Jays, the baseball squad won two World Series.

Peter lived modestly, moving in the late 1970s from a $90,000 townhouse, near but not in Westmount, to a similarly modest dwelling in mid-town Toronto. He darned his own socks and except for his valuable and exquisitely chosen art collection (Pellan, Chagall, Harris, plus an acre of Inuit sculpture) had no expensive tastes. "I'm just not secure enough to spend the kind of money my cousins do or to live in houses like theirs," he confessed. "A strong part of me keeps saying, 'My God, the money just came to me; maybe it could all disappear someday.'"

He came to maturity only of late, catching up to himself after marrying his third wife, Lynda Hamilton, a Vancouver management consultant, who fulfilled his quest for security and love. He spent the best decade of his life in their country place, a converted one-room school house north of Toronto, where his gentle nature was allowed to flourish.

Peter died just one day short of being awarded the Order of Canada, in a special bedside ceremony by Governor-General Roméo LeBlanc. The letters recommending him for the honour summed up his life. Conrad Black noted that he represented "the most human and constructive face of innovative capitalism." Jack Rabinovitch, his best friend, pointed out that Bronfman had contributed to "aspiring young artists." June Callwood, the Toronto social activist, praised "his inspiring decency, compassion and commitment."

The most significant letter came from cousin Charles Bronfman, Mr. Sam's son, the man whose inheritance Peter had so envied. "Peter," Charles wrote, "is a man who has carved a place for himself in Canadian history. He well deserves the recognition of being included in the Order of Canada."

Peter Bronfman had come home at last.

59

FOR THE LOVE OF ANDY

DURING THE THREE decades Andy Sarlos dominated Canada's financial markets, he operated according to his own rules and his own dimension. There was no one remotely like him. He paid more attention to the long arc of history than to the spurts and pulse of the Dow, valued friendship above profit and became the undisputed Canadian financial guru of his generation.

"His contacts were phenomenal," recalls Max Yamada, who worked for him. "Before joining his firm, I had run the largest U.S. dollar account in Canada for fourteen years and always got the first call from Wall Street. But after a week in Andy's office, I realized how business was really done. He could call literally anybody, and they'd always call back. Fast."

Sarlos was not the richest investor in the country, because he was a born gambler and enjoyed losing as much as winning. "If I was right all the time," he once told me, "it wouldn't be any fun. It's the risk that makes the market an exciting place to be." But he knew how to play the odds and in 1977 alone, the value of stock in his investment trust, HCI Holdings Ltd., more than tripled. At one point so many people wanted to buy shares in his firm that trading on the TSE had to be halted for four hours. During much of the 1980s, his trades accounted for 10 per cent of the TSE's daily totals. By then he was spending $8 million annually in brokerage fees, which made him the largest individual source of commissions on the Street. He seemed to be in on every deal that counted. In one transaction involving the Hiram Walker–Consumers Gas merger, he and his partners walked away with a $19-million profit.

He hypnotized his peers. "What's Andy up to?" everybody wanted to know. In the wine-bars and private clubs that ring Toronto's brokerage houses, where the senior analysts go to trade fables and lies, the talk was often about the source of his market magic. Why was this diminutive Hungarian, whose Establishment credentials were zilch, consulted by just about every big player in the country? Why did the likes of Peter Munk, Peter Bronfman, the Reichmanns in their days, Trevor Eyton and many others of equal rank scarcely make a major move without seeking his input?

The answer was simple. He gave advice the way a priest grants absolution—freely, and with no hidden agenda. That was unheard of on Bay Street, where contacts at his level usually mean leverage that can yield fees, big ones. Sarlos never marketed his friendships or his wisdom. "He was a giant of a man," Munk said of him. "A real prince who never said an evil word about anybody, and was more interested in making money for others than for himself. He was also very shrewd—on a human level, twice as shrewd as George Sorros. I can't even say how much I'll miss him, personally and in business."

To know him was to trust him. "Andy is Numero Uno with me," declared Gus Van Wielingen, one of Calgary's oil millionaires. "I don't mind giving Andy my chequebook any time. I'll even show him how to sign my name." As his network widened, Sarlos became a generous philanthropist, making significant donations to several Canadian universities. After the fall of Hungary's Communist regime in 1956, he contributed much time and money to help revive the economy of his former homeland, including the financing of a bank, department store, newspaper and the country's first modern shopping centre.

Playing the market, he always went to the source, whether it meant visiting rigs in the field and talking to the roughnecks actually drilling for oil or studying the sulphur market, because its supply-demand curve determines steel-manufacturing schedules, six months in advance.

He was a student of power and knew, for example, that CEOs of companies under threat of takeovers often act on the basis not of their disposable power, but of their disposable psychic energies. That trait made them vulnerable at pivotal moments, and despite his gentle manner, Sarlos knew when to move in for the kill. "Good traders," he maintained, "rely on what they hear; great traders assimilate the available facts, then act on the basis of their gut instincts and sheer nerve. Balls are as important as brains."

A Hungarian by birth and persuasion, Sarlos shared the national trait of being impossible to stop, once moving in a desired direction. (It's a well-documented fact that Hungarians will follow you into a revolving door, yet emerge ahead of you.) He loved Canada and was an incurable romantic.

The son of a Budapest grain-trader, he was drafted into the Hungarian air force, and arrested by the occupying Communists for plotting to defect to Yugoslavia. His subsequent imprisonment changed his life. "Death seemed a better alternative than life," he recalled, "because for a year, the guards always made you believe you'd be executed the next morning, and many of us were."

Sarlos later fought with bravery and distinction in the 1956 Hungarian Revolution, fled to Austria and eventually landed in Canada. After taking an accounting degree, he spent ten years in Labrador with Canadian Bechtel, then building the Churchill Falls power project. On Bay Street, his first venture was to buy out the falling Hand Chemical Industries, a small Milton, Ontario, firm which was going broke making fireworks, but had the advantage of a TSE listing and $1 million in its treasury. In the next five years he parlayed that seed money into $200 million.

But it wasn't uphill all the way. In the 1982 market crash, his company's stock fell from a high of $45 to 47 cents. He ended up with debts of $150 million. It was Sarlos's proud boast that he paid back every cent, instead of escaping, like most firms in his positions, into a "restructuring" mode, which would have saved him millions.

During the past decade or so, Sarlos continued to trade, but his role was more advisory. "Check it out with Andy," became the Street's war cry whenever a big deal was coming down. He never let up, though he suffered from increasingly serious heart trouble, undergoing three major operations, and was twice declared clinically dead.

The dignified and superbly organized way he died was typical of the man. On April 24, 1997, as he was leaving his office, he asked his chief assistant, Hal Jones, to close all his future positions. He was so weak he could hardly walk, but insisted on taking part that evening in a conference-call board meeting of Munk's Trizec-Hahn real-estate company, via his bedside telephone. Two days later he lapsed into a coma from which he never recovered.

The previous week Sarlos had dined out one last time with Peter Munk at the Toronto Club, and told him, "I am totally at peace with myself. I have had more lives than I deserved."

Perhaps, but Bay Street without Andy Sarlos will be an infinitely less interesting and much less compassionate place.

VIII SLOUCHING TO MILLENNIUM

SLOUCHING TO MILLENNIUM

"It's kind of like the early days of the universe after the Big Bang, when gases were congealing and galaxies were forming. No one is really sure how it will all sort out, and it's not yet clear where Earth is."

Tony Comper, president, Bank of Montreal,
commenting on the millennium,
quoted in Canadian futurist
Dan Tapscott's *Digital Economy*

WHEN BAY STREET bankers sound like Himalayan gurus, you know the world is turning upside down.

Welcome to the eve of the 21st century.

As the new millennium approaches, everyone becomes an armchair futurist. Yet, according to Yogi Berra, "the future isn't what it used to be." Any forecast beyond that wise observation is speculation, equal parts projection and fantasy. While some of the events and trends that will dominate the new millennium are already in place, most are beyond our imagining. Of those trends we can identify, and expect to continue, a few are comforting, some are exhilarating, and many more are nightmare-inducing.

The diagnosis of "pre-millennial anxiety" has become commonplace, yet at the core of this anxiety there will remain a great, even growing, excitement at being alive. This is human nature after all, as Ambrose Bierce observed in his wonderful *Devil's Dictionary*, under the entry for *future*: "That period of time in which our affairs prosper, our friends are true and our happiness is assured."

As we move into the next century, a new way of living will take hold in this country. On December 31, 1999, Canadians will feel the traditional flow of their lives being cut; what comes later will be very different from what came before.

Instead of remaining yoked to the civic virtues of deference and self-denial which have held us back for so many generations, Canadians will follow an ethic of personal fulfilment that stresses self-reliance, autonomy, questioning of established authority and orthodoxy, and the pursuit of a better *quality* of life, rather than a raised *standard* of living. Canadians will worship ideas, not heroes; will possess a lively sense of personal limits; and will come to rely on character instead of personality. Life in the 21st century will be what each of us makes of it, not what some government, corporation, church or even family wants us to become.

These trends are already in place, but the turning point of midnight, December 31, 1999, will provide these new attitudes with the necessary catharsis to establish them as generational values. Life unfolds according to a sequence of markers. Most of these way-points are personal, but some public events become the seedlings of a new collective culture: the birth, crucifixion and resurrection of Jesus Christ, the D-Day landings in Normandy, the assassination of John F. Kennedy, Montreal's Expo 67, or the magical goal by Paul Henderson that beat the Soviets at our national game—all, in their own way, helped define Canadian culture. But all will pale in comparison with the dawn of the new millennium.

When one year ends and another begins, people become both concerned and elated—worried about the change the future will bring, yet exuberant about the possibility of new beginnings. The annual ritual of death and renewal is magnified 1,000 times at the turn of a millennium. The immediate change will be more psychical than physical. Nothing will feel the same, because the millennium will have placed borders around our experience, no less real than the borders on a map. We will refer to events in the landscape of our memory as being either pre-millennial—as if the year 1999 were in some distant, hazy days of yore—or as post-millennial, referring to the day's headlines (or Web flash) and events up until the year 2999 as the present. All that's past will have become prologue.

Unless the warnings of some prophets, pundits and political scientists come true (of the three, the prophets have by far the better record for accuracy), this fresh approach will not stop history in its tracks. On the contrary, the last couple of decades have witnessed an unprecedented *acceleration* of history. In Europe, national borders which defended against invaders since Hannibal have fallen, to be replaced with the European parliament, as well as half a dozen new democracies. Ideological borders have been erased, their physical manifestation being the symbolic destruction of the Berlin Wall. The near-disintegration of Canada was the biggest domestic story of the decade, with Quebec appearing ready to raise an ideological and geographical curtain of its own.

Our system of two national parties, which between them have governed Canada since Confederation, was tested and found obsolete. Such bedrock institutions as the Canadian Red Cross, the Canadian Football League, Canada's military forces, organized religion, the British monarchy and most other touchstones that once regulated our lives will vanish as meaningful entities. Gone with them and many other, one-time reliable touchstones will be the certainty of being able to depend on the past as a guide to the future.

Even the rate of change is changing. Its quickening pace will cause Canada to spin around even faster on its axis. In Lester R. Brown's 1996 essay "The Acceleration of History," the ex-officio chair of the World Watch Institute observed that "people born since 1950 have seen more population growth in their lifetimes than during the preceding four million years; the world economy is expanding even faster, having increased by $4 trillion in the past decade, or more than from the beginning of civilization until 1950. The pace of change in our world is accelerating to the point where it threatens to overwhelm the management capacity of political leaders," he warned.

Yet, despite the massive political and social shifts we are bound to experience in the upcoming century, it is the lightning advances in science and technology that will most profoundly affect our lives. In the next decade, genetic engineering will begin to approach a miraculous state of grace which will eventually allow us to program much of the life we wish to lead. Disease will not be eliminated, but the contours of our wellness—or lack of it—will be foreseeable and medicine will be able to handle predictable problems. Inherited illnesses will be eradicated by injecting new genetic codes into developing embryonic cells. Scientists are also developing so-called "anti-sense" therapies that block certain malignant cells from developing, which may prove to be the best way of defeating cancer, AIDS, herpes and other chronic illness. Tissue transplants will advance cures for diabetes, muscular dystrophy, Parkinson's disease and Alzheimer's.

As more human reproduction takes place in test tubes or artificial wombs, sex will become strictly a recreational activity. On the molecular biology front, the limits of diagnosis will take incredible leaps. "I know people," wrote futurologist Graham Molitor recently, "who are developing a small card with 10,000 micro-wells on it. You'll be able to treat it with a drop of blood, and in a few hours have the results for 10,000 different disease diagnoses."

The intuitive leaps and cross-pollination of ideas that make scientific discoveries possible will be a pronounced feature of the 21st century, the result of global communications becoming as cheap as political promises, as fast as quicksilver and as simple as breathing. The most significant scientific breakthroughs will happen in computer technologies, which have made the communications revolution possible. Personal computers will accept voice commands and move information around the Earth, digitally and via satellite, at the speed of light. According to Bill Gates, the computer revolution merely provided the platform for the *real* revolution just around the corner—formation of a worldwide communications network. "We'll communicate with it through a variety of devices, including some that look like television sets, some like today's personal computers, some will look like telephones and some will be the size and shape of a wallet," he has written. "And at the heart of each will be a powerful computer, invisibly connected to millions of others." The effect of this change will be so wide-reaching, he adds, that the computer will be more than an appliance: "It will be your passport to a new, mediated way of life."

Gates has also described in some detail the requirements for a virtual-reality body suit, which would deliver one to ten million "tactels," or pinpricks of sensation, across the body's surface. This would trick the skin in much the same way rapidly changing still photographs trick the eyes into believing they are watching "moving" pictures. The result would be felt as a single continuous sensation, allowing users to experience their "virtual" bodies in cyberspace. "It will probably first be used to help people with physical disabilities," Gates has predicted.

Because of the size of its acreage, Canada is bound to be on the leading edge of the communications revolution. During the next decade, this country will be rewired with fibre-optic networks that will carry most forms of communication, becoming the 21st-century version of the vanished continental railroads. At the same time, artificial intelligence—an oxymoron for our times, given the scarcity of the real stuff—will become ever less artificial and ever more intelligent. Computers will not only learn how to think but how to *learn*, independent of human guidance. The micro-chip will take its rightful place among history's four greatest inventions—the others being fire, the wheel and hotel room service.

But it is the Internet and its many siblings that will have the most devastating effect on Canadian society in the next century. A fully operational, universal, digitalized information highway (of which the Internet will occupy but a single lane) will destroy much of the personal privacy we now enjoy. (Lock up your daughters and hire a hungry pitbull to guard your Web page.)

Not since Johannes Gutenberg printed his Mazarin Bible with movable type in 1455—rendering the mass distribution of the written word possible—has there been a communications revolution as profound as this. While both opened up new fields, in one crucial respect the information highway runs in the opposite direction from the Gutenberg revolution. Where cheap and plentiful Bibles allowed medieval folk *direct* access to the word of God, the Internet will allow people *mediated* access to the Almighty, or at least his digitalized equivalent. The *deus ex machina* will be the machine itself, providing its users with such credible "virtual" reality that it will challenge the attraction of the "actual" reality around them.

The virtual marketplace will eliminate the need for "real" real-estate agents, bank clerks, travel agents, stock brokers, and almost all other workers in the service sector whose employment is based on simple buy-and-sell transactions. These will be far easier handled at pit-stops along the information highway; but this raises the most complex legal problem of policing cyberspace: how will electronic transactions, expected to reach at least $100 billion by

2003, be taxed and regulated? A panel of Toronto jurists debating the issue recently decided that the only effective way to maintain legal control of cyberspace may be to punish tax dodgers and un-ethical business users with the ultimate sanction: banishment from the Net. (Perhaps they will be allowed their own virtual but separate reality, much as British prisoners were once sent to Australian penal colonies.)

Between now and the last day of December 1999, at Rotary luncheons, Canadian Clubs and fund-raisers across the country, speaker after unoriginal speaker will declare that the 21st century will belong to Canada. They will be wrong, just as Sir Wilfrid Laurier turned out to be wrong when he first said it. The next millennium will not belong to Canada—or to any nation east of Hawaii. This will be the age of the Asian Tigers and Dragons, the ripening of China as the world's dominant power.

In the scant four years from 1991 to 1995, the Chinese economy grew by a staggering 57 per cent, raising the per capita income of its 1.2 billion citizens by more than half. China will become the world's largest economy by about 2003, surpassing the United States as a generator of wealth, with many of its urban citizens enjoying higher standards of living than the richest of Americans and Europeans. The few remaining legacies of Communism will be dumped and Greater China will include not only Hong Kong, but Taiwan and Macao, as well as its moneyed and powerful diaspora. Shanghai, whose skyline already challenges that of Hong Kong, will emerge as the commercial headquarters for the People's Republic. A recent Canadian visitor to that city reports a construction binge unequalled anywhere, with eighty-five major new office towers reaching for the sky. As China's business mandarins come to dominate world commerce, that country's politicians, writers, artists and scientists will become internationally recognized, just as Solzhenitsyn, Sakharov and Khrushchev were during the flowering of the Soviet empire; or Mickey, Minnie and Goofy were during Pax Americana.

An integral part of China's industrialization will be an accelerated emphasis on education. China already has at least 200 million more high-school graduates than North America, and anyone who visits any Canadian campus quickly realizes how significant the

Asian presence has become. (Examination results reveal that their quality is even more impressive than their quantity.) As these young men and women return home to join the cadre of earlier, foreign-educated graduates, Chinese society is bound to become increasingly liberalized and free-wheeling, its citizens not afraid to voice their rights and grievances. Exposure to western society will raise the demand for political freedoms, but even more so for cars, televisions and home appliances. This will create a conflict of its own: China, for example, now builds an estimated 43 million bicycles a year, but for the first time since Mao, official policy favours the automobile. Bicycles are now banned in parts of downtown Shanghai and restricted during rush hours in other cities, raising fears of coming gridlock, pollution, energy consumption and further loss of croplands.

Escalating tensions could become unbearable between the bulk of China's largely rural population, which has lived through a half-century of Communist rule and remains deeply Maoist; and the newly educated urban class, which worships long limousines over the Long March. An astonishing 200 million peasants have already been uprooted from their communal farms by current market reforms and the chronic shortages of arable land. They are moving into China's overcrowded cities and no one knows how these internal exiles will earn their way in places that can't handle their existing growth rates. At the moment, ninety-five cities are already bursting with more than a million inhabitants and the birth rate will add the equivalent of Canada's entire population over the next two decades.

Demographers agree that the Earth's population will increase by at least 100 million per year in the early part of the next century. Although most of this growth will take place in what is now smugly called "The Third World," if the industrialized western democracies (including Canada) were to admit only 10 per cent of this population bubble, it would amount to 200 million additional people by the year 2020. This would transform the industrial powers beyond recognition. Not too many years after we celebrate the millennium, Canadians will discover that the Old Canada with its WASP ascendancy is not merely obsolete, it will have ceased to exist. The white Anglo-Saxons who once ruled this country will have become a visible minority; roast beef and Yorkshire pudding will be reduced to one of those exotic ethnic dishes that people munch on Parliament Hill every Canada Day, while watching the distant grandsons and granddaughters of our original Scots settlers perform listless Highland flings.

Despite its growing ties with Asia, both of blood and money, Canada will remain on the eastern periphery of the Asia region, and we may well count this as a blessing. Of the 8 billion people expected to inhabit the Earth by 2025, the 5 billion who live in Asia will produce at least a quarter of the world's goods. According to Ricardo Petrella, official futurist of the European Union, much of Asia's population at that time will be hived into fifty cities with 20 million inhabitants each. The environmental and social problems this could cause are beyond imagining.

Petrella, whose official title is Head of the Future Assessment in Science and Technology (FAST) program at EU headquarters in Brussels, makes some brutal predictions. He visualizes a world dominated by "a hierarchy of 30 city-regions linked more to each other than to the territorial hinterlands into which the nation-state once bound them. This wealthy archipelago of city-regions—with more or less manageable populations of 8 to 12 million—will be run by alliances between the global merchant class and metropolitan governments whose chief function will be to support the international competitiveness of the global firms to which they are hosts." (Petrella lists Vancouver as the only Canadian city to qualify as a 21st-century nation-state, though his rankings include Montreal-Toronto-Chicago as a "super region.")

The most frightening aspect of Petrella's vision is that beyond the walls of these wealthy enclaves, he foresees what he calls "impoverished lumpenplanets," where "peasants up-rooted from the land by free trade try to eke out an existence in violence-ridden mega-urban settlements of 15 to 18 million or more." That these marginalized classes would turn to crime (smuggling drugs, children, transplant organs and illegal immigrants) is obvious. But because these downtrodden classes will have access to CNN (by then, the Conrad News Network), they will have a media window on the prosperous city-states next door to them. Much as the television images of life in the decadent West helped to persuade East Berlin's residents to raze the Wall, future inhabitants on the wrong side of the Poverty Curtain are bound to incite civil disruptions of unpredictable intensity and duration.

Even if this depressing scenario proves to be wildly exaggerated, in the next millennium the chasm between rich and poor is bound to grow even wider. At the moment, the world's 358 billionaires control more wealth than 45 per cent of the Earth's population. As this imbalance becomes even greater, social unrest will increase. In response, the upper crust could share its wealth— but more likely they will retreat into guarded and gated fortress enclaves, where they will live in safety—and perpetual fright.

The climate of fear will feed another growth industry—personal security. Along with such everyday defences as watchtowers, dogs and armed response teams, the protection industry will expand into sophisticated aerial surveillance. The newest gadgets will include satellite images and helicopters with infra-red cameras that can detect the heat from a burning cigarette 1,000 feet below. The proving ground for such equipment is the Los Angeles Police Department, which already operates 50 Aerospatiale helicopters with 30-million candle-power spotlights to turn night into day, and a separate fleet of Bell Jet Ranger whirlybirds that can ferry SWAT teams into action at a moment's notice. It is only a matter of time, in the corporate world of tomorrow, before such services are privatized and offered to the highest bidders.

If all this weren't scary enough, seismologists predict that Tokyo and Los Angeles, both built on geographic fault lines, stand a good chance of being flattened in the first half of the next century. (In Hollywood's screen treatment of The Big One, some future Italian Stallion will whisper: "Hey babe, did ya feel da Earth move?") Apart from such acts of God, nature's battleground will be the great freshwater river systems.

The motor of economic growth was once fuelled by oil; in the next millennium, the precious fuel will be water. According to the World Bank, chronic water shortages affect 80 nations and 40 per cent of the world's population. The demand for water doubles every twenty years and much of it isn't where it's most needed. The main flashpoints in the water wars will be the militant demands for freshwater diversions from the rivers Jordan, Mekong, Ganges, Indus,

Tigris, Nile, Zambezi, Danube and the Rio Grande. Indeed, in a little-noticed watershed, the government of Mexico submitted a loan request in May 1995, to the United States. Unlike the widely publicized loan following the peso crisis of the previous year, however, the request was not for dollars but for water—some 2.8 million cubic metres from the Rio Grande. And even though the U.S. had shored up the Mexican economy a few months earlier with $20 billion, it refused the water loan. It was a chilling indicator of things to come. As Sandra Postel, director of the Global Water Policy Project in Cambridge, Mass., has written, "Only water scarcity threatens the three fundamental aspects of human security—food production, the health of the aquatic environment, and social and political stability."

She quotes an old Inca proverb: "The frog does not drink up the pond in which it lives." That wisdom is now forgotten in the Americas, and the water shortage will be felt closer to home. A 1987 Presidential Task Force predicted that one-fifth of the United States will suffer from severe water shortages by the millennium— which was then thirteen years away, not three—and supplies have been drying up ever since. With 10 per cent of the Earth's freshwater supply—more than any other country—Canada will come under enormous pressure to share its liquid resource with the American West Coast and midwestern states. Canadians will panic, tempted to abandon resistance and sell off their last bargaining chip. The thirst for water, not a French-speaking homeland, will be the greatest threat to the Canadian state in the coming century. Many years too late, Canadians will learn whether the water clause in the Canada-U.S. Free Trade Agreement was *really* about the American right to drink bottles of virgin spring water, or to drain Lake Superior.

Business in the 21st century will flourish, as free enterprise adapts to its global playground and takes over from an exhausted and largely bankrupt public sector. Apart from taking all the profits they possibly can, the main obsession of the transnational corporations will be how to minimize their taxes. With governments cracking down on tax havens, corporations will flee into a kind of Never-Never Land, a tax-free Shangri-La of their own invention. How will governments levy taxes on firms whose owners live in one country, build factories in another, sell their products in a third and invest their profits in a fourth, while not claiming corporate residence in any of them? Carl Gerstacker, a former chairman of Dow Chemical, once fantasized about purchasing "an island owned by no nation, that would serve as truly neutral ground, so that we could operate in America as U.S. citizens, in Japan as Japanese and in Brazil as Brazilians."

Outsourcing and co-sourcing will be the orders of the day. The vertically integrated company will go the way of the dodo bird, as companies fragment their operations and share resources with their competitors. The pacts among Canadian banks to share the cost of developing electronic banking are one good example. The life cycles of new products will become so brief that there will be no time for most new items to be manufactured by the companies that developed them. Instead, companies that achieve technological breakthroughs will license them, even to their fiercest rivals, and collect royalties. The average lifespan of new consumer electronic products will be reduced to sixty days.

A curious new phenomenon known as the "bimodal factor" will kick in, prompting very large and very small companies to flourish, while medium-size enterprises disappear. The trend has already taken root on Bay Street, where the giant bank-owned brokerages are booming and promise to grow even larger, while niche-driven boutique investment houses are also doing well. Of the mid-size firms, only Midland Walwyn survives. This trend will spread to every type of business, from auto manufacturing to computer software development.

The search for jobs will grow even more desperate in the 21st century, with Canadians (perhaps even Buzz Hargrove) finally realizing that the era of lifetime employment is truly over. By the millennium, most Canadians will either be overworked or under-employed, with eight million involuntary entrepreneurs working out of their homes or shared offices. The labour force will be further skewed as the country's traditional demographic balance is overturned. Within eight years, Canada will for the first time have more pensioners than children.

In a dramatic reversal of the Industrial Revolution, which pushed a craft-work society into the machine age, people will once again be thrown back on their individual talents and resources. That transition will be exhilarating, empowering and tough. Even working at home will come under pressure, as Third World entrepreneurs, with clicking computers and burning modems, offer to complete freelance assignments at a fraction of the going North American rates.

The closer we get to the year 2000, the clearer it will be that change has become the only constant in our lives. The millennial marker will grant us a pause in that long toboggan ride known as life north of the 49th parallel, a moment in time to focus on the future and assimilate the past—to find meaning in what we've been, so we can decide where we're headed.

To survive the pressures of the approaching millennium will require rare inner fortitude. The sense of individual vulnerability and collective ennui bound to taint daily experience can be reduced only through the strengthening of our inner spiritual resources. The indispensable lesson we must learn, on this tenuous cusp of the 21st century, is to remain open to new experiences, so that instead of worrying about the details of an unpredictable future, we allow our lives to unfold with hope and exhilaration.

Only by claiming our own future—and that of our immediate families and communities—will the human spirit prevail.

On that momentous midnight clear in 1999, when we greet the new millennium, we shall share an epiphany, a rare moment of mutual understanding. Amid our inflated hopes and fears, we will remember the firestorm of change that swept through our lives in the past two decades, and we will raise a glass of bubbly—"To the good old days ... "

IX BEARING WITNESS FOR MY COUNTRY

61

LOVE THIS LAND, NOT THE CONSTITUTION

CANADA'S DESTINY REMAINS circumscribed by a dozen suits bickering over constitutional crumbs in a loopy process that is as relevant to our daily lives as the mating habits of Brazilian killer bees.

We seem to have arrived at one of those rare junctures in Canadian history when we can sense the continuity of an age being severed. The constitutional contest has become a political endgame with no likely winners; national survival in any form short of a split Pakistan or an embattled Lebanon has become—but should not be—our highest goal.

In hard times, personal and national, Canadians have always found solace in the outdoors. Unlike most industrialized countries, where wilderness has been reduced to scenery, that glorious and beautiful hunk of geography to which we lay claim remains authentic. It is a place to which men and women feel rooted, where they can find spiritual sustenance, even if it's a toy cottage on a crowded lake.

Politicians should celebrate Canada Day by getting out of those stuffy Ottawa negotiating corridors where any radical new idea is as welcome as a pickpocket at a wedding. They should hit the back roads that lead north, west and east, away from the country of the mind, out into the real world.

There, they could recharge their brains and ventilate their lungs. They should give themselves a chance to taste the bite of salt air and watch the waves breaking against the rocks of Conception Bay in Newfoundland or pounding the beach at Bull Harbour on the northern tip of Vancouver Island. They should ride the rivers that cascade into the St. Lawrence or hike towards heaven in the Rocky Mountain foothills.

Best of all, they should live in a tent for a couple of nights, touch the earth and walk out into the summer dawn after a long rain. At that moment, they would feel the cathedral hush of a world freshly created, unsoiled by the selfish and self-perpetuating myths that have prevented this country from reaching its demonstrably bright potential.

The most influential thinker of our age, Marshall McLuhan, got it right when he observed that Canadians have a unique relationship with nature. "We go outside to be alone," he noted, "and we go inside to be with people, a pattern that is antithetic not only to Europeans, but to all other cultures." Just leaving the politicians alone with themselves and their consciences could have uncounted benefits.

It's high time the politicos realized that even if most of us really don't care which level of government administers what (since none of them will do it all that well anyway), we do care passionately about the future of our country. Few Canadians comprehend the subtleties of the constitutional negotiating process. It has gone on far too long and there are no guarantees that a new constitution, even if it's written on quality parchment and tied with a pretty red ribbon, would improve our lives. That doesn't mean Canadians are indifferent to what happens. They want Canada to endure, not as a constitutional cripple, but as a functioning entity capable of governing itself. It sometimes seems as if the lack of a new constitution is more disturbing than the Constitution itself—though we seemed to be perfectly fine while it was lodged in some dusty British archive for 115 years.

While just about every truth and tradition we've held sacred about this country in the past is in play as the feds and premiers attempt to nail together a new kind of country, one national characteristic remains immutable: Canada's outrageous size and geographical diversity.

This is not a country at all but a continent, which explains why it's so impossible to govern. How do you fashion policies that will meet the divergent personal imperatives of the Newfoundland fisherman, a Mississauga yuppie or an Oil Patch roughneck? It's just about impossible and always has been, but that doesn't diminish our potential—especially when measured against our size.

It's sometimes useful to recall the sheer immensity of the country. Laid over a map of Europe, Canada would reach from the west coast of Ireland across the Continent and stretch deep into Asia, east of the Ural Mountains. Ottawa would be located at about Kiev, the capital of Ukraine. Yet modern Canada's size has been reduced in its impact, through air travel, to the length of some in-flight, third-rate Hollywood epic.

There should be a law that Canadians would not be granted citizenship until they've crossed this country by car or, if they can find one, by train. That kind of odyssey would serve to remind us that even if we've always suffered from constitutional indigestion, our forefathers performed a series of miracles to originally settle this country. Exploring and taming Canada's resources has been a Homeric epic and it is only the poor quality of our history education that has failed to bring that truth home.

Even now, when we are ranked as one of the industrial world's seven leading nations, Canada's potential remains virtually untapped. After 125 years of selling off our natural wealth, still only about 7 per cent of the land has been permanently settled. Something like three-quarters of Canada's population is squeezed into 1 per cent of the country's territory, nearly all of it hugging the United States border. Most of our hinterland broods silent and inaccessible, beyond summer and beyond our reach, an empty land filled with wonders.

Apart from enjoying these geographical gifts, on this anniversary of Confederation we should pledge ourselves to becoming actively Canadian, instead of just living here. This country deserves that kind of commitment. That means, among other things, putting pressure on the politicians to hammer out a reasonable constitutional deal, and then get on with the more essential job of salvaging the economy.

Realities are most clearly viewed in retrospect. We often fail to appreciate the value of a relationship until it's over; all too often we underestimate how intense an experience can be until we look back in bittersweet remembrance. That's the way it is with countries. You seldom appreciate your homeland until you lose it.

And then it's too late.

62

CANADA IS THE SOLUTION,
NOT THE PROBLEM

IN 1867, WHEN THREE million inhabitants of four British colonies reluctantly joined in a federal union to be known as the Dominion of Canada, the issue was survival.

It still is.

Many fine theories have been spun about the endless conferences that led up to Confederation, but the most likely version of what happened runs something like this: revenues of the colonial governments that provided the rudimentary services that kept the people at bay and the politicians in pocket money were running out; the Yanks were in an expansionist mood, threatening the colonies' future independence; England's treatment of its North American holdings alternated between cynical disregard and benign neglect. Something had to be done. The fledgling politicians and opinion leaders of what would become the provinces of Ontario, Quebec, New Brunswick and Nova Scotia got drunk together in Quebec City, then got drunk together again in Charlottetown and finally decided they could grab more power for themselves by creating their own country than if they bought into the British or American systems—and bingo, Canada was born.

That may be a slight exaggeration, but you certainly wouldn't believe anybody could establish this crazy, horizontal-Chile-of-a-country, while stone-cold sober.

Ever since that initial July 1, when we first celebrated our birth, 130 years ago, we have been busy initially building and then shedding the ties that bind us from Atlantic to Pacific and back again. The north-south pull of economic gravity across the 49th parallel has always been more powerful than the east-west axis, held together by wishful thinking and Mel Hurtig. Most countries understand that the equation between national survival and economic efficiency doesn't always balance, but their citizens feel so strongly about the former that they are willing to sacrifice some of the latter.

Not to act in our own self-interest by strengthening the ties that bind us may seem strange. But then, we're Canadians. Our colonial roots combined with the effects of a killjoy Presbyterian conscience have cursed us with a perpetual inferiority complex. It has demanded that we don't have much fun and that we commit our psyches so deeply to local and regional issues that Canada has never worked very well.

Until recently, Canadians seemed proud of their feelings of inadequacy: whenever they walked into a room, they would inevitably race to sit in the most uncomfortable chair. Collectively, we acted as if we were determined to live out the snide put-down of comedian Dave Broadfoot, who once declared that "Canada is very important to the world, because if Canada didn't exist, the Chinese could sail right across and invade Denmark."

The governing perception Canadians have of themselves and the large land they inhabit is caught in our national motto: *a mari usque ad mare* (from sea to sea). The strength of this sentiment—that we connect the world's two great oceans—is one of the subliminal reasons so many Anglo-Canadians object to Quebec separatism. An independent Quebec would forever rend asunder the sea-to-sea metaphor that dominates our perception of the Canadian landscape. Ultimately, Canada's *raison d'être* lies in the possession of its land and water.

Still, some important ties still bind us together, and even if they've never seemed weaker, there remains a common determination among most Canadians—French, English and all of us others—that this country is worth preserving. Agustin Barrios Gomez, a former Mexican ambassador to Ottawa, got it right when he was asked what he thought of Canada, just before leaving his northern posting for home. "Canada," he said, "is the solution looking for a problem." That's precisely what we are. Yet the reason for such subtle optimism is hard to pin down, especially when counting up our national debt or watching Lucien Bouchard trying to tear the country apart.

The happy fact is that no matter how hard some Canadians try to make the worst out of the lousy economic and constitutional circumstances in which we find ourselves, most of us still subscribe to the notion that Canada is possessed of an extraordinary resilience. It must be. No other civilized nation on earth could withstand the venal maladministration inflicted on us by our politicians and still be around to celebrate the millennium.

Despite these and other problems, given the option of living somewhere, anywhere, else, most Canadians—even in Quebec—would probably agree that what we've got here is a daily miracle of a country. We more than meet the basic definition of a successful nation, as a body of people who have done great things together. This is a magnificently uncrowded land, enjoying personal and collective freedom as practised in few other lands. There are few class or caste boundaries to achieving ambitions and realizing aspirations. It's our incompleteness that attracts newcomers, because they feel there might be space for them. No wonder we're the envy of the world; no wonder so many people want to fashion new lives here.

Too often—as a nation and as individuals—we decry what we lack, instead of celebrating what we already have. Yet to most of the world's troubled citizens, Canada appears blessed with the mandate of heaven.

63

BEARING WITNESS FOR MY COUNTRY

THE LOCATION WAS cold—a bloodless, marble-lined chamber in the Victoria Conference Centre—but the occasion was inexplicably moving. The ill-starred Beaudoin-Dobbie Special Joint Parliamentary Committee on a Renewed Canada hit British Columbia's capital recently, and hardly anyone bothered to show up.

The tiny audience, which through the day frequently numbered less than the thirty members of the committee, consisted mostly of middle-aged, middle-class citizens feeling confused about a world they never made. As a group, they looked like the kind of people who write letters to CBC-FM classical disc jockeys, read consciousness-raising books by Joseph Campbell, grow alfalfa, and protest against the system by cutting their own hair. One or two obvious bigots, big men with cruel mouths—scars in bloodshot faces—bristled whenever Quebec or bilingualism was mentioned, but most of the listeners just sat there in quiet disbelief.

Their mood of incredulity was understandable.

Here we are, a country celebrating its 125th birthday, seriously debating the proposition of whether we should split apart or stay together—whether we should throw away all the impressive history we've made and become a burnt-out residue of warring provinces, diminished and alone.

That the burden of coming up with a formula to prevent this tragedy has come to rest in large measure on this creaky committee is a sign of how far we've slipped and how close we stand to the precipice. That is not to say that its members lack dedication or intellectual muscle. Senator Gerald Beaudoin, its co-chairman, is the

Wayne Gretzky of constitutional law, having turned his Gallic charm on a subject that defies levity and written half a dozen understandable books about it. The two-and-a-half-dozen men and women who make up the committee are as loyal and energetic a group of federalists as can be found anywhere, with the NDP rump—Lorne Nystrom, Ian Waddell, Lynn Hunter, Howard Mc-Curdy and Phil Edmonston—being particularly impressive.

Yet petitioners to the committee and its huddle of listeners sensed—and in some cases communicated—a certain unease, the feeling that history had bypassed these well-meaning legislators. They felt that the decisions that count would be taken elsewhere, in some unnamed Ottawa mandarin's cell, painted civil-service green, far from light and enlightenment.

The Victoria hearings had all the trappings associated with constitutional conferences: a press corps bored out of its skull, looking for the latest nut to propose that we get "the frogs to speak white" or tow Newfoundland out to sea; the consultants who collect fat fees for standing around looking glum and raising the odd eyebrow whenever someone mentions patriating the BNA Act. Also at hand were the simultaneous translators who are the ultimate proof of Canada's identity. This phenomenon surely defines us: watch any political conference on television when a participating male decides to speak French. Chances are his words will appear to come out of his mouth in English, spoken by a female translator—and vice versa. This transsexual, translingual image neatly catches the Canadian dilemma ...

Watching the proceedings, I felt that they should have been held in a public market or legion hall, some place that breathed signs of life and commotion, instead of this sterile conference centre, whose last occupants were probably detergent marketers or mutual-fund salespersons. That would have been symbolically important, because what's really taking place in this country is the unruly passage from mute acceptance of closed-shop authority to a militancy that questions all of the traditional power groupings. The once-smug citizens of a once-smug nation have staged a *coup d'état* against the idea of having decisions made for them by self-selected hierarchies.

For Canadians who have traditionally deferred to authority and behaved as if they thought it was daring to use an adverb, this amounts to a revolution. Our historical genius for compromise, for "muddling through," the willingness of Canadians to subjugate their regional concerns and personal feelings for the national interest, is dead. There aren't two solitudes in this country; there are thirty million.

In my own testimony to the committee, I speculated about the roots of Canada's problems—that most Canadians believe their country was born without actually having been conceived. There is a notion abroad that Canada just sort of simmered up and that we are, in effect, a residual state with no economic logic or the fulfilment of any manifest destiny.

We may be a loose federation of wildly diverse regions on the very margin of the civilized world, but despite their self-absorption, most Canadians still share the commitment to our nation as an entity, washed by three oceans. We may be angry with one another, but nobody is mad at Canada.

This country was built on dreams as well as appetites. It was put together not by bloodlines, kin or tradition, but by waves of newcomers of every seed and stock, determined to carve out new lives. Being Canadian has never been a nationality; it's a condition. When a citizen of Japan or Sweden declares that he or she is Japanese or Swedish, it is a definitive statement. When one of us admits to being Canadian, it's an act of faith, a matter of permissions, potentials and possibilities that will take generations to complete.

I believe that it's time we began to sing some songs in praise of ourselves. What we've got here is a daily miracle of a country that ever since 1867 has lived out the dictum that a "nation is a body of people who have done great things together." We have and will again.

Canada needs a hug.

Despite the disappointments and shattered illusions, it may be absurd to advocate innovation and reform Canada's political system.

But it's even more absurd not to try.

ACKNOWLEDGEMENTS

Most of the pieces in this book were first published in *Maclean's*, which I edited for more than a decade. For the past fifteen years or so I've been the magazine's senior contributing editor and columnist, writing on business and politics. I am grateful to Robert Lewis, the current editor of *Maclean's*, for his unswerving support and encouragement, and to Michael Benedict for his creative and sympathetic editing of my copy.

The Unknown Element was first published in *Saturday Night* magazine. Young Ken is from my book *The Merchant Princes*. The Naughty Reichmanns was published in *The Globe and Mail*. Citizen Hurtig; Fearless Mike; and Ah, Kim, We Hardly Knew Ye were carried by *The Vancouver Sun*, which, under the inspired guidance of Max Wyman, now publishes one of Canada's very best book-review sections.

For the inspiration of *Defining Moments*, I thank: Cynthia Good, my Penguin editor and literary guardian angel; Mary Adachi, whose blue pencil is faster than my computer; and Dana Doll, whose intelligence, care and imagination in assembling these articles made the venture possible.

P.C.N.
Kitsilano, B.C.